Everyday Handyman Secrets!

Tips From the Pros!

by Marc Gill and Myles Bader

Got a problem around the home, yard or garage?
If it's broken this book has the solution!

Everyday Handyman Secrets!
Tips from the Pros!

A special THANKS to Dr. Myles Bader, noted household author, for assisting Marc, and sharing his own handyman expertise. Dr. Myles H. Bader (Wizard of Food) has been a prolific writer of kitchen reference, household hint and cooking-secret books for over 20 years.

ISBN: 978-0-9882955-9-9
Printed and bound in the United States of America

10 9 8 7 6 5 4 3 2 1

Telebrands Press
79 Two Bridges Road
Fairfield, NJ 07004
www.telebrands.com

Please note: While this compilation of Handyman Secrets will solve many problems, total success cannot be guaranteed. Neither the author, publisher, manufacturer; nor distributor can assume responsibility for the effectiveness of the suggestions.

A Word from the Author

Hi there! Thank you for purchasing my book! Inside you'll find hundreds of simple tips, tricks and hints to make everyday jobs around the house, inside and out, easier!

My first DIY project was installing my own dishwasher almost 20 years ago. It took me 3 days.... no breaks! Just kidding. But the project did teach me one thing...that I wasn't very good at this. As a new homeowner, I realized how much money I could save by doing my own work and repairs around the house. I began seeking, asking for and collecting all sorts of fantastic ways to save time and money doing my own repairs, quick fixes and preventative steps all over my property. All of those helpful hints are in this book.

But I'm Not Stopping There!!!

I have also included countless terrific tips for saving time and money everywhere around your home, gathered over the years from professionals, friends and family all over the country. The result is an invaluable guide full of everything you'll need to tackle your do-it-yourself jobs, maintenance, beautifying projects, quick fixes.... and MORE. Big or small, this book covers it all!!

Enjoy!

Marc Gill

Table of Contents

CHAPTER 1

KITCHEN

CABINETS

SQUEAK, SQUEAK
To fix the problem of squeaky hinges on cabinets just use vegetable oil. Best to use a liquid spray oil, however, you can also use a silicon spray. Never use WD-40™ since it contains petroleum distillates that attract dust. Be sure and hold a rag under the area you are spraying to catch the excess oil.

SECRET TO REFINISHING WITHOUT SANDING
If you hate to sand cabinets and want them painted or then just use a degreaser and paint it on. Then wipe it off as per the instructions on the bottle. It will remove all the grease and grime allowing you to paint without sanding.

SCRUB-A-DUB-DUB
When the cabinets need to be cleaned, never use abrasive cleaners such as scouring pads or powdered cleansers. Just use liquid dish soap and water. Never use aerosol sprays that contain silicones or paste waxes. Also, be careful not to allow oven cleaners to touch the cabinets.

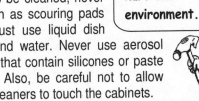

Aerosols hurt the environment.

HELP! I'M COMING APART

If you have a loose cabinet hinge you will have to drill out a larger hole. Be sure you don't go all the way through the cabinet. Glue in a hardwood peg, usually a ¼" dowel rod. When the glue dries, sand off the top making it flush with the surface of the door, and then re-drill your hole.

CALL THE CHIROPRACTOR, I NEED AN ADJUSTMENT

If the cabinet doors will not close properly, the door hinge is out of alignment and needs a small adjustment. Usually, one of the screws has loosened and needs to be tightened. If the screw hole is threaded and worn and can't be used, just force a toothpick or a matchstick in the hole and force the screw into it.

I'M GETTING A HEADACHE

If you are getting a headache from the cabinet doors banging when they are closed, the bumper pads are probably worn out and need to be replaced. All that is needed is to cut out a small round piece of felt and glue it on.

THINGS ARE NOT ON THE LEVEL

 If the cabinet doors are not level anymore it is probably the screws that attach the hinge to the frame that are the problem. Just loosen all the screws, then realign them and tighten them to fix the problem.

A STICKY SITUATION

When the cabinet drawers tend to stick it usually means that the drawer gliders are out of alignment, or you have debris in the tracks. Usually they just need to be sprayed with a silicon spray.

OUCH, GOT A DENT

If you get a small scratch or a small dent in your cabinets, just use some colored putty to fill it in then paint over it.

MY CABINET IS GROWING
Wood cabinets may swell up from moisture. This is usually caused by putting wet dishes away. It doesn't take very much moisture to cause a problem depending on how the interior wood is protected.

MUSTY ODOR BEGONE
If you have a musty odor in your cabinets, just sprinkle some baking soda around and allow it to remain for 1-2 days.

FIRE HAZARD!
Follow directions for self-cleaning ovens, especially if there are cabinets over them.

CONVECTION OVEN

HOW A CONVECTION OVEN WORKS
The standard oven and convection oven work in fairly similar ways.

The notable difference in the convection oven is that it has a fan that increases the distribution of the heat molecules providing heat to all areas more evenly and faster. Because of the fan and the efficiency of the heat circulation, a lower temperature is usually required.

- If you are going to use a convection oven, reduce the recommended temperature for a recipe by 25^0-75^0F.
- It is not necessary to pre-heat a convection oven. They heat up very quickly and evenly surround the food with heat.
- When baking in a convection oven lower the temperature by 50^0-75^0F to be safe or the baked goods may burn or overbrown.

COUNTERS

HOW CLEAN I AM.........
If you have a laminate counter top you have to be careful how you clean it. Just use a liquid detergent or a very mild abrasive cleaner and use a very light touch. If you really have a bad stain, use full-strength Pine Sol™.

GREAT SECRET

When it comes to refinishing an old wood countertop, just follow these hints: first sand any bad areas, then refinish with three coats of polyurethane for the best results.

Not a food-safe surface.

PAINTING OVER FORMICA IS WORK

If you are going to paint over the top of Formica you first have to sand lightly then apply Kilz™ paint and allow it to fully dry. Then you will have to add three colors of gray paint: light, medium, and dark then marbleize them together. Allow it to dry then apply five coats of polyurethane. Remember this will not be a food-safe surface.

CLEANING THE FANCY STUFF

If you have a Corian® countertop that needs to be cleaned, just use a gentle abrasive powdered bleach on a damp surface. Allow it to remain for 5 minutes before sponging it off, then rinse well and dry.

OUCH!

Hot pots, especially iron and aluminum should never be placed on Corian® countertops if the bottom of the pot is wet, since it may leave a mark on the surface that will be almost impossible to get off.

I DON'T WANT A SEPARATION

If the counter has separated from the wall it is usually caused by settlement and can be corrected by caulking between the countertop and the wall. Hopefully, there is just a small separation so that the counter does not have to be removed and reset.

GETTING DAMP DOWN HERE

If you have gaps in the calking around the sink it is usually caused by shrinkage and can be repaired by re-caulking or using seam filler.

MY MARBLE IS SCRATCHED

If you have a few small scratches on a cultured marble countertop they can usually be buffed off or polished.

PROTECT THE BUTCHER BLOCK

When you install a new butcher block counter it has to be properly sealed. It is recommended to use boiled linseed oil applying it with a paintbrush. Allow it to dry for 24 hours before applying a second coat then wait another 24 hours. Wipe the second coat off by rubbing with a clean cloth.

10

CURLING IRON PROBLEM

If you left your curling iron on the Formica™ countertop and forgot it while it was still very hot, it may have left a yellow burn mark. Providing that the burn is not too deep, it can be removed with a scouring cleanser. If it is deep, there is not much you can do about it.

SHOULD YOU EVEN BUY A FORMICA™ COUNTERTOP?

There are a number of disadvantages in buying a Formica™ countertop: abrasive cleaners will scratch and dull the surface, sharp knives will leave scratch marks, and a hot pot will actually melt the finish. Also, warping can occur if the area is wet for too long a period and the seams are too easily seen depending on the quality. Some will even fade in time.

FORMICA™ COUNTER CLEANSER

The following ingredients will be needed:

3 Tablespoons of white vinegar
½ Teaspoons liquid dish soap
½ Teaspoon of olive oil
½ Cup of very warm tap water
1   Spray bottle

Place all the ingredients in a spray bottle and mix thoroughly. Spray the counter and allow it to remain for a few seconds before wiping off with a damp sponge. Rinse the area well to remove all residues.

SHOULD YOU BUY A CORIAN® COUNTERTOP?

There are some advantages in having a Corian® countertop since they are fairly stain resistant and easy to clean and most scratches can be repaired. However, if they need repair it must be done by a professional. Also, they may scratch easily, and a hot pot will melt the surface finish.

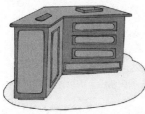

LOVE THOSE WOOD BLOCK COUNTERTOPS

This is one of chef's favorite countertops. They like "real" wood. It is very durable if cared for and cleans easily. Scratches can be removed by sanding. However, if you allow large amounts of water to remain on them, they may turn black and require sanding and re-sealing, which is expensive. Keep them dry and clean.

CERAMIC TILE COUNTERTOPS

If the grout is not kept clean it will become discolored and mildewed. Tile tends to chip and is not easy to replace. If you break a tile you need to drill holes and remove the tile, clean the area and replace with a new tile.

CERAMIC TILE CLEANER
The following ingredients will be needed:

Don't use chlorine bleach.

¼	Cup of white vinegar
1/3	Cup of household ammonia
½	Cup baking soda
7	Cups of warm tap water
1	Spray bottle

Place all the ingredients in a medium plastic bucket with a well-sealed cover and shake to mix thoroughly. Place the mixture in 2-3 jars, label and save. **Never add chlorine bleach to this mixture.** Use with rubber gloves to protect your hands and spray it on the surface to be cleaned.

FLAT BOARD = FLAT COUNTER
When installing a ceramic tile counter, to be sure that you have a flat surface, use a small perfectly flat board and place it over the tiles and tap gently. This will assure that all the tiles are set firmly and that the counter is level.

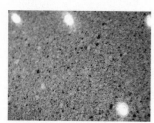

SOME OF MY GRANITE FAVORITES
Granite is one of the best countertops but it does require proper sealing. It is scratch resistant, hot pots can be placed on it and it is one of the best looking countertops. Another newcomer is Silestone™ made from quartz, which is harder than granite and does not need to be sealed.

GRANITE CLEANING TIPS
- Be sure to blot up stains immediately or they may penetrate the surface.
- To clean the surface use stone soap available in hardware stores, or use mild soap and water.
- Always use a soft, clean cloth and never an abrasive pad or steel wool.
- If you get a stain, try cleaning it with 2 tablespoons of dishwasher soap and water to prepare a thick paste. Place the solution on the stain and cover it with a piece of plastic wrap and allow it to stand overnight.
- If the stain is oil-based (grease, milk, etc) make the paste from hydrogen peroxide instead of the dishwasher soap.
- Acetone will remove ink stains from granite.
- For non-oil stains, try using molding and pure bleach made into a paste; then allow the paste to remain for 30 minutes before rinsing it off.

SPIT SHINE?

If you would like a quick shine on your countertop, just wipe it down with white vinegar.

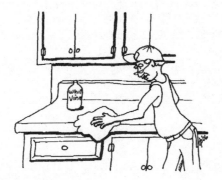

IS YOUR LAMINATE DULL?

You can brighten a dull laminate countertop by applying a coating of quality car wax. If you buff it off really good, very little of the wax will remain and you will retain the shine. It is safe to place food on the counter afterwards.

CROCK POT

The Crock Pot was invented in 1971 by Rival. Many consumers still question whether the pot is safe or a breeding ground for bacteria since it advocates all day cooking at a low temperature. The fact is that most slow cookers have settings that range from 170^0F to 280^0F.

Bacteria die at 140^0F, which is below the lowest possible temperature that can be used. However, if the lid is left off it may cause a problem with food not being fully cooked and harboring bacteria that is still alive.

To minimize the risk of food poisoning, do the following:

✓ All foods should be at refrigerator temperature. No frozen or partially thawed foods.
✓ Only cook cut up pieces of meat, not whole roasts or fowl to allow the heat to penetrate fully.
✓ Make sure that the cooker is at least half to two-thirds full or the food will not absorb enough heat to kill any bacteria.
✓ The food must be covered with liquid to generate sufficient steam.
✓ The original lid should always be used and should be tight fitting.
✓ When possible, allow the cooker to cook on the high setting for the first hour then it can be reduced.

- ✓ Never use the cooker to reheat leftovers. A number of bacteria are usually found on leftovers and it takes high heat to kill them.
- ✓ Always follow the manufacturer's directions for temperature settings.
- ✓ Never use a crock-pot to re-heat leftovers. The bacterial count will be higher and the food needs time at a higher temperature to kill them.
- ✓ Vegetables should be placed in crock-pots just before serving, depending on their thickness.
- ✓ All foods should be at refrigerator or room temperature before placing them into a crock-pot.
- ✓ Never put partially or frozen foods in a crock-pot.

CUTLERY

GENERAL INFORMATION:

One of the most important utensils in a kitchen is your knife. There are a number of different materials used in knife blades, many of which are relatively new and need to be evaluated as to which will suit you best. Make sure the handle is secured with at least three rivets. It should feel comfortable. Avoid plastic grips. When cutting foods, the best surface would be a soft wooden cutting board. Hardwoods and plastic boards tend to dull the blade faster and also reduce the life of the knife.

Carbon Steel

This is, by far, the best for keeping the sharpest edge and is the preferred knife for the serious chef. However, if the blade is not constantly kept dry it will rust. Acids in foods may also take their toll and turn the blade black, which can be transferred back to foods.

Super-Stainless Steel

This is not one of the better quality blades. Once it dulls and loses its original well-honed sharpness, it is almost impossible to restore to a decent level of sharpness. However, it does resist rust and staining.

Stainless Steel

Has the ability to resist rust and the acid effects from foods. Will take a sharper edge than the super stainless steel, but will dull and does not really take a very sharp edge.

High-Carbon Stainless Steel

This is the most expensive of the four types mentioned here and will not rust nor stain. It does not have to be washed and dried continually when in use. It can be sharpened to a sharper edge than either of the other stainless steel knives.

BE NICE TO YOUR KNIVES

When storing a knife, one of the best ways is to keep it in a wooden countertop knife holder that was made for the knife. However, not all wooden holders are quality ones and the holder should not have a hard surface for the blade to lie on. The higher quality holders will have a protective liner that allows the edge of the blade to rest free. When a knife is stored in a drawer with other utensils it will end up with small nicks on the blade and that will eventually ruin a high quality knife.

A SHARP INVESTMENT

When you purchase a knife it is an investment that you need to make. It is a kitchen tool that is indispensable and unless you buy a quality knife, you will not have it very long and will not be very satisfied with the results. Purchase either carbon-steel or high-carbon steel knives. The manufacturer should be a recognized name such as Trident, Wusthof, or Heckles. The blade and handle should all be one piece and the handle should not be attached to the blade. If the knife has a plastic hilt, it is not recommended.

GRINDING WHEELS ARE GREAT!

 The old grinding wheel was a very useful tool and was used to sharpen everything that needed sharpening around the house. However, the one method that should never be used on a good kitchen knife is that of allowing a coarse grinding wheel to be used. The blade will only last a few years and will become thinner and thinner. Rotating steel disks are not recommended either. The preferred method is the **"butcher's steel."**

This is just a rough-surfaced, hard metal rod with a protective handle. If the butcher's steel is used frequently it will keep the edge on the knife. If you have a problem keeping the edge it may mean that you are not using the sharpener as frequently as you should and you may have to use a **"whetstone"** to return the edge. The whetstone is made of silicon carbide (carborundum).

SHARPENING ANGLES

THE TOOL	THE ANGLE
Axe...	45^0
Carving Knife...........................	$15\text{-}20^0$
Draw Knife...............................	30^0
Drill Bits..................................	$24\text{-}32^0$
Hedge Hammer........................	$28\text{-}32^0$
Hockey Skates.........................	90^0
Lawnmower Blade....................	30^0
Plane Blade.............................	$25\text{-}30^0$
Pocketknife.............................	$15\text{-}25^0$
Scissors & Shears....................	80^0
Screwdriver.............................	90^0
Sickle & Scythe........................	30^0
Wood Chisel............................	$25\text{-}30^0$

DISHWASHER

GENERAL INFORMATION:
Dishwashers have at least one motor that is attached to  a pump that forces the water up into sprayer arms. When it is in the drain cycle it pushes the water and debris out of the dishwasher and into the sink that has the garbage disposer.

Larger food particles then wait for the next time you run the dishwasher to be reduced into minute particles that will go down the drain. Most European dishwashers have two motors, one for washing and the other for draining.

The latest dishwashers now have a soil-sensor, which checks the water to see if it is still containing debris from the dishes.

If the water is clean, the dishwasher will advance to the next cycle. This is a recommended feature when purchasing a new dishwasher.

SOMETHING SMELLS FISHY
Kitchen odors are frequently found in the garbage disposal and caused by food from the dishwasher. The best way to eliminate the problem is to run the garbage disposal for a few seconds after you finish washing the dishes.

WHOOPS! I'M OVERFILLING

If the dishwasher is overfilling with water then the float switch has gone bad and stopped functioning and needs to be replaced.

NOT UNDER THE SINK

It is best not to store the dishwasher detergent under the sink. It is too warm and moist there and it will cake-up too easily. If you are having a problem with caking up, buy a smaller sized box.

DISHWASHER IS SICK AND WILL NOT RUN

One of the main reasons that a dishwasher will not run is if water has seeped into the electronics burning out the timer or one of the other six control switches. It is best to call a repairman!

MY SOAP HAS NOT DISAPPEARED

When the soap dish or the rinse-aid dispenser does not empty it means that the timer switch has not sent a signal to the bi-metal switch that opens it and needs to be replaced. Or, it could be that you've filled the dishwasher too full preventing the soap dispenser from opening.

IT'S ALIVE! IT WON'T TURN OFF!

The dishwasher did not turn off when the door was opened during an active cycle. The door switches

may eventually get damaged or get debris in them and not function. This needs a service call to fix. Best not to let anyone near it unless they know how to change the switch.

HOW DRY I'M NOT...........

If the dishes are not drying completely, the drying fan has stopped functioning or is not functioning efficiently to do the job and needs to be replaced. It is usually found in the back right corner.

THE DISHWASHER IS HAUNTED - FUNNY NOISES

There are funny noises coming from the dishwasher. Sometimes funny noises can be eliminated by checking to see if a small object or a pit has fallen into the pump assembly.

WEEPING WATER

If you find water in the dishwasher when there shouldn't be any, this is called *"weeping water"* and is usually caused by a faulty fill valve, which will need to be replaced.

WHAT A PRETTY RAINBOW, BUT WHAT'S ON MY GLASSES?

Spotted glasses may be caused by a lack of water flow or from hard water.

If the glasses are getting a rainbow hue then it is probably from using too much detergent. This can also be caused by water not being hot enough. Try running the sink faucet until hot water starts running out, then start your dishwasher. Also, opening the dishwasher too soon after it has finished will cause this problem.

YUK! DIRTY DISHES

This is usually cause by obstructed water flow caused by poor loading of the dishes.

A HEATED SOLUTION

If the dishes are not coming out clean, try running the sink's hot water tap until it gets warm before you start the dishwasher. This will help the first cycle to have hotter water. If this doesn't work you need new nozzles.

GRANULES OR GELS
Most dishwasher manufacturers recommend that you use powders or granules and not gels. Gels tend not to perform as well.

APPLIANCES THAT DON'T LIKE EACH OTHER
To extend the lifetime of the dishwasher, never have it next to the refrigerator since both emit heat, unless you place an insulation panel between them.

ARE RUSTY RACKS YOUR PROBLEM?
If your dishwasher racks are getting rusty, purchase a bottle of rack touch up at any appliance parts department. New tine ends are also available.

TESTING YOUR SOAP
If you are curious to see if the water is hot enough for the dishwasher soap to dissolve properly, just run the hot water in your sink until it is as hot as it will get, then fill a glass and put a tablespoon of the soap in the water. If the soap dissolves before it gets to the bottom of the glass, the water is hot enough.

TANG™ YOU VERY MUCH
If your dishwasher is looking dingy and has deposits on the walls, just add 1 cup of Tang™ to the dishwasher and run it through a cycle. It will clean the interior and refresh the inside.

GETTING MOLDY IN HERE.........HELP!

If you use your dishwasher at least twice a week, you should have no problem with mold from the moisture. Residual water on the bottom will cause mold growth if the dishwasher is not used regularly and should be cleaned.

DISHES GETTING CHILLY, WHAT'S THE PROBLEM?

Some dishwashers put cold water into the dishwasher and the dishwasher must heat the water before it will start. This can take up to 30 minutes in older machines.

NOT TOO HOT OR ELSE

Your water heater should be set at 120^0F for the dishwasher to work at optimum efficiency.

BUBBLE, BUBBLE, HERE COMES TROUBLE

If your dishwasher is full of soapsuds and bubbles, you used the wrong detergent or tablet. Just place 2 tablespoons of vegetable oil into the soapy, water to break up the suds and sprinkle salt on the suds to disperse them. Placing ice cubes on the suds will also help to alleviate the problem.

IN-DEPTH CLEANING

For a thorough cleaning, place a bowl with 3 cups of white vinegar on the bottom rack and leave all racks in place. Do not place dishes in the dishwasher. Run the dishwasher through the wash and rinse cycle **ONLY**. Make sure that you _**turn the machine off before it goes into the drying cycle**_.

PUT A MUFFLER ON IT

If you want to quiet your dishwasher and have it on a cement floor, just place a piece of indoor-outdoor carpet under it to muffle some of the noise.

I'VE BEEN ETCHED!
If you place glasses next to each other and they are touching, they may get scratched permanently as well as not being thoroughly washed. Poor loading causes detergent to remain on the dishes.

SCRATCHES BEGONE
If you use a small amount of abrasive toothpaste on a cloth, you can remove minor scratches from glass.

EXHAUST HOOD (RANGE HOOD)

GENERAL INFORMATION:
Many range exhaust hoods really do not do a good job of eliminating steam, grease, smoke and food odors. Some hoods only re-circulate the air through a filter and return the air to the kitchen.

A range hood has to be vented to the outside to really be effective. Most re-circulating air vents can be converted to one that exhausts outside without too much trouble.

HELP! I'M WORKING TOO HARD
If the motor is getting smelly and hot, you will need to clean the fan blades with just soap and water. Dirty fan blades will restrict airflow and may cause the motor to overheat and catch on fire.

DIRTY WORK!
If you have a charcoal filter in your range-hood, it can be recharged, by placing it in a 450°F oven for 30 minutes (after completely cleaning the frame). If there is any grease left on the frame it may catch on fire or smoke up the house. Many activated charcoal filters cannot be cleaned and should be replaced once a year.

BE GENTLE NOW
Light bulbs in vents need to be removed and very gently cleaned with cool water and soap.

GET OUT THE GLOVES
If parts are greasy use ammonia and water to clean them. Never use abrasive pads or scouring powder on the vent parts. Metal grids need to be soaked once a month in ammonia and water.

FIRE, FIRE! LEAVE THE FAN ALONE!
If a fire starts on the range top, never turn the fan on over the range or you may pull the flames into the hood and into the house attic or ductwork.

THERE IS A GHOST IN MY HOOD

This is caused by the outside wind moving the damper and is a normal sound when it is windy.

It's not the wind!

FLOORING

GENERAL INFORMATION:

There are several types of kitchen flooring for you to choose from. The following are some of the more popular types:

> **Earthen Tiles** – These come in two forms: glazed and unglazed. You can even buy handmade ones with custom details. Most of the tiles are made from fine-grained clay and are machine-shaped and pressed. Glazed tiles are very resistant to stains and moisture, however, be sure and treat the grout with a liquid silicone sealer. Colored grout works best. These tiles cost $5 to $25 per square foot with installation costing $3 to $5 per square foot.

> If you are going to install earthen tiles over a deck, be sure and use ½" concrete backing board nailed over the deck and cement the tile to it. Use only grade 3 for kitchen floors.

> **Hardwood Floors** – This is normally ¾-inch tongue-and-groove planking. It has a warming effect on a room and will complement the cabinets and counters. The cost is about $6 to $8 per square foot and can refinished when it becomes worn. Be sure and seal the floor with three coats of urethane. The floor does not do well if water is allowed to remain and will buckle.

- **Kitchen Carpeting** – This thin, tough carpeting used to be very popular, however, it is not used very much anymore since it does not handle spills well and doesn't really fit in with today's kitchen styling. It is rubber-backed and does provide a soft, underfoot feel. It is very affordable and does come in stain-resistant.

- **Linoleum** -Linoleum can be manufactured by using a mixture of resins, (small particles of cork or wood fibers) and linseed oil that is adhered to a canvass, burlap or felt backing using high pressure. Never use a strong alkali-based cleaner on linoleum since they tend to ruin the linseed oil binder and may cause the floor to develop cracks, thus shortening the usable life of the flooring. Best to use a mild detergent solution and dry as soon as has been cleaned. A linoleum formula should never be used on a wood or cork floor.

SMALL, HOLE REPAIR
If you kept some scraps when the floor was laid, you are in good shape. Just grind up and powder the scraps then mix the dust with a small amount of clear shellac or white glue. Fill the holes and by the next day you will have trouble finding the holes.

- **Plastic Laminate Flooring** – This is a wood-grain plastic laminate, which contain silica sand and is harder than countertop laminates or hardwoods. It is bonded to plywood planks or squares. It simulates wood and is a tough floor.
- **Pre-finished Veneers** – These are pre-finished, tongue-and-groove plywood planks and squares topped with hardwood veneers. Most of these are installed as floating floors. The planks are glued together along the tongue-and-groove joints and then laid over a foam pad. Urethane finished veneers cost about $3 to $6 per square foot installed. The top of the line, however, has a super-hard acrylic-plastic sealant forced deep into the veneer, making it more resistant to scratches and dents.
- **Resilient Flooring** – This comes in either vinyl-sheet goods or tiles and is very affordable. The prices range from $6 to $40 per square foot with installation running from $4 to $8 per square foot. There are two types of this flooring: layered and full-depth. The layered has a printed vinyl fused to white, fibrous or foam liner. The second type is inlaid, which has colored composition particles extending the full depth of the flooring.

The recommended type is the inlaid since there is no surface layer that can be punctured, snagged or will tear more easily. The price is dependent of the thickness of the wear layer. If you plan to place this type of flooring over existing flooring, it would be best to have a professional do the job.

> **Stone Flooring** – These are permanent floors and are marble, slate or granite. They are susceptible to scratching, especially marble. Granite is the most durable and floors run from $12 to $30 per square foot plus installation.

Kitchen Carpeting

SHELF IT!
You can use leftover linoleum to line pantry and cabinet shelves. It will make cleaning the shelves easier.

STICKY PROBLEM
To remove tar, just place some dry ice on the tar and wait for it to harden then scrape it off.

DON'T USE A HAMMER AND CHISEL
The easiest method of removing old flooring is with a heat gun. It will still be a messy job, but it will get done. If you are working to remove tiles, a hair dryer will work just as well.

I'M COMING APART AT THE SEAMS
If the seams of your kitchen carpeting are starting to come apart, it would be best to handle this problem as soon as it appears and before the edges start fraying. There are two ways to correct the problem depending on the location. If the problem is in a high traffic area, pull back the area that has come loose and use carpet glue on the part that has come up. Be careful not to get the glue on the carpet, so don't use too much.

If you use too much and it seeps through when you place a medium weight on the area, you may ruin the carpet. If the problem is at the wall, just use double-sided carpet tape.

FILLER'UP
A gouge can be fixed using almond-colored kitchen and sink caulking and use a small amount of food coloring to try and match the floor color. It won't remove the gouge, but it won't be very noticeable.

DON'T USE RUBBER BACKING!
Never use foam or rubber-backed mat or rug on a linoleum floor or it will cause permanent discoloration.

CURLING TILES?
If one of the tiles has started curling on the edges, use a blow dryer on high heat and warm the tile, just enough to soften it. Raise it and place fresh glue down then press it back into place and put a heavy weight on it till it dries. Be sure that there is no glue seeping out or whatever you place on it to hold it in place will be there permanently.

FREEZER CHEST

GENERAL INFORMATION:

All modern day freezers are now automatic defrost freezers that do not need to be turned off and defrosted. When frost builds up in the freezer it automatically melts. The more food you have in the freezer, the more efficient the freezer's energy usage. It will take more energy to keep a half empty freezer cold than a full one. The automatic defrost freezers have a timer that turns off the freezer every 6-8 hours and turns on the defrost heater.

Some models also have a timer that can be set to run the defroster at a specific time of the day. The water from the defrosting then goes into a pan under the freezer and is evaporated by either a fan blowing warm air over it or by the heat of the compressor.

NOT A NICE PLACE TO BE
If frost is building up in the freezer, the timer is not working. It may not be sending the signal to the heater motor or the heater motor is not working. One of the two will need replacement. The condenser coils may also be dirty and need cleaning. You can do the coils, but let a repairman do the rest.

OUCH! I GOT FREEZER BURN
Freezer burn is actually dehydration that is caused by the food being exposed to the air in the freezer. Food in supermarket wrappings are not airtight and if frozen for more than a few days the food need to be re-wrapped in as airtight a wrapping as possible.

HOW COLD IS COLD?
Your freezer should maintain a temperature of 0^0F to 8^0F.

If you immediately turn the freezer on and fill it with food it will take about 24 hours to reach this temperature. It is best to leave a new freezer on for 24 hours before placing food in it.

IT FEELS LIKE A ROLLER COASTER IN HERE

The temperature of your freezer should never fluctuate more than a few degrees to keep foods at their best. The temperature should be kept at least 0^0F or below for the best results. Thawing and re-freezing is the worst thing you can do to foods. Every time the temperature drops in the freezer, some of those small ice crystals will convert to larger ice crystals and little by little, the dish will be ruined.

TO FILL OR NOT TO FILL

It is best to keep your freezer at least half full to maintain a constant temperature.

FROSTY, THE FREEZER.....

When frost builds up on the walls of a freezer that is not frost-free it needs to be thawed out if it reaches about 1-inch thick.

GETTING COZY IN HERE

If the freezer is not getting cold enough or is not freezing it may be due to a number of different problems. The compressor is not functioning, you may have a refrigerant leak, or the timer is not working properly. Need a repairman!

However, if the freezer is running and not freezing properly or developing frost near the top, check the door seal and be sure that the door is sealing properly. In time the seal will need to be replaced. Depending on the climate, the rubber seal will deteriorate and cause abnormal leakage. The magnetic strip may also become loose and not hold the door shut tight.

HELP! MY TEXTURE IS CHANGING

When you freeze foods, you are actually freezing the water that is in the food cells. As the water freezes it expands and a number of the cell walls rupture releasing their liquid, which then freezes into ice crystals, thus resulting in the food becoming softer. These changes in texture are more noticeable in fruits and vegetables since they have higher water content than most other foods.

Certain vegetables such as tomatoes, lettuce and celery are so high in water content they literally turn into mush when frozen. When cooked products are frozen, their cell walls are already softened therefore they do not burst as easily. This is especially true when high starch vegetables such as corn, lima beans and peas are included in dishes.

MICROBE ALERT, MICROBE ALERT

Most microorganisms are not destroyed by freezing and may even be present on fruits and vegetables. Blanching does help lower the microorganism count significantly but enough of them do survive and are ready and waiting to destroy the food as soon as it thaws. Inspect all frozen foods, which may have accidentally thawed by leaving the freezer door open or from an electrical failure. The botulism microorganism does not reproduce at 0^0F.

Cold doesn't bother us microbes!

QUICK, FREEZE ME FASTER

The damage to foods when freezing them can be controlled to some degree by freezing them as fast as possible. When foods are frozen more rapidly, the ice crystals that are formed are smaller and cause less cell wall rupture. If you know you will be freezing a number of items or a food that you really want to keep in good shape, try setting the freezer at the coldest setting a few hours before you place the food in. Some freezer manuals also will advise you switch shelves that are in the coldest area.

FREEZING FOOD TIPS

+ Foil containers are best for freezing if you are going to go from the freezer to the oven.
+ Only freeze baked goods that are low in moisture. Breads must be wrapped very tightly.

- Foods that contain spices will not freeze well and retain the flavor of the spice.
- Vegetables must be blanched before freezing.
- Frozen fruits do not retain their flavor.
- Remove fat from meats and they will freeze for a longer period of time.
- Remove all poultry innards before freezing.
- Low fat fish freeze better.
- The higher the fat content of dairy products the better they will freeze.
- Cheese will freeze well.
- Most sauces freeze well.

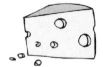

PROBLEMS AFTER FREEZING FOODS

Apples	Becomes mushy and may turn dark
Celery	Becomes soft and only good for cooking
Cooked egg whites	Turns rubbery
Cooked macaroni and rice	Mushy, loss of taste
Cheese in blocks	Tend to crumble too easily
Cheese, crumbled	Soggy
Cucumbers	Limp, waterlogged, poor flavor
Custards	Gets watery
Cream cheese	Become grainy and crumbly
Cream pies	Gets watery
Custard fillings	Separates, watery
Egg whites (cooked)	Soft, tough, rubbery
Fried foods	Loss of crispness, soggy
Gelatin	Weeps
Grapes	Becomes soft and mushy
Gravy	Need to be re-heated if fat separates
Icings made with egg whites	Weepy
Jelly on bread	Tend to soak into the bread
Lettuce	Loses shape and very limp
Mayonnaise	Separates
Meringue	Toughens
Milk sauces	Tends to curdle or separate
Onions, raw	Watery and limp but OK for cooking
Potatoes, Irish	Soggy when frozen in soups or stews
Potatoes, raw	Texture is lost and they may darken
Radishes	Texture is poor and they become pithy
Salad greens	Lose crispness

Sauces with milk or cream -- May separate
Sour Cream -------------- Separates, watery
Tomatoes, raw ----------- Watery and tend to lose their shape
Whole milk -------------- Separates
Yogurt ------------------ Separates

GARBAGE DISPOSAL

GENERAL INFORMATION:
The disposer works by using a small motor, which powers a flywheel that throws the garbage into a shredder producing a pulp that will easily flush down the drain. There are two major types of garbage disposal units. They are the batch feed, which is activated by turning a stopper, and the continuous feed operated by turning on a wall switch.

CLICK, CLICK???????????
If you try to use the disposer and it didn't turn on, try pushing the small red button on the bottom of the disposer. Sometimes a jam will cause the unit not to work at all and it may appear to be an electrical problem. However, removing the jam and pressing the red button usually works.

UNFRIENDLY DISPOSER FOODSTUFFS & ???????
There are a number of foods that will cause a jam and stop the disposer. These include garlic skins, celery strings, cornhusks, potato peelings, tea bag strings, silverware, children's toys, etc.

AVOIDING A CLOG
Certain peelings will clog most garbage disposals. The best way to avoid a problem when you need to peel potatoes or other vegetables is to place a funnel down the garbage disposal to block the debris.

PEEK-A-BOO
If you look down the sink into the unit with a flashlight and see a foreign object use needle-nosed pliers to remove it. If the object is jammed into the blade use the "L" shaped metal tool (Allen wrench) found under the sink. Place the small wrench into the hole on the bottom of the disposer and turn it to release a jam before removing the foreign object. The small wrenches are available at any hardware store but should come with your disposer.

THERE'S SOMETHING SWIMMING IN THERE

If the disposal is not draining, try a plunger and be sure it is seated well before trying to push it down a few times. If this does not work you will have to remove the curved trap under the sink and clean it out.

IS YOUR FOOD FLYING AROUND THE KITCHEN?

If food is flying out of the disposer you have not placed the rubber stopper over the hole. The stopper should have small holes in it to allow water in. If this is not the problem, call Ghostbusters!

COLD SOLUTION

To sharpen the blades of a garbage disposer, just place 3-4 ice cubes into the disposer, and run it for a few seconds. This should be done once a month if the disposer is used regularly. To freshen it, grind lemon peels in it.

A LITTLE BIT WILL DO YA

Never place any type of chemical drain cleaner into a garbage disposal. If you need to get rid of odors use a small amount of white vinegar.

DEATH BY DRAIN CLEANER

Drain cleaners should never be placed in the side of the sink that has the disposer or it may be damaged.

SEASONING THE DISPOSER

Just pour ½ cup of table salt in the garbage disposal then run with water as usual. This will clean and freshen up the disposal. However, if you prefer you could pour ½ cup of baking soda in the drain and flush it with very hot water.

RUN WATER, DURING AND AFTER

Most people are aware that you should run water while running the disposal, however, you should also run the water for 30 seconds after it has finished running to be sure that all the garbage has cleared the pipes.

OUCH, OUCH, THAT'S TOO HOT

Always use cold water when running the garbage disposal.

KEEP ALL YOUR FINGERS

Never place your hand into a garbage disposer. Always use a needle-nosed pliers kept under the sink to remove foreign objects.

HOT WATER DISPENSER

GENERAL INFORMATION:

This unit works with a control valve that is on top of the sink and dispenses hot water. The heating element is under the sink and heats the water to a temperature that is set by the factory. If the heating element goes bad it is best to replace the entire unit since a service call and repair will usually cost more than a new unit.

TRICKLE, TRICKLE

If you are not getting enough water from the tap then the line is partially clogged and will need to be removed and flushed out. There may also be a leak in the line so check under the sink for water spillage.

COLD TEA IS NOT VERY GOOD

If the water is not getting as hot as you would like, then you will need to read your manual and reset the temperature control, which was set by the factory. If a plumber is installing a new unit, be sure they adjust the temperature control to the desired temperature before they leave. If you installed the unit, check to see if you attached it to the cold water line. The temperature of water coming out of a unit should be $190^{0}F$, which is enough to give you a nice burn.

HALF-A-CUP WILL NOT DO
These under the sink units can only supply a few cups of water at a time.

ICE CUBE MAKER

GENERAL INFORMATION:
The ice cube maker is a small appliance that is in the freezer compartment of the refrigerator and continually makes ice cubes. The icemaker works by signaling the water-fill valve to send water to the filling the tray. When the water thermostat signals the water-fill unit that the tray is full, it stops sending water. When the ice cubes reach a certain temperature there is a signal sent and the tray empties.

BAD ICE CUBE, BAD ICE CUBE
If your ice cubes have an off taste or smell bad then they have probably picked up refrigerator odors and have been in the icemaker too long. Even if the water is filtered this will still occur.

NO STICK ICE CUBES
If you are making a lot of ice cubes for a party and place them into a bag in the freezer ending up with a big glob of ice there is a solution. Next time just place them into a brown paper bag before putting them into the freezer and they will not stick together.

KICK IT!
If the icemaker won't make ice cubes there are a few things you can do. First, check and see if it has accidentally been turned off. There is a thin, coat-hanger metal bar on the right side of your icemaker. When the bar is up, the icemaker is off. If the bar is down the icemaker is on. If the bar is up, slowly lower it and the icemaker should work.

A common icemaker problem is freeze-ups. Next time this happens just use the hair dryer to defrost the problem. This problem won't occur if you release a few ice cubes every few days.

CALL THE FILTER CHANGER
If you start detecting a bad taste it may be from an old worn out filter and should be changed. These filters should be changed every 6 months.

HOW CLEAR I AM................
Cloudiness in ice cubes is caused by entrapped air bubbles. If you want clear ice cubes boil the water first and make them in an ice cube tray.

KITCHEN SINK

NEED A LITTLE REPAIR

Best to buy a new one!

If your sink is scratched and chipped it can be resurfaced for about $300; however it is only guaranteed for about a year. A spray-on epoxy coating can be applied but only holds up well for bathroom sinks and bathtubs since they are not used as much as the kitchen sink. Buy a new sink! However, most hardware stores have a do-it-yourself kit that works great and can give you something to do.

CAN FALL ASLEEP WAITING

Waiting for hot water at the kitchen sink can waste thousands of gallons of water every year. The solution is the purchase a Chilipepper™ hot water appliance. It is a small pump that speeds up water from the hot water heater to the sink.

DRIP, DRIP, DRIP

Leaky faucets can be expensive when you start to figure that one drip per second over the course of a year will consume about 400 gallons of water. It only takes a few minutes to replace a washer or tighten the faucet insert.

THAT'S TOO TIGHT

It is not necessary to turn faucet handles all the way off, just until the water stops flowing. If you force the faucet all the way as far as you can, you may compress the gasket and eventually make the faucet leak.

OR USE YOUR MOUTHWASH

Odors in the sink can usually be eliminated by running very hot water down the drain or placing 2 tablespoons of baking soda in the drain and allow it to remain for a few minutes before running the hot water.

If this fails place 1 cup of white vinegar in the drain and allow it to remain for 20 minutes before flushing with hot water.

STEEL SINK RUST REMOVER

Prepare a thick paste of baking soda and warm water and allow it to remain on the stained area for about 2 hours then buff the entire sink with the paste using a damp, soft cloth. Rinse with cool water.

ALL STOPPED UP AND NOWHERE TO GO

After trying a "plumber's helper" with no success, try the following method. Remove all standing water so that you are able to pour the ingredients into the drain. First pour 1 cup of baking soda, 1 cup of table salt, and ½ cup of white vinegar into the clogged drain. These will start dissolving any organic matter and grease away immediately. Allow it to stand for 5 minutes then flush 1-2 quarts of boiling water down the drain.

KA-POOSH

If you have ever tried plunging a double sink, it may have been a very unpleasant experience. Next time you try to clear the drain, be sure and have a helper unless you have very long arms. The helper needs to place a rag or stopper into the other drain so that the water will not rush up and out as you plunge. If you have a dishwasher that drains through the disposer use a "C" clamp and two wood blocks to seal the drain hose, which will keep the water from backing into the dishwasher.

MICROWAVE

GENERAL INFORMATION:

The microwave contains a small transmitting antenna similar to the one a TV station might use. The microwave oven converts the house current into an extremely high voltage, which feeds the "magnetron." The magnetron converts the current into radio waves, which cause the liquid molecules in the food to vibrate at a fast rate causing friction and generating heat for cooking.

This process usually results in short cooking times, which retains the nutrients. The water content of the vegetables will determine just how well they will cook. Microwave ovens should have a movable turntable so that the food will not have "cold spots." This can result in the food being undercooked. If you wish to brown foods in the microwave, be sure and use a special dish for that purpose. The dish should always be preheated first for the best results. If you don't have a browning dish, try brushing the meat with soy or teriyaki sauce.

A steak will continue cooking after it is removed from the microwave and it is best to slightly undercook them.

Some foods are not meant to be placed in a microwave such as breads, since their internal structure is composed of many air pockets. The structure breaks down easily in the microwave and the bread becomes tough.

WHEN WAS THE MICROWAVE OVEN INVENTED?

In 1946 Dr. Percy Spencer, an engineer at Raytheon Laboratories, was working with a magnetron tube, which produces microwaves. He had a candy bar in his pocket, which he went to eat and found that it had melted. There was no heat source for that to occur. The only thing he could think of that would cause this to

occur was the magnetron tube he was working with. He then tried placing a small amount of popcorn near the tube and the popcorn popped in a few seconds. He then tried focusing the beam through a box at an egg, which exploded on one of his associates much to both of their surprise. The result was the first microwave oven called the Amana Radar Range™ introduced in 1977. The use of the word "radar" was used since the actual beam was invented in England and used as microwave radar to detect Hitler's planes in 1940.

DON'T GET ZAPPED

Microwave doors may become misaligned, especially if you tend to lean on them occasionally. They will leak radiation and should be checked periodically with a small inexpensive detector that can be purchased in any hardware store.

OUCH!

If you microwave a dish with a lid, be sure and aim the lid away from you when you are opening up the container. Escaping steam and spillovers are common causes of injuries.

SAFETY FIRST

If a child accidentally turns on the microwave, damage may occur. To avoid a problem, just keep a cup of water in the microwave when it is not in use.

KA BOOM

Microwave ovens are just as safe as a regular oven. However, make sure you never place a sealed container in a microwave.

MICROWAVE MAGIC?

A microwave oven actually works by emitting high-frequency electromagnetic waves from a tube called a "magnetron."

This type of radiation is scattered throughout the inside of the oven by a "stirrer." The "stirrer" is a fanlike reflector, which causes the waves to penetrate the food, reversing the polarity of the water molecules billions of times per second. This causes them to bombard each other and creating friction that heats the food.

NOT A GOOD SIGN
If you hear a hum, the magnetron is probably bad or you have a bad high voltage diode.

IT LOVES ME, IT LOVES ME NOT
If the microwave shuts off periodically, check to see if the fan is running. If the fan is not running when it shuts down there may be a short in the wiring. Another reason may be that the air intake grill is plugged up with dirt. Use an old toothbrush to clean the grill.

THE DANGEROUS TEA BAG
Never place a tea bag in the microwave! The metal staple holding it together can ruin a microwave oven.

DO I, OR DON'T I MICROWAVE IT?
Microwave cooking is less expensive than most other methods of cooking, however, it is only desirable for certain types of foods. If you are baking a dish, it will rise higher in a microwave oven. However, meats do not seem to have the desired texture and seem a bit mushy. When it comes to placing something frozen in the microwave, it will take longer to cook since it is difficult to agitate the water molecules when they are frozen.

BAD MICROWAVE, BAD MICROWAVE
If all seems normal and the food is not being cooked it may be a loose high voltage wire, a bad solder joint on the board, magnetron problem or a power relay problem. It is best to bring it to a repairman.

ANOTHER FUNKY PROBLEM
The display is counting down and no cooking is taking place. This is usually a bad door switch or a faulty relay.

DON'T BLOW A FUSE
If the microwave goes dead it is usually a faulty door switch that has blown the interior fuse.

TAKE IT FOR A RIDE
If the fan does not run, the microwave needs to be taken in for service since the fan is needed to cool the magnetron.

FUSE BLOWN?
The fuse will sometimes blow if the sensor senses overcooked burned food. This can easily be fixed by replacing the fuse.

FILL 'ER UP
Used microwave food containers should be saved and used for leftovers; just fill, freeze, and re-heat. It is always wise to check and see if a dish is microwave safe and will not melt. Just place the container next to a ½ full cup of water and turn the microwave on high for about 1½-minutes or until the water is boiling. If the dish is hot when you touch it, you will be able to cook with it.

EXPLODING FOODS
Certain foods will explode in a microwave, especially if they have skins that will not allow the water that is expanding to be released. These include eggs, potatoes, squash and any food that has a shell or tight skin.

NEATNESS COUNTS
If you don't clean up the microwave regularly the spills will cook onto the surface. To remove them easily, just place a sponge dipped in water or a small dish with ½ cup of water in the microwave and cook on high for about 2 minutes then wipe up.

WHY THE GLASS TRAY?
Glass trays are placed in the bottom of all microwave ovens to catch spills and raise the food up off the floor of the unit allowing the microwave energy to hit the bottom of the food.

MIXERS

SOLVING MIXER PROBLEMS

MOTOR DOESN'T RUN OR IS SLUGGISH

1. **Food mixture is too thick** – Either use higher speed or thin out mixture. If you keep trying, the motor will be damaged.
2. **On/off switch dirty** – Remove the housing and clean switch as well as all contacts using #400-sandpaper.

MOTOR RUNS BUT BEATERS DO NOT TURN

1. **Motor runs but beaters will not turn** – Beaters may not be locked into gear shaft.

MIXER MAKING TOO MUCH NOISE

1. **Beater hits bowl** – The beaters should just clear the bottom of the bowl. If they don't then you need to adjust the height by unplugging the unit and removing it from the stand. Lift up the hinge and turn the screw to raise or lower the hinge.
2. **Beaters striking each other** – If beaters are damaged or wobbly when they run, they need to be replaced. If the gears are misaligned, unplug the mixer, remove gear cover and realign gears. The base-plate or the gears themselves may be marked to aid in alignment. If there are no markings insert the beaters into the gear shafts and use the beater blades as a guide.

OVENS

HELLO IN THERE

If the oven does not come on it may be due to loss of electrical power, clock may not be set to manual, a burned wire connection, bad selector switch, fuse blown, circuit breaker kicked off, or a defective thermostat.

IT'S GETTING DARK IN HERE

If the oven bake light comes on but the oven is not heating up it may be from a defective bake element, a bad thermostat, or a burned wire connector. Usually it is the bake element and will need to be replaced, or the oven has a bad thermostat that needs replacement.

OVERNIGHT SENSATION
To make oven cleaning both easy and efficient, all you have to do is sponge on a generous amount of household ammonia and allow it to remain overnight. Let the oven air out the next morning then wipe it clean with a damp sponge.

HOW CLEAN I'M NOT.............
If the self-clean feature is not working it may be due to the panel cover for the door glass not being in the right position, the door was not locked, clock improperly set, defective thermostat, the self-clean switch is not closing, or a defective clock. Usually it is one of the easier problems and should be easily solved.

STOP! YOU'RE KILLING ME
If you have a self-cleaning oven, be careful not to use any type of oven cleaner or the finish will be removed and the oven will no longer be self-cleaning. You can use window cleaner or a mild detergent. Also, if you leave the racks in the oven while it is going through the self-cleaning cycle it will discolor the racks.

HELP! I'M COOKING
If you have ever wondered why you can place your hand into a hot oven and not be burned, the answer is simple: air does not conduct heat well. However, if you leave it in there long enough it will come out medium-well. Water conducts heat more efficiently and will easily burn you.

THE SPEEDY OVEN
If the oven is cooking too fast and at a higher than normal temperature it may mean that the thermometer is not calibrated, it has a defective thermostat, the selector switch is bad, or the bake/broil switch has gone bad. Time for a repairman to be called!

TIMING IS OFF
When the timing is off, it could be that you have a bad clock, defective selector switch, bad wire connection, or you don't know how to operate the unit.

SOMETHING'S OUTTA WACK
The oven door is getting too hot, which is usually due to defective door seals, poor insulation or that the door hinges are out of alignment.

RACK 'EM UP
Oven racks and smooth porcelain surfaces can be easily cleaned with a pumice stone in the oven.

LOOKS SPOOKY IN THERE

The red glow in the oven is the "glow-bar," which glows red-hot. When it reaches a specified temperature the gas jets will open. If the igniter is faulty it will not reach the proper temperature and the gas will not be released.

TICK, TOCK, TICK, TOCK

When the range burners work and the oven won't work, it is usually due to the clock being set wrong.

DON'T USE OVEN-CLEANER

Oven cleaners should never be used in self-cleaning ovens.

MY BROILER IS SICK

If you are having problems with the broiler not broiling, the broiler element has burned out and needs replacement.

IT'S NOT THE 4TH OF JULY

If you ever see sparks coming from the oven, unplug the oven from the wall immediately. After you unplug the unit see if you can tell where the sparks came from so that you can replace the part or call a serviceman.

CLEANING-UP

The majority of aerosol oven cleaners contain sodium hydroxide (lye), which is also found in drain cleaners. When lye is sprayed on burnt fats and carbohydrates it converts them into soap that is easily wiped off with a damp cloth. It would be best to use a number of the newer products that use organic salts and are less dangerous.

REMEMBER TO TURN IT OFF

If you have an oven that is not equipped with a self-cleaning feature then just preheat the oven to 200^{0}F and turn it off. Place a small bowl with ½ cup of ammonia on the center shelf then close the oven and allow it to stand overnight. The next day, open the oven and allow it to air for 30 minutes in a well, ventilated kitchen then wipe up the mess with a warm, damp paper towel.

BAKED GOODS ARE BURNING

There are a number of reasons that this may happen. You may be using dark utensils, which will absorb too much heat or the utensils are too large for the product. You can also have a blocked exhaust vent.

SOGGY BAKED GOODS, YUCH!

This is usually caused by the oven not being hot enough or the oven thermostat needing to be reset. The thermostat may have to be recalibrated.

IS UNEVEN COOKING A PROBLEM?

Probably being caused by a defective door gasket or one that is worn and needs to be replaced.

POTS & PANS

GENERAL INFORMATION:

There are a number of materials that are used to manufacture pots and pans, many of which do not really do the job adequately. Remember, the thicker the gauge of the metal, the more uniformly it tends to distribute the heat. The finish on the metal will also affect the efficiency of the cookware. The names of product lines of a number of cookware companies for 2013 have changed, but the materials have, for the most part, remained the same.

POOR PAN, ONLY HAS A 50:50 CHANCE

There is only a 50:50 chance of saving a non-stick pan that has had an oil fire in it. However, there is one possible solution: try making a paste from baking soda and water and applying it to the pot, and then allowing it to remain overnight. Apply mild pressure the next day and hope for the best.

CLEANING NON-STICK POTS

For the most part these plastic coated pots are easy to keep clean. However, they do stain and may over time develop a buildup of grease and oil. If this occurs it will adversely affect the efficiency of the non-stick surface.

To clean the surface, just mix 2 tablespoons of baking soda with ½ cup of white vinegar in 1 cup of water and clean the pot by placing the ingredients into the pot. Place the pot on the range and boil it for about 10 minutes. Wash the pot, then rub vegetable oil on the surface of the plastic coating to re-season it.

I'VE FLIPPED MY LID
If you lose a top knob to a saucepan lid, try placing a screw with the thread side up into the hole then attaching a cork on it.

Poor pot, he has a screw loose!

GET OUT THE HAMMER AND CHISEL
If food gets stuck to a pot, just fill the pan with warm water and place a fabric softener sheet in the water then allow the pan to soak overnight.

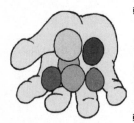

GOOD USE FOR MARBLES
If you want to keep the water level up in your double boiler, just place a few marbles in the bottom of the boiler. When the level gets too low they will start to rattle.

YUCKY ALUMINUM POT
If your aluminum pot is discolored, just fill the pot with water and add 1 tablespoon of cream of tartar and boil for about 20 minutes.

BRASS &COPPER POTS

BRASS AND COPPER POTS FOR EVERYDAY USE
Most brass and copper pots and utensils may have a lacquer coating that should be removed before using the item to hold or cook food in. If the item is just for decorative purposes, than the lacquer coating should not be removed and the item just cleaned with lukewarm water with mild detergent. If the item is to be used with food, than the lacquer must be removed by placing them into a bath of 1 cup of washing soda mixed into 2 gallons of boiling water. After a short time the lacquer will just easily peel off.

Brass and copper will not react with any food and are safe to cook in. Copper is one of the best heat conductors and is preferred by many chefs. Copper pans, however, should only be purchased if they have a liner of tin or stainless steel to be safe, otherwise they may leach metals into the food.

When you cook in glass, remember to reduce the oven temperature by 25^0F.

One of the worst types of cookware is the thin stamped stainless steel pots with a thin copper-coated bottom. The copper coating is approximately 1/50th of an inch in thickness and too thin to distribute the heat efficiently and uniformly.

The *"real"* copper cookware provides excellent heat distribution on the bottom as well as the sides of the pan. The copper, however, needs to be kept clean and if black carbon deposits form to any degree it will affect the heat distribution significantly. These pots are usually lined with tin which must be replaced if it wears out otherwise excess copper may leach into the food causing a health risk. Foods that are high in acid will increase the release of copper. The metal ions in copper will also react with vitamin C and reduce the amount available.

SHINE THAT COPPER
A great cleaner for copper can be made from a paste prepared from white vinegar, salt and all-purpose flour. Another method is to spread catsup on the copper and allow it to remain for 10 minutes before wiping it off.

BRASS AND COPPER CLEANER
The following ingredients are needed:

½	Fresh lemon or
2	Tablespoons of lemon juice
1	Tablespoon of salt

Place the salt in a shallow dish and dip the exposed end of the lemon in the salt and use to scrub the stained area. Another method is to make a paste of lemon juice and salt and use a cloth dipped in the solution to clean the brass or copper surfaces. If the pot has a green spot, use a solution of ammonia and salt to remove the area that has turned green. Gloves should be worn when using ammonia and always try not to breathe the fumes and work in a well-ventilated area.

ENAMELED COOKWARE

While the enamel does resist corrosion, it is still metal coated with a thin layer of enamel. The coating is produced by fusing powdered glass into the metal surface, which is in most instances cast iron. The cookware can chip easily if hit against another object and can even shatter if placed from a very hot range into cold water.

GLASS COOKWARE

Rapid temperature changes may cause the glass to crack or break in many brands. Glass has a very low "heat-flow" efficiency rating and when boiling water is poured into the glass cookware, the actual heat that is transferred from the boiling water to the bottom of the cookware will travel slowly back to the top of the pot.
Because of this, the bottom of the pot will swell and the top of the pot does not expand creating a structural type of stress and a crack is very possible. Corningware® and Pyrex™ in that order would be the only choices for glass cookware, since both will resist most stresses.

ALUMINUM

The majority of cookware sold in the United States in 2012 was aluminum, which is an excellent heat conductor. Current studies report that there is no risk from using this type of cookware unless you are scraping the sides and bottoms of the pots continually, allowing aluminum to be released into the food. Rarely does anyone do this. Excessive intake of aluminum may lead to Alzheimer's disease. Aluminum cookware stains very easily, especially if you are using hard water to cook with. Certain foods, such as potatoes, will also cause the pans to stain easily. If you cook a high-acid content food such as tomatoes, onions, wine or if lemon juice is used in aluminum, it will probably remove some of the stain. If a pan is already stained when the acidic foods are cooked, it may transfer the stain to the food possibly turning your foods a brownish color.

Aluminum pans also tend to warp if they are subjected to rapid temperature changes, especially if they are made of thin gauge aluminum. If they are made of a thick gauge, they will have excellent heat-flow efficiency and will not rust, thus making the thick pan the best pan for use as cookware. Water and cream of tartar will clean aluminum.

Just fill the pan with water and add 1 tablespoon of cream of tartar then boil for 15 minutes before washing. Lime-soaked pickles should never be made in an aluminum pot even though the instructions state that aluminum is recommended. A chemical reaction takes place, which is not healthy.

ALUMINUM POT, BURNED-ON FOOD REMEDY

The following ingredients will be needed:

1   **Tablespoons of baking soda**
¼   **Cup of warm tap water**

Place the warm water over the burned area, then pour the baking soda on top of the water. Allow the solution to sit for 12 hours before cleaning off.

CAST IRON/CARBON STEEL

A Cast Iron/Carbon Steel pot may only supply a small amount of iron in elemental form to your diet, but not enough to be much use nutritionally. Certain acidic foods such as tomato sauce or citrus fruit may absorb some iron but not enough to supply you with adequate daily supplemental levels. Iron does, however, conduct heat fairly well. These are both non-stainless steel, iron-based metals that have a somewhat porous, jagged, surface. These pots need to be *"seasoned."* To accomplish this, you need to rub the cooking surfaces with canola oil and heat it at 300^0F for about 40-50 minutes in the oven, then allow it to cool to room temperature before using. The oil has the ability to cool and seal the pores and even provide a somewhat nonstick surface. Another factor is that when the oil is in the pores, water cannot enter and possibly cause the formation of rust.

These pots should be washed daily using a mild soap and dried immediately. Never use salt to clean the pot, since this may cause rusting. If a cleaner is needed, be sure it is a mild one. Iron pots tend to release metal ions that react with vitamin C and reduce its potency. Cast iron pots can be cleaned by just filling the pot with warm water and dropping in 3 denture-cleaning tablets. Allow the pot to sit for 1 hour. This method will not affect the seasoning. To remove rust, just use sand and vegetable oil and rub lightly.

CAST IRON POTS

To clean burned-on food from a cast iron pot, just mix sand and vegetable oil in the pot and scrub with steel wool. Be sure and re-season afterwards.

COOKING TO RE-SEASON

If you need to re-season your cast iron pot, just use it to fry food. The hot oil will do the job. Best to rub the pot lightly with vegetable oil before putting it away after you clean it.

CAST IRON POT CLEANER

Mix the following ingredients together in a small bowl:

1	Teaspoon of ascorbic acid (vitamin C)
2	Cups of tap water

To remove rust from cast iron pots, just briskly rub the area with a paste made from the ascorbic acid and water. If the rust spot still persists, try allowing the mixture to remain overnight.

CLAY POTS

Remember to always immerse both the top and the bottom in lukewarm water for at least 15 minutes prior to using.

BRRRRRR, IT'S CHILLY IN HERE

Always start to cook in a cold oven and adjust the heat after the cookware is placed into the oven. If sudden changes occur, the cookware may be cracked.

NAUGHTY, NAUGHTY

Never place a clay cooker on top of the range directly on the heat.

GLASS COOKWARE

Best to use a commercial cleaner made specifically for glass cookware. Burned on grease can be removed using ammonia. Never use an abrasive cleaner.

NON-STICK

These include Teflon™ and Silverstone™ and are made of a type of fluorocarbon resin that may be capable of reacting with acidic foods. For 2012 there were a few minor improvements but basically stay with the top brands. If you do chip off a small piece and it gets into the food, don't be concerned it will just pass harmlessly through the body. Never allow any brand of "non-stick" surface pan to heat to a high temperature dry.

The pan may release toxic fumes if heated above 400°F for more than 20 minutes. This could be a serious problem for small pets and birds. Proper vegetable oil seasoning of most pots will produce a non-stick surface without risk and last for months.

These non-stick surfaces are the result of a chemically inert fluorocarbon plastic material being baked on the surface of the cookware or other type of cooking utensil. Silverstone™ is the highest quality of these non-stick items.

The food is actually cooked on jagged peaks that protrude from the bottom, which will not allow food a chance to stick to a smooth surface. The surface is commercially *"seasoned,"* producing the final slick surface. The major contribution of a non-stick surface is that of allowing you to cook without the use of fats, thus reducing the calories of foods that would ordinarily be cooked with fats. The less expensive non-stick cookware usually has a very thin coating and will not last very long with everyday use. With heavy usage and continual cleaning, the coating will eventually wear thin.

TEFLON SURFACE CLEANER

The following ingredients will be needed:

3	Tablespoons of baking soda
3	Lemon slices
1	Cup of hot tap water

Place the baking soda and the lemon slices on the stained area, then add the water to cover. Simmer the pot on low heat until the area appears clean.

STAINLESS STEEL

To be a good heat conductor, they need to have a copper or aluminum bottom. High acid foods cooked in stainless steel may leach out a number of metals into the food, which may include chlorine, iron, and nickel.

I'M ALL STREAKY

If your stainless steel is streaked, just clean with olive oil or club soda.

STAINLESS STEEL POT CLEANER

The following ingredients will be needed:

| 1 | Tablespoon of household ammonia |
| 1 | Pint of cool tap water |

Place the ingredients into a container and mix well, then apply to the stainless steel pot.

MULTI-PLY PANS

The bottoms of these pans usually have three layers. They are constructed with a layer of aluminum between two layers of stainless steel.

NO HOT SPOTS HERE!
Stainless steel does not have the hot spot problem and the heat will be more evenly diffused by the aluminum.

RANGE TOP

GENERAL INFORMATION:
Electric range tops have visible coil burners or may be a *"smooth top"* that has the burners integrated into the glass surface top. The range tops have a coiled wire beneath the burner area, which conducts electricity heating up the burner or surface area.

LIGHT 'EM UP, IF YOU CAN
If burners don't light chances are that the small holes for the gas to go through are plugged and need to be cleaned out with a very fine piece of wire.

SURE IS DARK IN THERE
If the ovens will not light it may be due to a circuit breaker problem, or the oven fuse blew. It could also be due to clock settings being touched by someone not familiar with the oven, or a short in the wiring.

NOT GOOD!
If the burner will not lower and stays on high heat, the switch control is bad and will have to be replaced.

I WORK WHEN I WANT TO
If only one of the burner elements works intermittently you have a worn or bad contact in the receptacle that the element plugs into.

NEVER CLEAN THESE WITH A HARSH CLEANER
The burner top is usually aluminum and should never be cleaned with an oven cleaner. However, with any type of oven cleaner make sure that there is good ventilation or they may burn the lining of your mouth and throat.

NOT VERY ATTRACTIVE
If you wipe down your walls with a mild solution of white vinegar and water occasionally the walls will not attract grease.

GASPING FOR OXYGEN
One of the best fire extinguishers is baking soda. The oxygen supply is cut off and the flame goes right out. Always keep an open box in the cupboard next to the range.

PUT A LID ON IT
A fire in a pan can easily be put out by just placing a lid over the fire, thus cutting off the oxygen supply.

WAX ON, WAX OFF, WAX ON, WAX OFF
To make cleaning up easier, just rub the top of the stove with a car wax occasionally and it will stop the grease from sticking to the top.

REFRIGERATOR

GENERAL INFORMATION:
The refrigerator is one of the most complex appliances in the kitchen. There are a number of thermostatic controls, ice and water dispensers, automatic defrosters, compressors, condensers, metering devices, evaporators and lighting. In normal operation very little ever goes wrong with a refrigerator, however, the more electronics we are presently placing in them, the more problems are occurring.

BAD REFRIGERATOR, BAD REFRIGERATOR
When the refrigerator is not automatically defrosting and frost is showing up, the defrost heater, which is located just underneath the cooling coils, behind the back panel has stopped working and probably needs replacement.

GETTING WARM IN HERE
If the refrigerator is not cooling this is one of the more serious problems and you may have to replace either the compressor or the condenser, or the capillary tubes may have plugged up and are not allowing the refrigerant to flow.

Another solution to the lack of cooling may be that the thermostat has gone bad interrupting the electricity flow to the compressor, which stops the cooling process.

HERE A DROP, THERE A DROP
If you have a leaky water dispenser, you will need to replace the water valve. The water pressure may also be too high.

NICE WATERFALL
If water is running down the back of your refrigerator it means that the drain tube is blocked and the water is unable to get to the tray to be evaporated and needs to be cleaned out. You will have to remove the drain tube and blow air into it to clean it out.

IS YOUR HAIR STANDING ON END?
If you were shocked when touching the refrigerator there is a bare wire touching somewhere and it needs to be found and fixed! Best to unplug it first!

HATE TO TAKE SIDES
The refrigerator is cold and the freezer is not working or vice versa. If one side is cold and the other is not, it means that one of the temperature gauges is stuck or broken and will need to be replaced. May or may not be a job for you depending on the age of the refrigerator.

STOP RACKS FROM RUSTING
Because of the moisture in a refrigerator, the racks may rust. To prevent this, just coat the racks with floor wax.

FROST-FREE DIRT
Frost-free freezers that don't ice up can still get dirty and collect odors. The easiest way to clean them is to use ½ cup of isopropyl alcohol in 1 quarts of lukewarm water. The alcohol has the ability to loosen and icy matter and allow you to sponge away the dirt and odors. You won't even have to dry the surface since the alcohol will evaporate very quickly.

COVER UP
To cover a scratch on your refrigerator or freezer, try using the same color enamel paint. This really works great and will last a long time.

CLEAN LIVING

If you have a problem with mildew forming in your refrigerator, just spray the insides with vegetable oil. Spray the freezer after it has been defrosted and next time it will be easier to defrost.

SLICK IDEA

If you have a problem with ice cube trays sticking to the bottom of the shelf, try placing a piece of waxed paper under the tray. Freezing temperatures do not affect waxed paper.

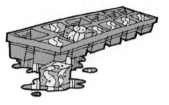

KEEP YOUR FIZZLE IN

The refrigerator is a good place to store many chemicals such as hydrogen peroxide. It will stay active for a longer period of time. Nail polish is another chemical that likes the cold and will go on smoother.

HOW SWEET IT IS!

To eliminate refrigerator odors just leave ½ a lemon in the refrigerator. Old coffee grounds in a cup or a few charcoal briquettes works great too. You can also place a few drops of "real" vanilla on a cotton ball and place it into the refrigerator.

LOST LUSTER

Washing and scrubbing the refrigerator will eventually cause the finish to become dull. To liven it up and bring back the shine, just wash the surface with a mild solution of white vinegar and water. Use a cloth to apply the solution for the best results.

CLEAN GASKETS LAST LONGER

Refrigerator door gaskets need to be cleaned regularly with a borax or baking soda solution only. The stronger detergents may cause the gasket to deteriorate faster.

A CLEAN COIL IS A HEALTHY COIL

If you clean the coils underneath or on the back of the refrigerator you will have a substantial energy saving. Purchase an inexpensive **condenser cleaning brush** and be sure to clean the front plate. The backing, which is usually cardboard, is very important to the running of the refrigerator and keeps air being pulled over the hot condenser keeping it cool. If this cover is gone the compressor will eventually burn out.

TESTING THE DOOR FOR LEAKAGE

The door gasket will wear out eventually and cause cold air to leak out. To test the gasket, place a dollar bill between the door and the gasket and close the door. If you can't remove the bill, the gasket is OK. Another method is to place a 100-watt work light in the refrigerator, close the door, turn off the kitchen light and look for the light around the rubber seal. If you see the light, replace the gasket.

I'M GETTING DIZZY

It is best not to move a refrigerator on its side unless you really have to. The oil may come out of the compressor and run up the cooling lines.

CAN I PLACE A REFRIGERATOR IN THE GARAGE?

Not a problem unless it is a self-defrosting and the garage temperature drops below 50°F. When this occurs the oil may become too thick and cause a compressor failure.

IT'S GETTING CROWDED IN HERE!

Best not to pack your refrigerator too full or it will restrict air circulation and give you poor cooling conditions. Freezers, however, can be packed full with no problem.

PRODUCE DRAWER SECRET

If you have a two produce drawer refrigerator, keep one drawer with ½ -inch of water in the bottom and keep your green, leafy produce in this drawer. It will not hurt the workings of the refrigerator and will keep the greens crispy longer.

UNDER REFRIGERATOR CLEANING

Try using a yardstick with a thin cloth wrapped around it that has been dampened with water and white vinegar. This will work easily under the refrigerator as well as behind it. You may have to move the yardstick around and repeat the process a few times to get the whole area clean.

REFRIGERATOR FRESHENER

The following ingredients will be needed:

	Teaspoon of baking soda
1	Teaspoon of lemon juice
2	Cups of very hot tap water
1	Spray bottle

Place the hot water into a spray bottle then add the ingredients and mix well. A light mist sprayed inside the refrigerator next time you clean it out can remain on the walls and shelves. Allow the mixture to dry for a few minutes. This spray freshener can be used anywhere you need a freshener.

SMALL ELECTRICAL APPLIANCES

BLENDER/MIXMASTER

PAPER MACHE TRICK
Next time you do paper mâché and require a little more detail than the standard strips and paste, try ripping up an old phone book into 1 inch strips then placing strips in your blender. Shred it into tiny little pieces. You will need to add a little water as the pieces get smaller or they will start to float above the blades. Squeeze out the excess water, add some glue or paste to the results and it will become a lot like sticky clay. Be careful not to make it too thick. Remember this is just for extra detail since paper can develop mold.

SAVE THOSE OLD SOAP BARS
Stop throwing out those miniature pieces of soap. Just pulverize them in your blender to create a powder that will be perfect for washing delicate fabrics.

CLEAN ME OR LOSE ME
To keep your blender and mixer working great, be sure and lubricate all moving parts, with a very, light coating of mineral oil (not vegetable oil).

This should be done every 3 months. Before you use a measuring cup to measure a sticky liquid, try spraying the inside with vegetable oil and the liquid will flow more freely.

A CLEAN BLADE IS A HAPPY BLADE
Food tends to get caked in the bottom of the blender around the blades and is difficult to clean off. Just fill the blender halfway with hot water and add 2-3 drops of liquid soap. Turn the blender on high for 30 seconds. The face of the blender is also a difficult area to clean, especially around the buttons. A nailbrush does a really good job.

✓ Make sure that you clean the blender after you use it. The best method is to fill the container ½ full with warm water and a few drops of detergent. Cover it and run it on low speed for about 5 seconds. Clean the base with a sponge but never immerse it.

✓ The blade will easily jam on most blenders and special care must be taken to avoid the problem if the machine is used regularly. Every few weeks you need to take the time to disassemble the container unit (jar bottom, sealing ring and the blade) and then wash the parts in warm, soapy water.

✓ Never use scouring powder or steel wool pads. The glass jar can be washed in the dishwasher, but not the other parts.

✓ Never store food overnight in the glass container.

✓ Never insert utensils into the blender while it is running.

✓ The container must contain at least 1 cup of liquid before adding any ice cubes to the container.

✓ The blades may be very sharp so be careful when the blender is running and when you wash the blades.

✓ If the blender is laboring when processing a heavy load, place it on a higher speed.

✓ If the blender ever stops while it is blending, turn it off immediately or you may cause damage to the motor.

✓ Never place hard frozen cheese in the blender or it may break the blades.

FIXING A JAM-UP

Blade assemblies easily get jammed when you do not use the blender for a period of time. If the unit is disassembled regularly this should not occur. The nut can be unscrewed to disassemble it. If there are tabs around the nut, just bend them out of the way and replace them after you clean the shaft. To free the shaft, gently rap it on a board.

BREAD MACHINE

GOING INTO LABOR

If you hear the motor laboring too much when you are sending something through the machine, allow the machine to rest for 20 seconds before continuing.

HAVING A CRACK-UP

The bread has a crack around the top and sides. The solution is probably that the dough is too dry. Try adding 1-2 tablespoons of liquid. If the machine is programmable, increase the rising time.

I'M TOO CRUSTY

Set the crust control to light or choose the sweet bread setting. You can also remove the bread from the machine 5-10 minutes before the bread cycle ends. Reducing the amount of sugar sometimes helps as well.

A NO, NO

Most bread machines are timed for the use of dry yeast. Compressed fresh yeast should never be used in bread-baking machines.

CRANK UP THE MACHINE

If you use a bread machine and want the finest all-natural flour money can buy, try calling (800) 827-6836. King Arthur Flour is located in Norwich, VT and offers a unique strain of white, whole-wheat flour.

STOP! YOU'RE KILLING ME

Remember that adding extra salt, fresh garlic, cinnamon or sugar to the dough may slow down or even stop yeast action.

GET A HAMMER & CHISEL

If you have a problem with the paddles sticking to the shaft, apply a small amount of vegetable oil before you add any ingredients to eliminate the problem.

OUCH! I HIT MY HEAD

If the top of your bread is raw, it means that the bread has risen too much and hit the top of the bread machine.

SECRETS OF THE BREAD MACHINE

• Use only flour from hard wheat that has not been treated chemically.

- If you use a delayed cycle, never use fresh eggs and fresh milk. Use powdered eggs and milk.
- Never add any ingredients including hot butter unless it cools or you may kill some or all of the yeast.
- Always check the dough after 5-10 minutes in the first kneading cycle. You may need to add more liquid depending on the weather.
- Dry weather may require additional moisture.

- If you are using sweet dough, place the dough in a plastic closed bag in the refrigerator for about 12 hours to allow extra rising time.
- For all heavy flour, such as whole wheat, buckwheat, rye, etc. Use the whole-wheat cycle.
- Any bread that is low in sugar or fat should use a shorter knead time cycle, such as the French bread cycle.
- If the breads are high in fat and sugar or you are using ingredients that burn easily, use the sweet bread cycle.
- To prevent soggy crusts, remove the pan and the bread before the cool down cycle starts and allow the bread to cool for 15-20 minutes.
- The flour used should contain at least 12 grams of protein per cup.
- Dry yeast needs to be stored in an airtight container since it absorbs water easily.
- If you replace whole-wheat flour with ¼ cup of gluten flour it will give the bread better texture.

The flour to liquid ratio should be 2½-3 cups of flour to 1¼ cups of liquid. In the summer (due to higher humidity), however, you will need a little more flour and in the winter use a little less.

- The machine can be opened to check the dough as it is being kneaded, but don't touch the dough.

When using a machine with a delayed cycle, never place fresh ingredients in such as eggs, milk or cheese. Bacteria may have a field day and give everyone food poisoning.

- Always soften butter at room temperature before adding it to the recipe.
- If you use too little yeast, the bread will not rise properly.
- If you use too much yeast, the bread will rise and then collapse.
- Time the completion of the bread to about 1-hour before you will be eating it.
- If the bread is undercooked and somewhat gummy on the inside, the bread did not rise sufficiently.

> The ratio of salt to flour in bread is ½ teaspoon of table salt for each cup of flour used. Some recipes call for less salt, but it would be best to use the ½ to 1 ratio.

- The dough should be pliable around the blades. If it's chunky then it is too dry and additional liquid is necessary.
- For a great, nice sweet loaf, just double the amount of yeast; cut back on the salt; use 1/8 teaspoon of vitamin C powder; use the longest cycle on your machine or remove the dough and form it by hand before baking it in the oven.
- If your bread machine does not have a cooling off cycle, be sure and remove the loaf as soon as it finishes baking.
- High-protein flour will produce high-rising bread.
- Whole grain flours will produce denser, heavier breads.
- If the bread rises, then collapses in the middle, you have used too much liquid.

> Salt is used in bread for flavor and bread can be made without salt if you're on a salt-free diet. Remember, however, that salt inhibits yeast and the dough will rise quicker if you don't use any salt.

- In most cases, bread machine dough is better than hand, kneaded dough.
- Use special instant yeast for sourdough or for sweet breads.
- Most bakers who use bread machines prefer instant yeast, either regular instant or instant gold for most all-purpose baking needs.
- If you add raisins or nuts to the machine, it would be wise to add 1-2 teaspoons of additional flour. This helps the dough *"open up"* more easily.
- Never use rapid-rise yeast in a bread machine.
- Normally 1-2 teaspoons of sugar is added to a 1-pound bread.
- Any kind of sugar can be used in bread machines. That includes corn syrup, molasses, honey and all other syrups.

> The best flour for bread machines is King Arthur's unbleached, all-purpose, high-protein flour.

- A one-pound bread machine can handle 2-3 cups of flour.
- A 1½ -pound bread machine can handle 3-4 cups of flour.
- Almost all bread recipes can be made in a bread machine.
- Whole-wheat flour may not be the greatest flour nutritionally as once thought. The additional fiber tends to cause a percentage of the nutrients obtained from the whole wheat to be flushed out of the body.
- Whole wheat is fine for additional fiber and texture.

Lots of bad bacteria here!

CAN OPENER
DE-GUNKER

To clean your can opener, try running a piece of paper towel through it. This will pick up the grease and some of the gunk.

TIPS FOR PROPER USE & CARE

✓ Be sure and unplug the power cord before removing parts or when cleaning the opener.

✓ Under no circumstances ever immerse the opener in water.

✓ Best to clean the cutting wheel (or the blade) and the shaft regularly. Use hot sudsy water and never use a scouring pad on the opener or any other abrasive cleaner. The cutting wheel is very sharp so be careful.

✓ Some cans that have a heavy rim may cause the opener to stall. If this happens, just grasp the can and move it counterclockwise to assist with the cutting action. If there is a large dent in the rim, try opening the can at the other end or start the cut just after the dent.

✓ Never try to open aerosol cans.

✓ Knifes must be clean and completely dry before trying to sharpen them.

✓ All can openers are designed with built-in protection from overheating. If you are sharpening a number of knives and the motor stops, you have been overworking the sharpener. It should cool down in about 10-15 minutes and you can resume sharpening.

✓ Never sharpen a blade that has a serrated or scalloped edge or it will ruin the knife.

✓ Make sure you remove the housing and clean out any metal fillings if you do a lot of sharpening.

COFFEE MAKER
THE STORY OF COFFEE

The coffee tree is believed to have originated in Central Africa where the natives would grind the coffee cherries into a powder and mix it with animal fat, then roll it into small balls, which they would take with them on long journeys or hunting trips.

Raw coffee is high in protein (until it is diluted with water) and when combined with the fat provided adequate calories and a stimulant. The first factual information relating to the actual drinking of the beverage is by the Arabs in the Middle East.

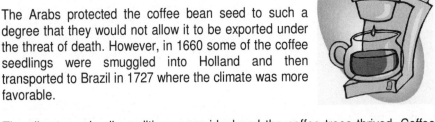

The Arabs protected the coffee bean seed to such a degree that they would not allow it to be exported under the threat of death. However, in 1660 some of the coffee seedlings were smuggled into Holland and then transported to Brazil in 1727 where the climate was more favorable.

The climate and soil conditions were ideal and the coffee trees thrived. Coffee trees need an annual rainfall of over 70 inches of rain with every tree only producing about 2,000 *"coffee cherries"* to make one pound of coffee. The United States consumes 50% of the world's coffee, which amounts to 400 million cups every day. The average coffee drinker drinks 3 cups per day. Eight out of 10 adults drink at least one cup of coffee daily.

Coffee prices have risen dramatically since 1994 due to major frosts in Brazil, which destroyed 1 billion pounds of coffee, about 10% of the world's coffee supply.

ROASTING THE BEANS

Raw coffee beans must be roasted to change an unappetizing seed into a beverage that is desired by 80% of all adult Americans. Roasting shrinks the bean about 15% and increases its size by 50% in a process similar to popcorn popping without the full explosion.

The longer a bean is roasted, the darker it becomes. Darker roasts do not necessarily produce a stronger coffee. The following are the steps the bean is subjected to during the roasting process.

1. The roasting process applies heat to the bean in such a manner as to assure that every surface area of the bean receives the same amount of heat. Even heating is important.
2. The heat is applied at the lowest temperature to perform the roasting and for the shortest period possible.

TYPES OF ROASTS

Light City Roast
The bean is not fully matured with a cinnamon color instead of brown. The flavor is somewhat weak.

Standard City Roast

Most popular roasted bean sold in the United States. It may be sold as the American roast or just the brown roast. The beverage that is brewed is somewhat dull and a little on the flat side.

Full City Roast

Popular roast on the East Coast! It is roasted for a slightly longer period than the standard roast, which produces a darker cup of coffee. The coffee bean is a dark brown with no hint of oil on the surface. Most specialty coffee shops on the East Coast will carry this roast.

Brazilian Roast

No relation to Brazilian coffee. The bean has been roasted a bit longer than the full city roast and the coffee has a darker color and a flavor that starts to taste like a very dark roast.

French Roast

The bean has an oily appearance on the surface and the color is a somewhat dark, golden brown. The coffee has a smooth rich flavor and is easily distinguished from the lighter roasts.

French/Italian Roast

It is also called Spanish or Cuban roast. The bean is roasted darker than the French roast and this coffee makes excellent espresso.

Italian/Espresso Roast

Darkest roast possible without carbonization of the bean or roasting it to death. The bean has a shiny, oily surface and looks black.

I'M SPOUTING COLD WATER INSTEAD OF HOT

Current is not passing through the main heating element or something is blocking the flow. If there is no blockage the main heating element will need to be replaced. This is a job for the repair shop.

PROBLEM SOLVERS FOR DRIP-TYPE

1. **Brewed coffee does not stay warm** – The keep-warm element is not working and either the element or the switch will need to be replaced. If the element has gone bad it is best to just purchase a new coffeemaker.

2. **Coffeemaker is sputtering, leaking or steaming** – It is due to either the rubber tubing that is used to join the heating unit to the reservoir and outlet tube, or the water passage is being blocked by a buildup of mineral deposits. Either replace the rubber tubing or clean out the mineral deposits. Loosen the residue with a needle or toothpick then run through brewing cycle with a mixture of half water and half white vinegar. Then run it through twice with clean water.

3. **Coffeemaker is shocking user** - This is caused by a frayed power cord, an electrically live component grounded to a metal part or leakage current due to faulty insulation. If you think it is leakage current it needs to go to the shop.
4. **Coffeemaker is blowing fuses** – Probably from an electrical overload and the coffeemaker just needs to be on a different outlet. If the problem is in the internal wiring, take the machine in for repair.

TASTE THE DIFFERENCE
Never use soap in a coffee maker. Always clean it with a solution of 50% white vinegar and 50% water. Allow it to run through a complete cycle then refill it with cold water and let it run through another cycle.

ELECTRIC BLANKET

TIPS FOR PROPER CARE & USE

✓ When the blanket is turned on, never fold it, lie on it or place anything on it, especially a pooch.
✓ Never place the control near the radiator or windowsill since it should have a normal airflow.
✓ Never dry clean the blanket, just launder it by hand using lukewarm water and a mild soap (check the label first for washing instructions).
✓ Best to set the temperature to high then lower it to the desired temperature.
✓ All electric blankets are mothproof and do not need to be stored with mothballs.

FOOD PROCESSOR

MAKE DRESSINGS & DIPS
Food processors have the ability for making mayonnaise. In the cap of the feed tube, there's a little tiny hole. If you add the oil through the hole, it flows into the eggs at just the right pace to be absorbed and turned into mayo.

It also works great for making a mustardy or creamy salad dressing like Caesar, pesto, or an oil-based dip.

ZAP IT WITH SOAP
To keep your food processor clean, try running a small amount of liquid dish soap through it then rinsing thoroughly.

IRON

REMOVING WAX FROM LINENS
A steam iron is the perfect tool for lifting melted wax from linens. Just lay a couple of paper towels over the wax and press them with the iron allowing the wax to transfer to the towels as it melts. Be sure and move the towels each time you pick up the iron to prevent re-depositing the wax.

FLUFFING UP CRUSHED CARPET AREAS
If you are moving a piece of furniture and you have compressed carpet areas where the furniture used to be, the cure is simple! Just use a spoon to loosen the fibers up then hold a hot iron over the area and let the steam fluff up the carpet area.

IRON ON VENEER
A steam iron is perfect for applying iron-on veneer edging or patches. The heat from the iron will activate the glue on the veneer then all you have to do is cut the veneer to the size you need, cover it with a piece of heavy paper or a cloth to protect the surface, then press it with your iron to activate the glue.

IRON MORE EFFICIENTLY
Put a layer of aluminum foil under the cover on your ironing board, as the heat from the iron will reflect off of the foil and help you iron twice as fast!

DON'T GET STEAMED UP OVER STEAM
When your steam iron stops steaming it is probably clogged with mineral deposits. The best way to remove the deposits is to place white vinegar in the water reservoir then place the iron flat on an oven rack and plug it in. Set the steam setting and by the time the steam starts coming out, the mineral deposits will have dissolved.

SEASONING YOUR IRON
If your iron is leaving small black marks on the clothes sprinkle a small amount of salt on a piece of paper then run the warm iron over the salt to clean the bottom. This will also eliminate starch buildup on the bottom on an iron. Toothpaste will also remove starch.

WHERE OH WHERE HAVE MY LITTLE HOLES GONE?

If the holes in your iron are all clogged up with hard water deposits, just mix a solution of 1/3rd cup of white vinegar and 1 tablespoon of baking soda and blend well. Pour the solution into the iron and heat the iron just until it starts steaming. Turn it off and empty it then fill it with warm water to rinse very well. Empty and rinse a few more times. Then run the steam on a piece of old rag to remove any residue.

TOASTER

WHAT HAPPENS WHEN YOU TOAST BREAD?

A French chemist first discovered the browning reaction of toast. He discovered that when bread is heated a chemical process takes place that caramelizes the surface sugars and proteins turning the surface brown. The sugar then becomes an indigestible fiber and a percentage of the protein (amino acids) loses their nutritional value. The toast then has more fiber and less protein than a piece of bread that is not toasted.

The protein is actually reduced by about 35%. If you're making your own bread, you can increase the amount of protein by just reducing the amount of regular flour by 2 tablespoons and replacing it with an equal amount of quality soy flour.

HERE YE, HERE YE, TOASTER SHOCKS USER

If you are having a shocking experience with your toaster, the power cord is probably frayed and needs to be replaced. However, if there is a current leakage problem you need to take the toaster to a service center for repair.

MY TOASTER IS BLOWING FUSES

Possible circuit overload and you just need to move the kitchen appliances around to different circuits. However, it may be a bad power cord or even a short circuit inside of the toaster.

GOING DOWN, BUT NO TOAST

Best to see if the power is on, or if the cord or plug is broken. If none of the easy fixes work then it is probably the main switch inside the toaster and it needs to go to the toaster shop.

TOASTING BUT COLOR IS NOT RIGHT

The thermostat is broken or out of adjustment. Check and see if color control is set properly or if it has loosened and needs to be tightened.

The other reason could be that inside of the shell is stained and needs to be cleaned with bicarbonate of soda (best to unplug it first). You may have a broken heating element and if so it goes to the repair shop.

TOAST IS BURNING UP AND WON'T POP UP, BAD TOASTER!

There are a number of possible problems such as the heating element is broken and you just need to buy a new toaster. Or the main switch is broken and can be replaced or just the thermostat is broken or out of adjustment.

TOASTER OVEN

WARM DINNER PLATES

When serving steak, be sure and warm your dinner plates for 5 minutes at 170°F. The toaster oven will warm at a lower temperature than a conventional oven.

YUK! MELTED PLASTIC

When plastic melts on your toaster oven you need to handle the problem immediately. Turn the oven off and allow it to cool then remove the plastic with acetone (nail polish remover). Make sure that the area is well ventilated since the fumes may be hazardous.

WAFFLE IRON

GREAT GRILLED CHEESE

A waffle iron is designed to make a great grilled cheese sandwich. It is better than a frying pan since the waffle iron creates dimples in the bread, which increases its surface area and gives it a nice crunch. The waffle iron also divides it into four pieces, making it convenient for child-sized portions or snacks.

TRASH COMPACTOR

GENERAL INFORMATION:

When you place trash into a compactor, close the door and then press the start button, the motor will start and cause a set of reduction gears, or operates a belt-pulley system, that lowers the ram. The ram exerts high pressure on the trash and flattens it. As soon as the ram reaches its set point, the motor reverses and raises the ram back up to the top.

SQUEEZE HARDER

If the compactor does not work, check the wall socket first then the ground fault interrupter (GFI) and the switches. This includes the door, key or micro switches. Try plugging some other appliance into the socket to be sure it is working.

DAMN RAM

If the ram gets stuck or has gone down and won't come back up, there may be a broken drive belt, chain, or one of the gears has broken.

Grandma broke it again!

MY DRAWERS ARE STUCK

If the ram partially comes back up and the door opens making a vibrating noise, the garbage is not being rammed down evenly and you have a large object that is not being crushed or broken up.

GET OUT THE CROWBAR

When the drawer is hard to open, it means that there is food or an object is stuck and needs cleaning out. If damage has been done then you may have to replace the tracks or rollers.

CLEAN OUT THE ATTIC

You can put any type of garbage into the compactor that you would normally throw into your trashcan in the home.

KILL THOSE BUGS

Use a good bacteria-killing cleaner or a de-greaser to regularly clean the compactor, especially the surface head of the ram. Compactors are breeding grounds for bacteria.

UTENSILS

GREAT, GRATER TIP

Cleaning the grater will never be a problem if you use a small piece of raw potato before trying to wash it out. Sometimes a toothbrush comes in handy, too.

WATER PURIFIER

GENERAL INFORMATION:

There are numerous methods of home water purification systems. If you decide to purchase a system, be sure to investigate the different types and the availability of service for that particular system. A number of units only produce a minimal quantity of pure water, which would not be sufficient for many families while other units do not provide the level of desired filtration.

The most common unit for a home is the reverse-osmosis filter system.

This is one of the most popular units sold in the United States and utilizes a duel sediment filter system. The system is effective in removing up to 90% of the minerals and inorganic matter. The system works by forcing water through a thin membrane, which removes the inorganic metals. Most units only produce a few quarts of pure water a day.

PURE AS THE DRIVEN SNOW
One of the best ways to be sure is to purchase a test kit from a hardware store or check with your local water company.

SCIENCE OF WATER TESTING
This test will determine if any bacteria are present in your drinking water. Sugar is a food supply for bacteria and they will become very active and feed on the sugar and multiply. Place the sugar in a cup of water and place the cup in a sunny location. If the water becomes milky after about 2-3 days the bacteria are very active.

WHERE'S MY REPLACEMENT, I'VE BEEN OVERWORKED
The cartridge filters should be replaced twice a year for the average home.

NOTE: Never hook a reverse-osmosis unit to an icemaker since it does not generate enough water pressure to operate the water inlet valve properly.

OTHER TYPES OF WATER FILTRATION:

Activated Charcoal Filtration Units
A number of the more popular units filter the water through activated charcoal filters. This method is very efficient in filtering out insecticides, pesticides, chlorine, and organic matter. However, this type of filter is not very effective in filtering out bacteria and un-dissolved metals, such as lead, copper, iron and manganese.

Filters need to be checked regularly and changed or the system will be useless. If you do choose this type of unit, be sure it does not contain silver to neutralize bacteria. Silver is not that effective and a percentage may end up in your drinking water.

Chlorination
Systems that utilize chlorine to kill bacteria usually produce water with a somewhat off-taste and odor to the water.

The system must be functioning properly at all times or there is the possibility of the chlorine forming a dangerous element.

Multi-Stage Filtration

These units are one of the most effective and usually recommended above most other units. They utilize a number of filtration methods such as a pre-filter, which will remove iron, rust, dirt particles, and sediments as small as 5 microns. They also have a lead-activated carbon filter, which removes lead and chlorine as well as a carbon block filter to remove chlorine, improve taste, remove odors, and most organic impurities.

Micro-strainers

A good method of filtration, however, it is not able to remove most nitrates and nitrites. It will remove almost all chemicals and bacteria.

Distillation

Distillation is one of the most effective methods of filtration. Water is boiled producing steam, which is then cooled to produce water vapor, which is then trapped. However, certain gasses are not removed through this method. The more efficient distillers utilize activated charcoal filters as an additional organic material remover. Be sure and de-scale your distiller regularly or the efficiency will be greatly reduced.

Aeration

Radon gas is a continuing water contamination problem, especially in the Midwest United States. An aeration filter is the most effective type of filter to resolve this problem. A survey conducted by the Environmental Protection Agency estimated that over 8 million people are at risk from radon contamination.

Ultraviolet Radiation Purifiers

These types of filters are very effective in filtering out bacteria and are normally installed on wells in conjunction with other types of filtration units. This system does require a constant electrical line voltage. It does not remove cyst contamination.

Ozonators

These filters are being used more extensively than ever before and are frequently found on swimming pools built after 1992. They utilize activated oxygen that is capable of purifying and removing bacteria without chlorination. Recommended more for swimming pools rather than drinking water since the system may produce bromate, which may be related to tumors of the kidney.

Carbon Filters

These filters utilize carbon to attract the contaminants, which then adhere to the carbon.

They are useful in removing odors, improving the taste of water, and eliminating organic chemical compounds. Their drawback is that they do not remove heavy metals.

Magnetic Water Conditioners

Since all home appliances or equipment that use water build up scale over a period of time, these conditioners are a must for the homeowner who wishes to protect their investment with a minimum of repairs from water scale damage.

These systems do not affect water purity, however, they condition the water magnetically altering the physical characteristics of water-borne minerals. The mineral will no longer be able to cling to the insides of the water pipes and no scale can be formed.

MISCELLANEOUS KITCHEN TIPS

FILE IT AWAY

If you have a problem with limited space, try using a metal vertical file holder to store your cutting boards and baking sheets. This will keep them in an orderly fashion.

WRAPPING THE REMOTE

Many kitchens have TV's or radios that are operated using a small remote control unit. When working in the kitchen with all sorts of flour and ingredients, it would be best to wrap the control in plastic wrap, which will still allow you to use it while keeping it clean.

RE-USABLE TISSUE BOX

After you use up all the tissues, try using the empty box to hold plastic bags or plastic garbage bags.

TIE THEM IN A KNOT

When you throw away dry cleaner plastic bags or supermarket bags, it would be safer to tie a knot in them so that children can't get into them.

UGLY CUTTING BOARD

If your cutting board is stained, just mix 2 teaspoons of household bleach in 2 quarts of water and scrub till it's clean. Allow it to soak for a while if it is really bad. Be sure and rinse several times with very hot water to get rid of all traces of the bleach.

GRAND OPENING
Next time you need to open a stubborn jar, try using a piece of plastic wrap around the top for a better grip. You can also use a pair of rubber gloves or place the jar, top down, into a dish of hot water to release the vacuum seal.

SERIOUS STICKINESS
To solve the problem of sticky rims from honey or other sticky food, just place a piece of plastic wrap between the lid and the rim before you screw the top back on. Another method is to wipe a small amount of vegetable oil around the rim before you place the lid back on.

BAD FOAM
Using brass or copper utensils in the fryer will react with the oil and create foam.

THE TRAVELING KNIFE
If you have to bring a knife with you and need to travel a distance, just place the knife inside a roll of paper towels. It will accommodate an 8-10" blade without extending out the other end.

KEEPING BRUSHES IN TIP TOP CONDITION
Small brushes used around the kitchen, especially basting brushes are very difficult to get clean. These brushes are usually dipped in oils and sauces and it is almost impossible to remove the stickiness. Just wash the brushes very well in hot liquid soapy water, rinse well and shake dry. Place the brushes with their bristles pointing down into a cup and fill the cup with coarse salt until the bristles are covered.

The salt will draw moisture out of the bristles and keep them dry and in good condition ready for the next use. The salt is easily shaken off.

NO-SKID CUTTING BOARD
Always place a rubber mat under her cutting board so that it wouldn't slip.

AN EYE-OPENER

Small items such as boxes, jars and extract bottles tend to get lost in the cupboard. If you want to see those items easily, just stack 2X4 pieces of lumber that have been cut to the right length to create different heights in the cupboard or cabinet. This will place the items higher than the others.

STOP FALLOUT

Small kitchen utensils such as cake testers, pastry tips and other small items tend to fall through the holes in the silverware container. To avoid this problem, just place a small sponge pot scrubber in the bottom of the container.

PROTECTING THE SINK

When you are washing a heavy pot in the sink and you don't have a protective rubber mat, just place some wooden spoons under the pot to protect the sink from scratches or chips.

WARM THOSE DISHES

Serving meals on warm dishes is really the way to go. All you have to do is place the dinner plates in the dishwasher on the dry cycle to heat the plates. This is especially good when serving steak, since as the steak cools it may get somewhat tough.

NAILING DOWN THE SILVERWARE TRAY

Silverware trays are always moving in the drawer and usually end up in back of the drawer. Purchase some florist's clay and place a small piece under all four corners and in the center of the bottom of the tray to keep the tray in its place.

EXTRA COUNTER SPACE

When you need a little more extra counter space, just open a large drawer and place a cutting board on top of the drawer.

OIL SPILL!

When you spill oil on the kitchen floor it can be quite a mess to clean up. Next time it happens, just sprinkle a thick layer of flour on the area and wait a few minutes for the flour to absorb the oil. Use a dustpan and broom to clean up the flour then spray the area with a degreaser window cleaner and wipe up the balance with paper towels.

GOOD USE FOR KEY HOLDER
Try placing a small plastic key holder on the inside of a cabinet door or on the cupboard wall to hold your measuring cups and spoons.

SAVING THE COUNTERS
Many countertops cannot handle hot pots being placed on them. To save your countertop and to provide you with more space to place hot pots, try using an inverted baking sheet on the counter as a big trivet.

DRIP, DRIP, MESS, MESS
When you have to pour melted butter, hot oil or any liquid that would ordinarily make a mess from a pan by dripping, just pour off the hot liquid and continue turning the pan through one full rotation over the container you are pouring into. Eventually the pan will be right side up again forcing any drippings to end up back in the pan instead of dripping down the sides of the pan.

BURNER PROTECTION
Next time you brown meat or pan fry on the stovetop, try placing inverted aluminum pie plates over the burners to protect them from the splattering grease. The pie tins can easily be cleaned and used.

IN THEIR PLACE
If you need to add ingredients with one hand and use the mixer with the other hand, then the bowl you are working with may have the tendency to move around. If you want to stabilize the bowl make a circle with a damp kitchen towel and place it under the bowl.

SPLATTER ELIMINATOR
When using a hand-held mixer it tends to make a mess, especially when you are whipping cream. To eliminate the problem, just place a piece of parchment paper over the bowl with an extra inch or so around the bowl and make two holes in the center of the paper. Feed the mixing blades through the holes and mix away.

REDUCING SPLATTER
When you are frying, try placing a large wire-mesh strainer over the pan to stop the splatter. This is especially handy if you have the different sizes to fit over a variety of pans.

SHARPENING THE VEGETABLE PEELER

You can use a paring knife to sharpen your vegetable peeler. Scrape the backside (not the cutting blade) between the blades of the vegetable peeler to remove the burrs. Then scrape the front side of the vegetable peeler using the back tip of the knife.

EASY DOES IT

A nick on the rim of a glass can be easily removed with an emery board. Don't use a nail file or sandpaper. They are too coarse and will scratch the glass and ruin it.

SOAP WORKS AS WELL

If you are having problems with sticky drawers, try rubbing a candle along the tops of the runners.

BAD SCOURING POWDER, BAD!

Scouring powder will scratch the surface of most appliances. Best to use small amount of baking powder mixed with water.

ODOR EATERS

A number of foods are capable of removing odors. Vanilla extract placed in a bottle top in the refrigerator will remove odors, while dry mustard is commonly used to eliminate onion odors from hands and cutting boards. Other solutions include leaving a small cup of used coffee grounds on 2 shelves.

An excellent method of removing odors from the kitchen is to keep a few washed charcoal briquettes in a shallow dish on top of the refrigerator. Frying a small amount of cinnamon will chase all odors from the home.

GETTING IN SHAPE

Butcher blocks will not only harbor bacteria deep down in the cracks but are also difficult to clean. They need to be washed with a mild detergent, then dried thoroughly and covered with a light layer of salt to draw any moisture out that may have gotten into the crevices. The wood can then be treated with a very light coating of mineral oil. Make sure it is only a light coating since mineral oil may affect the potency of a number of vitamins in fruits and vegetables.

TIME SAVER

Keeping a grater clean so that you can continue to work and still grate a number of different foods is an old chef's secret. A chef will always grate the softest items first then grate the firmer ones.

NOT A CRACK-UP
A trick used by antique dealers to remove hairline cracks on china plates or cups is to simmer the cup in milk for 45 minutes. Depending on the size of the crack the protein (casein) in the milk will fill in the crack.

NOT A FASHION STATEMENT
A great idea used by professional cooks worldwide is to keep a small plastic baggie handy, in case you have both hands in a food dish or dough and need to answer the telephone.

GLUE REMOVER
The glue on any type of contact paper will easily melt by running a warm iron over it or using a hair dryer on high heat.

MEASURING UP
If you want to use the fewest utensils possible, first measure out all the dry ingredients then the wet ingredients. By doing this you can use the measuring spoons or cups for double-duty.

SLIPPERY SUBJECT
When preparing a pan that needs to be greased, try saving your salt-free butter wrappers or use a fresh piece of bread. Remember salt butter wrappers may cause foods to stick.

ONE FOR THE GRIPPER
If your drinking glasses are slick, try placing a wide rubber band on them so that the children will get a better grip.

HANDLE ME CAREFULLY
Refrigerator handles are a prime source of bacteria, lurking and waiting to cause a problem. It is best to clean the handle everyday (at least once).

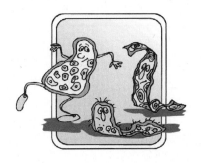

KEEP IT A BIT CHILLY

Check the temperature in the refrigerator at least every other month to be sure that it is holding 40^0F and the freezer is at 0^0F. Best to be safe than sorry!

MOVE OVER, GIVE ME ROOM TO BREATHE

Remember for your refrigerator to be efficient the food you store has to have room to breathe. Cool air must be able to circulate around the food freely.

CHAPTER 2

BATHROOM

BATHTUB

HAVING A CRACK-UP

If you are getting cracks in the caulking around the bathtub, the cracks are probably from settling. To fix the problem, remove the cracked old caulking with a putty knife being careful not to damage the porcelain or tile around the tub. Do not use the strip caulking  that comes in a roll. This is very difficult to install. Place in new waterproof caulking then allow it to dry overnight before using the tub. It is best to purchase a bead cleanup tool to help complete the job.

BOY, AM I DISCOLORED!

Most discolorations are from hard water stains. Try covering the bathtub with paper towels that have been soaked in full strength white vinegar. Remove the towels after 2 hours and you will be amazed at the result.

GETTING GLAZED

If your bathtub needs to be re-glazed it would be best not to purchase a kit from the store, as they do not hold up well. Call a professional re-finisher.

THERE'S A FUNGUS AMONG US

To remove mold and mildew from around the tub, I recommend using a solution of one cup of bleach to three cups of water.

If this does not work well increase the bleach until it does the job. Wear rubber gloves and rinse the area well before using the bathtub.

KEEP IT ON YOUR HEAD!
If you get hair coloring stains on a porcelain tub and on the tile, just use a mild solution of bleach and water and allow it to remain for a while before washing it off.

TOO MUCH MOOD
If you want to get burnt marks from a candle off a cultured marble tub, just sand it off with a fine, then an ultra-fine, piece of sandpaper. After sanding use a polishing compound and make sure that the surface is wet while you are sanding.

ARE THE EXPENSIVE BATHTUB CLEANERS REALLY NECESSARY?

Most bathtub cleaners advertise that they contain powerful disinfectants that will kill bacteria as well as cleaning off the soap scum and dirt residues. While they do contain disinfectants, the bacteria killing action only lasts for about 3-4 hours and then the bacteria comes right back.

RUST IN THE BATHTUB
Rust stains may appear in metal tubs and can be cleaned with a paste prepared from borax powder and lemon juice. If this fails, try a commercial preparation.

CABINETS

HERE A SPOT, THERE A SPOT
To solve the problem of water spotting on a wood surface in the bathroom, check with your local hardware store. They have a product that can be applied on the wood surface that will provide a protective shield.

FAUCETS

I'VE BEEN EXPOSED
To stop the damage to metal faucets from exposure to moisture, paint the bathroom fixtures with a special clear epoxy paint found in most hardware stores.

GO RENT A JACKHAMMER
To remove hard water residue from faucets, you will need to use a non-acid bathroom cleaner, which will not damage the faucets.

SIMPLE SOLUTION
To remove the handles from the faucets, just pop out the decorative insert with a thin screwdriver point.

STEP BY STEP METHOD OF CHANGING A SINK FAUCET

* ❖ Turn off the water supply under the sink or at the main water supply to the house.
* ❖ Turn both spigots on to release any water leftover in the lines.
* ❖ Remove the water lines running to the faucets using a crescent wrench.
* ❖ Use pliers to remove the two plastic nuts holding the faucets on.
* ❖ Remove the faucets and use a scraper to remove any residue on the sink area.
* ❖ Roll some plumbers putty into a long roll, about the thickness of a pencil. Place the putty on the sink in the shape of the new faucet.
* ❖ Place the new faucet on the putty and press down to seal the faucet to the sink.
* ❖ Replace the plastic nuts under the sink that came with the new faucet.
* ❖ Place the new plastic flexible water lines back on and do not over tighten.
* ❖ Remove any excess putty.
* ❖ Unscrew the aerator and open both spigots before turning the water back on. Any debris will then be released before you put the aerators back on.

DON'T MESS UP THE CHROME
Wrenches have teeth that will damage chrome pipes and scratch them. Before you use them on a chrome pipe, wrap two layers of black plastic electrical tape around the jaws.

FLOOR

BLACK TILE A NO, NO
The secret to getting watermarks and scratches off black tile is to use a marble polish and a non-acid cleaner for the marks.

THE BEST FLOORING
Use either tile flooring or Pergo™ flooring.

HAIR DRYER

15 UNUSUAL USES...

1. It can quickly set icing on a cake, the air and heat of a hair dryer can speed up the process.
2. If your cake is sticking to the cake pan, use your hair dryer on the bottom of the pan then invert it, it should drop right out.
3. You can use a hair dryer on an ice carton to soften ice cream for easy scooping.
4. Freezer defrosting is easy with a hair dryer (Be careful of puddles of water and the dryer.)
5. Automatic ice-makers can get jammed with frozen ice; relieve that with a long blast of hot air.
6. Remove contact paper from shelves by heating it with the hair dryer and gently working the edges up. It also works for bumper stickers and other sticky things.
7. Use a hair dryer to dust hard-to-dust items.
8. Heat crayon marks until softened then scrub with hot water and detergent.
9. Old photo albums with magnetic pages can get stuck, just unstick them with a blast from the hair dryer.
10. Spot-iron wrinkles by lightly dampening the area and then heating the wrinkles with your dryer.
11. Wet boots, shoes, and sneakers can smell really bad if left to dry slowly. To alleviate the problem, just dry them with your hair dryer.
12. Winter can bring frozen windows and locks, just thaw them with a hair dryer.
13. Window screens collecting dust and pollen? Blow it back to where it came from!
14. Removing bandages can hurt more than the wound; just soften the adhesive with a hair dryer first to ease the discomfort.
15. If you have trouble keeping hot compress hot, just keep your hair dryer by you and reheat as necessary.

DOING THE TWIST
You can keep hair dryer cords from twisting up by using ponytail holders on them.

CAN'T BREATHE
If the motor keeps overheating and turning the dryer off, check the exhaust area and clean out the dust that has accumulated blocking the airflow.

SHOWER

GENERAL INFORMATION:

One of the major problems with showerheads are clogging from hard water deposits and using too much water. Most new showerheads only use 2.5 gallons per minute compared to as much as 5 gallons per minute in older heads. Replacing the old head can save as much as $60-$150 on your water bill, and energy savings depending whether it is gas or electric. You will save about 1200 gallons per year in the average home.

COUGH, COUGH, I'M ALL CLOGGED UP
If the showerhead is clogged with hard water deposits, you will need to remove the head and soak it in white vinegar overnight in a plastic bag or just place the vinegar in the bag and attach it to the shower head with rubber bands. If the holes are clogged badly, you may need to use a strong piece of thin wire and push it through each hole.

CLEANSER FOR SHOWER NOZZLE RESIDUE
The following ingredients will be needed:

1	**Cup of white vinegar**
1	**Teaspoon of lemon juice**
1	**Cup of very hot water**
1	**Spray bottle**

Place all the ingredients into a small bowl and mix well, then sponge on the showerhead and clean with an old toothbrush.

THE WEEPING SHOWER DOOR
If the shower door tracks are not draining properly, the weep holes may be clogged. Use a pipe cleaner to clean them out.

POLISH THOSE SHOWER DOORS

If the soap and scum buildup is really bad you will have to use full strength white vinegar. After you clean the doors, wipe them down with furniture polish that contains lemon oil. If the film is really heavy, use a steel wool pad soaked in dishwasher liquid and the glass will sparkle.

WHITE CRUD

Soap buildup on shower doors can be eliminated if you squeegee off the door after every shower.

INSECURITY

If your shower rod becomes loose, you should be able to tighten it by adjusting the tension by turning the ends. If that doesn't work, buy a new rod, it's probably worn out!

A LITTLE DRIP WON'T DO YA

If your showerhead drips, then the head is dirty or defective and needs cleaning or replacement.

A SHARP IDEA

The best way to clean a marble shower, if you have a bad area, is with a razor blade providing it is wet.

CLEANING FIBERGLASS

It needs to be cleaned regularly with a disinfectant and a white nylon scrub sponge.

SINK

WHOOOOOPS

Whenever you work in or around the bathroom sink or really any sink, be sure and place the drain in the closed position. Small parts and tools may fall into the drain and be a pain to retrieve.

Really important! Make sure to close the drain when putting on a piece of jewelry over the sink.

SLOW STREAM, A PROBLEM?

If the water flow from the tap is too slow, it is usually caused by the aerator at the tip of the faucet being clogged. Unscrew the aerator and clean the screen with an old toothbrush then rinse thoroughly.

AIR GOT IN THE LINE

If water is splattering out of the tap, there is probably air in the lines. Just open all faucets in the home for five minutes to release the trapped air.

BOY, AM I LOOSE

If you have a water leak under the sink it is usually caused by loose plumbing fittings that just need to be tightened.

NO MORE STAINLESS SINK STAINS

In order to remove spots from a stainless steel sink, all you have to do is rub the spot with automobile rubbing compound. It will also leave a thin layer of wax to spot future spotting.

DON'T BE ABRASIVE

Never clean a stainless steel sink with any type of abrasive cleaner or steel wool. The best thing to use to clean the sink is baking soda. Vinegar will remove water spots.

STEAM ROOMS

GENERAL INFORMATION:

Steam rooms are usually made from tile, acrylic or glass enclosures. The humidity is 100% and the room is filled with steam.

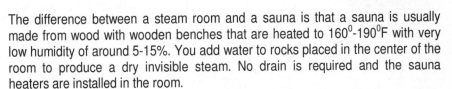

The temperature can get between 98^0-118^0F. A drain is required as well as a gasket around an airtight door system. The steam generator is installed outside and usually very close to the room. After the room has been used, it should be allowed to air out or dried, otherwise mold will form very quickly.

The difference between a steam room and a sauna is that a sauna is usually made from wood with wooden benches that are heated to 160^0-190^0F with very low humidity of around 5-15%. You add water to rocks placed in the center of the room to produce a dry invisible steam. No drain is required and the sauna heaters are installed in the room.

SEEING THE LIGHT

Mirrors can be brightened by rubbing them with a cloth dampened with alcohol. Alcohol will remove a thin film of oil that is left from cleaning agents.

A WASTE OF A COOL ONE
If you wish to "frost" a bathroom window use a solution of 1 cup of "Lite" beer mixed in 4 tablespoons of Epsom salts then paint the mixture on the window, it will wash off easily.

TILE COUNTER

GENERAL INFORMATION:
One of the problems with tile is the buildup of soap scum. A small amount of white vinegar or lemon juice on a cloth will solve the problem.

A POOR SETTLEMENT
When grout cracks appear between the tiles it is usually caused by settlement or shrinkage and can only be fixed by removing the old grout and re-grouting.

HERE YE, HERE YE, SOAP STAINS GROUT
Grout stains are usually caused by moisture and soap stains. It could be stopped by wiping down the tile after bathing or turning on an exhaust fan.

HOW LOOSE I AM..............
If the soap dish loosens up there is no way to tighten it without removing it and re-installing it. Make sure you caulk it well!

TOILET

GENERAL INFORMATION:
Most toilet problems are simple to repair and should be easy for you to tackle. Any replacement parts are available at any hardware store and the parts that may need replacement are easily accessible.

Toilets are made of either porcelain or ceramic and are acid resistant, which is good since most of the commercial toilet cleaners contain either an acid or ingredients that turn into acid when they come into contact with water.

Needless to say if you swallow most commercial toilet cleaners it will most likely lead to your demise in very short order. If you use one of the following formulas and there is still a ring that persists, try using a pumice bar to remove the ring. Just dampen the bar and gently rub the surface to avoid scratching it. A **"00"** piece of sandpaper will also do the trick.

MAKING TOILET BOWL CLEANER

The following ingredients will be needed:

1	**Cup of hydrogen peroxide**
1	**Tablespoon of household ammonia**
2	**Quarts of warm tap water**

Place all the ingredients into a bucket and mix well. You will need about 1 quart of the solution for each toilet. Pour the solution in the toilet and allow it to remain for about 30-40 minutes before you scrub and flush. If this is done weekly, residues and discoloration should not occur. ***Store properly – POISON.***

INEXPENSIVE TOILET BOWL CLEANER

The following ingredients will be needed:

1	**Cup of white vinegar**

Place the vinegar into the toilet and allow it to remain for 8-10 hours then scrub.

BRRRRRRRRRR, I NEED A WRAP

Moisture on the toilet tank is caused from the tank sweating because of the cold water in the tank coming into contact with the warm tank. This causes condensation, which can run on the floor or get on the walls. To solve the problem, just purchase a terrycloth tank cover and it will absorb the moisture. You can also install a mixing valve to warm the water as it enters the tank.

REMOVING THE SEAT OF THE PROBLEM

If you have a problem removing a toilet seat with corroded bolts you will need to place some penetrating oil on them and allow it to remain overnight or saw the bolts off with a hacksaw. When placing the new bolts on use a small amount of petroleum jelly on the new bolts.

THE TOILET'S RUNNING AWAY

The water level in the tank may be too high and the float arm stem may need to be adjusted downward. Lift the cover of the tank and remove it. Pull the float upwards, but do it gently. If the water shuts off then you will have to adjust the float position. This should be attempted before attempting to change or replace the rod. Turn the water supply off and adjust the float position by bending the rod until it is ½ inch lower. Then turn on the water and flush the tank. Only half the float should be covered by water.

MY TOILET RUNNETH OVER

If the toilet is backing up and overflowing there is probably an obstruction in the line and the toilet needs plunging. Turn off the water using the water valve at the bottom of the toilet to stop the flow of water. Then plunge away and good luck. Hopefully, it's not one of the kid's toys that stuck.

SOUNDS SCARY IN THERE
When the toilet starts to make strange gurgling and dripping sounds, the flapper is probably warped and needs to be replaced.

FILLER-UP
If the toilet bowl will not fill properly there is usually a simple solution. Either the water supply has been turned off or the strap to the flapper may be broken or has come loose.

WATER LEVEL IS NOT ON THE LEVEL
The water level of the toilet seems lower than other toilets I have visited. You probably have a 1.6 toilet that is designed to use less water.

In this type of toilet, the amount of water is determined by the size of the bowl. A low water level can also be caused by a toilet that is poorly vented or has a clogged vent.

PHEEEEW, SKUNK ALERT
When your toilet starts to smell like a sewer it may be caused by a low water level in the toilet bowl allowing sewer gas from the system to enter. A loose toilet can also release the sewer gas.

THERE ARE GHOSTS IN MY BATHROOM
If the toilet flushes and no one is in the bathroom, this is referred to as "phantom flush" and usually caused by the design of the refill valve. What it is telling you is that your toilet has a leak in the flush valve. The only other cause is if the refill tube is not cut to the proper length.

POP, POP, FIZZ, FIZZ ALKA SELTZER WILL CLEAN TOILETS

Just drop 2-3 Alka-Seltzer™ tablets in your toilet and wait 20 minutes before scrubbing with a toilet brush. Between the citric acid and the bubbles it will work great.

WHAT DO LARGE TOILET CLEANING TABLETS REALLY DO?

The bowl-cleaning tablets that are placed into the toilet tank are not going to clean your toilet. They are only designed to slow down the process of hard-water buildup, which contains imbedded dirt and debris. They contain a strong chlorine bleach compound or quaternary ammonium chloride. Both are strong disinfectants and have good cleaning properties. Some products, however, may be so strong that they will cause scaling of any metal surface in the tank and may cause the toilet to clog up.

METHOD OF REMOVING A TOILET

1. Best to empty the toilet first! Turn off the water supply to the toilet and then flush the toilet and hold down the handle to empty it. Sponge out any water that is left in the tank.
2. Use an adjustable wrench and disconnect the water supply line from the shut-off valves. Keep a towel handy since there may be some water left in the line.
3. Remove the tank, making the toilet bowl lighter to remove and reducing the risk of cracking the toilet or bowl. This is an important step if you are only removing it and then reinstalling it to repair a leak around the base or putting in a new floor.
4. Remove the two bolts at the bottom of the tank that secure it to the bowl. Inside the tank you will need a screwdriver in the head of the bolt and a pair of tongue and groove pliers to hold the nut on the outside of the tank to remove the bolt.
5. Remove the decorative plastic or ceramic caps that are covering the two nuts that are securing the toilet base to the floor.
6. Remove any plumber's putty from around the nuts and base with a plastic scraper or even an old credit card, and remove the nuts. If you see any corrosion around or on the nuts, be sure and apply penetrating oil to soften the corrosion. Hopefully, you won't have to cut the bolts off.
7. Rock the toilet back and forth to loosen and break the seal. If you are alone, straddle the toilet and bend your knees when removing the base.
8. Put on the rubber gloves. You will need to keep the sewer fumes from entering the house by placing a big rag with a string tied to it down the hole. The string is to help you remove the rag if it gets too far down the drain.

9. Use a plastic putty knife and remove the wax residue from around the drain opening. If you plan on reinstalling the old toilet, be sure and clean the wax from the flange (underside of toilet) using the plastic scraper.

METHOD OF INSTALLING A TOILET

1. First you will need to pack plumber's putty around the old or new bolts to keep them in an upright position. This step will not be necessary if they have a plastic stabilizer.
2. Place the toilet bowl on its side and press a new wax ring on the horn. Only use just enough pressure for the ring to stick.

3. Pull on the string and remove the rag from the drainpipe, lift the toilet bowl and place it into position with the holes fitting on the bolts.

4. After you replace the toilet, rock it back and forth carefully while applying a small amount of downward pressure on the base in order to seal the bowl and the wax ring. Sit on the toilet to seat it solidly.

5. Now you need to install the washers and floor bolt nuts and tighten them by hand. Then you need to gently tighten them with an adjustable wrench, alternating from side to side, tightening the base a little at a time. If you over tighten the bolts it will crack the base.
6. Connect the supply line to the water inlet pipe under the tank. Best to replace the line with a new flexible braided steel line.
7. If the old tank was removed from the old toilet and you are going to reinstall it, be sure and place new rubber washers under the tank bolt heads before you secure the tank to the bowl.
8. Now connect the supply line to the shut-off valve and just hand-tighten. Check for leaks by turning the water on and allowing the tank to fill with water. Then flush a few times. Tighten any connections if necessary.
9. Providing that there are no leaks, run a bead of silicone caulk around the base to keep mop water from going under the toilet.

OUCH! YOU'RE SCRATCHING ME

Some toilet brushes have metal rims holding the bristles used to scrub the toilet. Be sure and replace the brush as soon as you start seeing wear on the bristles or the metal will scratch the porcelain and it will be a bear to clean off.

CHAPTER 3

FAMILY/TV ROOM

FISH TANK

The following are some of the answers to questions that I feel might be asked.

TAKE THE TEMPERATURE
The average temperature of a tropical aquarium will depend on the type of fish that are placed in the tank. It will also depend on what part of the world the fish comes from.

THE STRAIGHT INFORMATION
Substrate is very important in a fish tank! If you are using salt water, use a carbonate substrate designed specifically for salt water.

SCRUB-A-DUB-DUB
A question that I frequently get asked is if you have to give a new fish a bath before adding it into your fish tank? A bath does not remove any parasites if they are present. It is best to quarantine the fish in a separate tank for a period of time to be sure they are healthy.

IT'S GETTING DARK IN HERE
If you are setting up a new tank, only add one fish and plants to begin the tank cycle. The water should clear up in two weeks. If it doesn't, stop feeding the fish for three days and change 20% of the water.

BEWARE OF THE GIANT OSCAR

If fed properly and well, Oscars will grow at about one inch per month until they reach several inches in length. They need at least a 55-gallon tank to do really well.

BROWN-OUT

To get rid of brown algae, the tank probably needs more light. If you have a fluorescent bulb it should be changed every 6 months or it will lose its effectiveness.

IS IT SUPPOSED TO BE GREEN?

Pea-green algae is a problem. Just reduce the amount of fish food and add live plants. The plants will compete with the algae for nutrients that are in the water.

KEEP A LID ON IT

It is best to always keep a lid on the aquarium so that objects cannot accidentally fall in or the cat can't get to the fish. Some fish are even jumpers and can end up on the floor.

THERE'S AN ALGAE AMONGST US

Algae of all types usually grow because of too high a nutrient content in the water. If the problem persists, add some plecos and they will eat the algae. Algae can also grow faster if the tank is placed in direct sunlight for too long a period.

HUMMMMMMMMMMMMMM

The aquarium motor should be very quiet and the hum barely noticeable. If the hum starts to get louder than normal, it would be best to have a spare motor handy since it may be ready to go bad.

TANKS MUST BE SEASONED
Never purchase the tank and the fish at the same time. The tank should be set up and allowed to season for a few days before adding any fish. You need to be sure everything is working properly, especially the filters, heater, etc.

THAT'S AN EYE-OPENER
Fish don't close their eyes because they don't have eyelids.

AND AWAY WE GO..........................

It is not necessary to leave a light on in the house if you go away on vacation. If you have a planted tank, the light should be on a timer. If there are no plants the light can remain off as long as you do not have baby fish.

INCHING ALONG!
There is an old saying that if you have a 25-gallon tank, you should keep 25 inches of fish in the tank. However, the one-inch per rule is not a good rule and should not be adhered to. Certain species of fish need more water than others.

GET RID OF CHLORINE
Be sure and always eliminate the chlorine in the water before adding it to the fish tank. Just allow the water to remain at room temperature for 3-4 hours and the chlorine will dissipate into the air. Commercial preparations are available if you don't want to wait.

CAREFUL WHAT YOU ADD
Many fish are killed every year by people placing items into the tank that they think looks pretty. Shells you buy from the dime store or the ones you pick up on the beach may be contaminated with parasites, bacteria or lacquer and kill the fish. Shells from the beach need to be thoroughly cleaned and sterilized before being added to a tank.

CLEANING A FISH TANK
Place some non-iodized salt on a sponge and clean away. Make sure that the salt is not iodized... or no more fish. Make sure that the fish are out of the tank and the tank is rinsed well.

SAVE THE OLD WATER
Don't throw the old water out when you are changing the water in the fish tank. Use the water to water your houseplants since it is an excellent fertilizer.

FLOORING

REPAIR A LOOSE VINYL TILE
Vinyl floor tiles can sometimes slip out of place. If this happens just cover the tile with aluminum foil, then run a hot iron back and forth over the area. The heat will re-activate the tile adhesive. Then just stack a couple of heavy books on top to hold the repair down for a couple of hours. Safety tip: Remember aluminum foil can get hot so don't get burned.

FIX BROKEN OR DAMAGED VINYL
A steam iron can also be used to help remove a broken one. The same principle applies: using heat to reactive the glue. Lay the aluminum foil over the tile and run the iron over it to loosen the adhesive. Then use a wide putty knife to remove the tile. A little white vinegar will remove any adhesive residue then just replace with a new tile.

HOW ABOUT A RAINBOW
Light color flooring, whether wood or vinyl, will reflect light and the room will not need as much lighting. A darker surface floor will reflect very little light, meaning that more lighting will be required.

MAKING A ROOM LOOK LARGER
Furnish the room with lighter color furnishings.

LIGHTING

FLOURESCENT LIGHT PROBLEM SOLVER

Tube flickers or partially lights
- Rotate the tube and make sure that it is seated properly in the sockets.
- Replace both the tube and starter if the tube is discolored or if the pins are bent or broken. Starters are only found in older units.
- Replace the ballast if it is not more expensive than replacing the entire unit. In many instances the ballast costs as much as the entire unit.

Tube will not light
- Be sure that the wall switch is working properly and repair if needed.
- The tube may not be seated properly and may just need to be rotated a little.

- If the tube is discolored or if any of the pins are bent or broken, it is best to replace the tube and starter to be on the safe side.
- Replace the sockets if they appear to be chipped or if the tube does not seat properly.
- Replace the ballast or the entire fixture depending on the cost.

Loud humming noise and black substance around ballast
- Replace the ballast or the entire fixture depending on the cost.

WHAT IS BALLAST?
Ballast is a special transformer that regulates the flow of 120-volt household current to the sockets. The sockets then transfer the power to the metal pins that extend into the tube.

SOMETHING WEIRD GOING ON
If the florescent lights are getting dark on the ends, just reverse the ends to extend their life.

COUGH, COUGH
When fluorescent lights seem to getting darker it usually means that the bulbs have not been cleaned and dusted regularly.

SAVING MOOLAH
New low wattage light bulbs are excellent! They produce high quality light and reduce the heat entering the room. This will make it easier to cool a room in the hot summers.

FORGET THE GROW LIGHTS
The new fluorescent light bulbs that have become popular in the last 2-3 years will work just as well. They are less expensive to operate and will last about 10,000 hours. These new lights provide the blue end of the light spectrum, which is what the plants desire.

SLIDING GLASS DOORS

LITTLE DAMP IN HERE
Condensation should not be found between window and sliding glass door pane. If you know the manufacturer, they should be contacted since the panes should be sealed for life. There is no way to repair the problem.

TRACK DOWN THE PROBLEM
If the door tracks have become worn and not working well it would be best to replace the entire door. The tracks are usually an integral part of the door and the cost would be prohibitive to try and fix only the tracks.

PUSH HARDER IF YOU DARE
If the doors are too hard to push, first try and adjust the rollers. The adjustments are either on the sides of the door or on the bottom rail of the door. You may have to remove the door and clean the track. Silicone spray may also work.

DAMN LATCH
The mechanism needs an adjustment.

HINTS TO KEEP THE SLIDING DOOR SLIDING EASILY

> Occasionally clean the track. Dirt and debris will build up inside the track and cause a problem. Use your vacuum crevice tool to get inside the groove.
> The track should also be cleaned using a cup of white vinegar in a bucket of soapy water. Scrub the track well and use a toothbrush to get into the small cracks if necessary.
> Adjust the roller height, which may get loose and move over time. The adjusting screw on a wood door is on the inside bottom edge. On aluminum doors you can find it on the inside vertical edge. It should only take a few turns to adjust it.
> For security, cut a piece of ½ inch round doweling and place it in the door track when you are away from home.

STEREOS

These are complex pieces of equipment that do need a certain amount of care to keep them working at optimal levels. The equipment is too complicated to repair once it breaks down, however there are a few prevention tips that will keep them working more efficiently.

- ❖ Be sure and keep the components clean.
- ❖ Oxidation of the electrical contacts on receivers is one of the most common problems. Clean the contacts with a contact cleaner including all jack inputs and speaker terminals.
- ❖ If you are getting a hum from the speakers, make sure that all connections are tight and that the grounding wire is connected to the right terminal. You can also hook the grounding wire to the screw in the plate of an electrical outlet. All components should be plugged into their own outlet.
- ❖ Multiple outlet boxes will sometimes cause a hum if there are too many units plugged into them.
- ❖ If the speaker is not working and the connections are clean and tight then check the speaker wires and possibly replace them. If the run is very long to the speakers, the wires need to be thicker.

TELEVISION SETS

A NO, NO

Be sure and never use an aerosol spray or a liquid cleaner on a TV screen. Be sure and unplug the set when cleaning the screen. It is best to use an anti-static dryer sheet.

BAD BIRD!

One of the more frequent problems with reception is from birds landing on a TV antenna and putting it out of line.

WOOD FURNITURE

SCRATCHES AND HOW TO REMOVE THEM

- **Dark Wood** – Try filling the scratches with shoe polish that matches the lightest shade of the finish. You can also rub a walnut in the direction of the scratch over the scratch.
- **Cherry Wood** – Try using cordovan or any reddish shoe polish that comes close to matching the wood color.
- **Oak Wood** – Use a tan or natural shoe polish or iodine that has been diluted 50% with denatured alcohol.

INSTANT COFFEE SCRATCH REMOVER
Prepare a thick paste of instant coffee and water then rub it into small scratches and nicks to hide them.

OAK FURNITURE REVIVER

The following ingredients will be needed:

½   **Cup of soda ash**
1   **Quart of warm tap water**

Place the ingredients into a small bucket and mix well, then clean the furniture with a soft bristle brush and rinse with cool water. You need to dry with a clean, dry, soft-cloth.

HOW TO REMOVE WATER DAMAGE

- Moisten a clean cloth with denatured alcohol or turpentine and try rubbing the spot out lightly.
- Mix a small amount of baking power with water and make a paste. Rub the mixture on the stained area in the direction of the wood grain very lightly.
- If all else fails, try rubbing the area hard with a solution of rottenstone and mineral oil made into a paste. This will remove the stain but leave the area dulled until you polish it.

HOW TO FIX CIGARETTE BURN MARKS

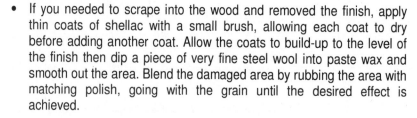

- If the burned area is just into the finish it will be easy to clean by wrapping a small piece of very fine steel wool around your finger and gently rubbing the area.
- If you notice the burned area has blisters, just hold a small knife blade at a right angle to the burned area and scrape the area lightly in a side-to-side motion. After the burned area is removed, use a piece of very fine steel wool to rub the area until smooth. If there is any finish left, just polish and wax the area.
- If you needed to scrape into the wood and removed the finish, apply thin coats of shellac with a small brush, allowing each coat to dry before adding another coat. Allow the coats to build-up to the level of the finish then dip a piece of very fine steel wool into paste wax and smooth out the area. Blend the damaged area by rubbing the area with matching polish, going with the grain until the desired effect is achieved.

HOW TO REMOVE INK STAINS ON WOOD

- If the wood is not sealed, ink will penetrate deep into the wood and you may never get it out.

94

- If the finish is protected with wax, blot it up immediately before the ink can penetrate the wood.
- Clean the surface using a damp cloth and never rub the area.
- Try rottenstone or a wood oil as soon as possible if the stain persists.
- Make an oxalic acid solution using 2 tablespoons of acid to 1 pint of warm water then use an eyedropper and place a few drops on the area. Only allow the solution to remain for a few minutes before rinsing off.

HOW TO CLEAN A CLOUDY SURFACE ON WOOD

Grease deposits from cooking or an oily cloth that has been rubbed on the wax finish usually causes this. Use a furniture polish that contains a solvent to clean the area.

HOW TO GET RID OF WHITE MARKS ON WOOD

DID YOUR FRIENDS OR FAMILY LEAVE YOU A RING?

When a family member or friend places a glass that is damp or has condensation on a waxed wood surface it may leave a white ring or spots. If the surface is cleaned off within a short period of time, the spot may be easily removed. However, if it is allowed to remain it will leave a stain that may be more difficult to remove. A mild abrasive made into a paste will usually remove almost any ring or watermark.

The paste can be prepared from any natural oil - which includes olive oil, petroleum jelly, margarine, and even butter, combined with baking soda or salt. In many instances toothpaste, especially the powdered variety, can be used with excellent results. After you remove the stain, be sure and apply a good coating a polish.

CAUTIONS WHEN STRIPPING WOOD FURNITURE

- Be sure that the product is biodegradable.
- Does it have a childproof cap?
- Is it flammable?
- Will it clean up with soap and water or do you have to use a dangerous solvent?
- Do you need special tools?
- Do you have adequate ventilation if the vapors are toxic?
- Avoid strippers that contain methanol, toluene, methylene chloride, acetone, and dibasic esters.

ADDITIONAL PROBLEM SOLVERS

- Sometimes these are a result of a liquid containing alcohol (medicine, alcoholic beverages, or perfume) being placed on the wood. Try a solution made from equal parts linseed oil, turpentine, and vinegar.
- Try a cleaning-polishing wax.
- If all else fails, try rubbing lightly with 0000 steel wool and rub with the grain. If the furniture has a high-gloss finish then do not use steel wool.
- Try using a paste made from powdered pumice or a mixture of rottenstone and linseed oil.
- If you are sure that it was caused by alcohol, try using household ammonia on a damp cloth. Do it quickly then clean with non-sudsy water.

FILLING OAK WOOD CRACKS

The following ingredients will be needed:

Fine starch flour
Thick brown shellac

Place the ingredients into a container and mix well, add enough of the brown shellac to the starch to make a paste. After it has been applied and dried, sandpaper the surface and rub with a soft cloth dampened in oil and thin shellac.

THE COPS HATE THIS TRICK

To stop seeing fingerprints on a freshly waxed surface, just rub a small amount of cornstarch into the surface. This will remove any excess wax and keep the surface from showing up any fingerprints or smudges.

FILLING CRACKS IN MAHOGANY

The following ingredients will be needed:

4	**Ounces of beeswax**
1	**Ounce of red lead**
	Yellow ochre

Place the beeswax in a double boiler and melt, and then add the red lead and enough ochre to produce the desired color. Remove from the heat and allow it to cool. Use the mixture before it hardens and is warm enough to work.

WOOD FURNITURE RENEWAL

The following ingredients will be needed:

1   **Parts linseed oil**
1   **Part turpentine**

Place the ingredients into a small bowl and mix well. Using a woolen rag, rub a light coating on the furniture that needs restoring. Immediately dry off with another woolen cloth.

DON'T KNOW HOW TO GET RID OF YELLOW STAINS ON LIGHT WOOD

- Unfortunately as light wood furniture ages, direct sunlight may cause areas of yellowing. Nothing can be done except to keep light-colored furniture out of the direct sunlight.

TIPS ON CHOOSING A WOOD STAIN

Gel stains
This is the easiest method for beginners to use since it adheres to vertical surfaces and will not run. It will not raise the grain but too many coats will cause darkening. The drawbacks are that it is expensive and difficult to clean up as well as having a limited numbers of colors.

Oil-based stains
This is the traditional stain. However there are concerns about the effects of the petroleum vapors and the environment. It is best used to touch up or do re-staining. It is permanent, will not fade, and doesn't raise the grain but additional coats will darken. It is somewhat difficult to clean up, has an unpleasant odor and is flammable.

One-step stain & finish
This is the fastest method of finishing wood if you are not too fussy about the exact color that is achieved. Used mainly on door and window casings with good uniform results and will not raise grain. The final color is not too deep and will not build up the color.

Penetrating oil stains
These products protect wood as well as stain it and may be called Danish oils or rubbing oils. Good for high traffic areas that have attractive grains. It is easy to apply and doesn't raise the grain. Additional coats will darken and the colors are limited. Somewhat expensive oil!

Water-based stains
They are replacing oil-based stains since they are easier to use and safe for the environment. Used on floors and most other woodwork as well as children's toys.

It is easy to clean safe to use and additional coats will darken. It raises wood grain and will not penetrate too deep but does require a finish coat.

TIPS ON CHOOSING CLEAR FINISHES

Danish or Tung oil
Can penetrate the wood and harden the grain with moderate resistance to stains, scratches, and burns.

Very good resistance to water and alcohol! Usually hand-rubbed and will need 2-3 applications to get a deep, rich color. It dries in about 8-12 hours.

Lacquer
It provides a fast drying finish that will produce a smooth finish and is used on the majority of furniture. It is best to spray many thin coats and allow the last coat to dry out for 2-3 days before rubbing with fine steel wool. Comes in a wide variety of finishes!

Natural-resin varnish
Will resist scuff marks and is available in many colors as well as clear and used for outdoor applications. It is best to apply with a varnish, cheesecloth or artist's brush. Should be applied thin and used with the recommended solvent. The finish is from high-gloss to satin to low-gloss. The drying time is 2-3 days and maybe a little more if it humid.

Shellac
Will form a hard finish, however, it is easily dissolved by alcohol and can be easily damaged by water. It is available in either clear or pigmented! It is best to use a small brush with a chisel tip and thin with alcohol solvent. Make sure that you protect the top with a coating of paste wax. The finish will come out with a high gloss and if desired can be dulled with steel wool. Drying time is about 2½ hours and you should allow 3-4 hours between coats.

Oil-based polyurethane
Has good mar-resistant qualities and is durable but will yellow over time. If used with a fairly dark stain the yellowing is not that noticeable. Apply with a natural-bristle brush and be sure that it has a chisel point or use a lamb's wool applicator. The finish is from high glossy to dull sheen. It has a drying time of 1-2 hours and make sure that you leave about 12 hours between coats.

Water-based polyurethane
Not as durable as oil-polyurethane, however, it will not yellow, but will need additional coats later on. Apply with brush or use a lamb's wool applicator. The finish is from high-gloss to satin. Allow 3 hours for the first coat to dry and 5-8 hours for the second coat to dry.

SMOOTH IT OUT BETWEEN COATS

Always allow varnish or shellac to fully harden then use fine sandpaper or fine steel wool to level the surface between the coats. This will also help the next coat adhere better. Clean off all dust and any debris before applying the next coat.

VENETIAN BLINDS

GIVE THEM A SHOWER

If you want to clean your blinds with the least amount of effort, just hand them in the shower and let the shower do the work. They will even drip dry there. If you wipe them with a dryer sheet occasionally they won't attract dust.

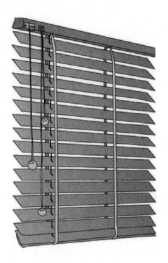

CHAPTER 4

THE KID'S ROOMS

BEDDING

GENERAL INFORMATION:
Since children tend to play in the dirt, climb trees, and play many games that lead to them becoming dirty and carrying dirt and allergens into the home, it is important to clean the bedding in a child's room frequently.

BUGS GALORE
Wash the bedding at least once a week in 130^{0}F water. Place a mattress cover on the mattress that will not allow dust mites to get into the bedding. Mite-proof mattress covers are readily available. About 45% (about 44 million homes) of all bedding in the United States contains dust mites.

NIGHTY NIGHT
For babies the crib mattress should be firm and should be tight-fitting. Make sure that the bedding cannot be dislodged.

For older children always purchase a new mattress that has good support. Never purchase a used mattress under any circumstances.

CARPETING

GENERAL INFORMATION:
The carpeting is capable of holding many allergens as well as the bedding and should be washed and vacuumed regularly. The carpet is also housing a number of biological pollutants that may be coming from the chemicals used in the manufacture of the carpet.

DESIGNING SPACE FOR CHILDREN

GENERAL INFORMATION:

INFANTS & TODDLERS

- ❖ Need safe spaces that can be explored.
- ❖ Must have sturdy furniture.
- ❖ Toys that keep their interest for prolonged period.
- ❖ Constant supervision.
- ❖ Toys that are safe for their age group.

PRESCHOOLERS

- ❖ Need adequate open space to play in.
- ❖ Furnishings should be sized for the child and their environment.
- ❖ Toys or learning equipment must relate to their age group.
- ❖ Should be responsible for their room and space.
- ❖ Have a safe area for them to explore and to promote their independence.

ELEMENTARY AGE CHILDREN

- ❖ Area to study and complete projects.
- ❖ Board to display their artwork and special school projects.
- ❖ Safe storage for collections.
- ❖ Area for special pets.
- ❖ A degree of privacy.

TEENAGERS

- ❖ Privacy.
- ❖ Area where they can be with friends.
- ❖ Computer desk and bookshelves.
- ❖ Ability to organize their own space and belongings.

ELECTRICAL SAFETY

GENERAL INFORMATION:

All electrical outlets in young children's rooms should be covered with a plate that utilizes the screws in the original plate to secure the plate. Cords to lamps need to be secured to the outlet with a special device found in hardware stores for that purpose.

NEVER USE PUSH-IN PLASTIC SOCKET COVERS!

FIRE SAFETY RULES

GENERAL INFORMATION:

The importance of teaching kid's fire safety and what to be aware of around the home or what to do in a fire emergency is very important. Fires in the home, while not common occurrences, do cause thousands of injuries and death to children every year.

Children are at risk from fire dangers and are not aware of them and what to do when various problems arise. Different rooms and times of the day relate to a variety of dangers. In a school setting many of the factors relating to fire safety are not taken seriously enough because of the number of students in the class and distractions. Most fires occur between midnight and 6AM.

> ➢ Don't allow children to play in the kitchen when parents are cooking since hot water can be spilled, a range top may be hot, or an oven may have a hot door.
> ➢ Kids should only cook when an adult is present.
> ➢ Never allow children to wear long sleeves when cooking.
> ➢ If food catches fire in a pot, don't move it! Just cover it and turn off element.
> ➢ Always sleep with bedroom door closed so that heat and smoke won't hamper your escape.
> ➢ If there is smoke stay close to the floor and crawl to window or exit.
> ➢ Never hide, so that firefighters can find you.
> ➢ Have an escape ladder in your room if bedroom is on second floor.
> ➢ Practice home escape plan.
> ➢ Never leave a child alone in a room where there is a candle burning or a lit fireplace.
> ➢ Know what the smoke alarm sounds like with a test.

STEAMING THE NAP UP

Indentations from furniture can be raised back to its original level by using a steam iron. Hold the iron just above the indentation (don't touch the carpet) and allow the steam to penetrate the area. The carpet nap should rise back up again. If this doesn't work, place an ice cube on the area overnight.

FURNITURE

A GOOD SEPARATION

The slats and spindles in a baby's crib should be spaced no more than 2 3/8th apart. Be sure that there are no slats missing or the baby will escape. Also, there should be no more than 1" between the edge of the mattress and the crib wall.

BUNKEM-UP

Bunk beds are not recommended for children under the age of 6.

LOCATION, LOCATION, LOCATION

A child's bed can be placed anywhere in the room as long as it is not near the window. Children have broken windows with their feet by accident more often than most people realize.

HERE KITTY KITTY

Pets tend to leave a number of potential allergens around the room. These include hair, dead skin, saliva, urine or fecal drops, dander, and even pollens from outside. Cats are actually more high risk than dogs when it comes to dander, hair, and allergens.

That's one thing we have over cats!

DANGER LURKS IN A LOCKED TOYBOX

The toy chest should never be the type that locks when closed. There should not be any type of a catch on the chest. However, the chest needs to have a safety hinge installed so that it does not close on the child's fingers.

LOOK OUT BELOW

Make sure that the dresser you purchase has drawer stops so that the drawer does not come out easily and fall on the child.

PETS IN THE BEDROOM

We will be good.

GENERAL INFORMATION:

Pets are capable of causing allergic reactions in susceptible children or adults. If your child suffers from allergies or symptoms that may be related to airborne allergens then your family pet may be the problem. Many pets sleep or interact for many hours in your child's bedroom. The proteins from animal droppings are capable of sensitizing children and may cause an allergic reaction or an asthmatic attack. If you think that a pet is the problem verify it with your family physician with allergy tests.

PET RULES

1. Leave the pet outside if possible and play with them there and change clothing before going in the house.
2. Wash the pet regularly. This only provides a temporary solution. Pets can be bathed once a week.
3. If the problem was identified as being related to the pet and the pet is now living outside, be sure and thoroughly clean the home including the walls, steaming the carpet, upholstered furniture, and removing any bedding and dishes the animal used.
4. Wash any clothing that had contact with the pet.
5. If all else fails, find the pet a good home.
6. Remove all of the pet's toys from the house.
7. Wash all children's stuffed animals.
8. Keep pets away from any fabric-covered furniture.
9. If you suspect that the pet is causing allergies, make the bedroom a "pet-free" zone.

ROCK-A-BYE-PET

Pet is sleeping on the bed. Many people like their pets sleeping with them on the bed. When the weather is cold, they like having the warmth of a pet alongside them. It is best to have a washable cover on the area that the pet sleeps on to catch the dirt, dander, and hair.

SAFETY & TOYS

GENERAL INFORMATION:
Every year hundreds of children are injured or killed by toys! Parents must realize that there are dangers in allowing certain aged children to play with certain toys. Supervision is necessary even with toys for some older children. While manufacturers try to produce products that are safe, it is almost impossible to produce a product that will be 100% safe for all children. Unfortunately, when a problem is found after manufacture it is sometimes too late to pull the product from shelves until after the children have been injured.

YOU BETTER BEWARE, YOU BETTER CARE.............
Common problems include choking on small parts, strangulation, loud noises that affect hearing, toxic materials in toys, and even projectiles. The law requires labeling of choking hazards in toys for small children. Be sure and look for the label.

TOY RULES

> Supervise children when you give them any toy with a cord or piece of elastic attached to it. Yo-yos can be dangerous depending on the age group using the toy. Strangulation and injuries to eyes, face and neck have been reported using yo-yo water balls.
> Try not to purchase toys that create too much noise. About 15% of children between the ages of 6-17 are presently showing signs of hearing losses.
> Be aware that some plastic mouthing toys may contain harmful chemicals from a group of chemicals called "phthalates." Craft clays and play cosmetics may pose a problem.
> If buying on the Internet, be sure that the warning labels are displayed on the web site. Almost 75% of toy sellers do not show the label. Check with www.recalls.com
> Hand-me-down toys may not be in good condition and pose a risk factor.
> Never give a small ball with a diameter less than 1.75 inches to a child under 3 years of age. Look for the choking hazard label.
> Balloons at a party can be a potential choking hazard.

> Toys in vending machines may not display a warning label.
> Projectile toys are rated to be amongst the most dangerous on the market.
> Do not allow a child to reach a crib mobile.

AND AWAY WE GO...............
Injuries occur frequently from scooters. Be sure and purchase safety gear for scooters, bikes, and skates.

FREEZE THE LITTLE BUGGERS
To keep stuffed animals free from dust mites place the stuffed animal in a large plastic bag and place the bag into the freezer for 24 hours once a month.

CHOKE TEST
Use a cardboard toilet paper roll and place the toy into the tube. If it goes into the tube it is too small for children under 3 or older children if they place objects in their mouth frequently.

STORAGE

GOING DOWN UNDER
Try and use the space under the child's bed for storage. The easiest way is to use drawers that are made to go under the bed with special rollers.

NO CLUTTER HERE
There an easy storage method so that a child's room does not look cluttered all the time. Just use plastic lidded storage boxes, which can be stacked and make great storage containers.

UP, UP, AND AWAY
There are many items that can be hung from the ceiling or special shelves that hang from the ceiling can be easily installed.

WINDOW COVERINGS

GENERAL INFORMATION:
Pull cords from window coverings have become a concern in relation to children strangling. Almost 200 deaths have been reported from children strangling on pull cords. Most deaths have been in children under the age of five.

THE HANGING CORD

Deaths are caused by cribs being placed too close to the cords. Young children should never be left alone in rooms with hanging cords or climbing on furniture to look out windows.

SUGGESTIONS FOR A SAFE ROOM

➤ If you have horizontal blinds you need to cut the cord above the tassel, remove the equalizer buckle, and add a separate tassel at the end of each cord. You could also cut the cord above the equalizer buckle then add a breakaway tassel, which will come undone if a child becomes entangled in the loop.

➤ If you have pleated or cellular shades leave the cord near the head rail in place. Cut the cord just above the tassel and add an additional tassel at the end of each cord. If the shades expose a loop cord when raised, be sure and keep the cord above a level that a child can reach.

➤ If you have vertical blinds, a continuous loop system or drapery cords you will need to install a cord tie-down device. It should be permanently attached and you should have the tie-down attached to floor, wall or window jamb.

➤ If cords can be affixed so that they are never in the reach of children some of the above measures are not necessary.

To get free tassels call (800) 506-4636

CHAPTER 5

I'll get out of your favorite chair as soon as you finish my doghouse!

PET'S AREA

BATHING

GENERAL INFORMATION:
It is best to brush your pet before giving them a bath to get all the tangles out and any debris that is caught in their fur. Also be sure and avoid getting water in pet's ears since they could easily get an infection.

WHOOOOOOPS
If your dog keeps slipping in the bathtub, be sure and place a rubber mat in the bathtub for the pet to stand on. Only use that mat for the pet.

HAIR WE GO AGAIN
To keep dog hair from clogging up the drain, cut a piece from an old screen and place it over the drain. You can also use a tea strainer if it is a small drain opening.

BAD DOG, BAD DOG
Urine will cause unsightly yellow burn areas on a lawn and one of the best ways to solve the problem is to prepare a solution of 1 cup of baking soda in 1 gallon of water and saturate the areas every 3-4 days. Urine is high in acid and the baking soda will neutralize it since it is a base. The dog will also not be able to recognize the spot again.

BIRD FEEDERS & HOUSES

DOES THE COLOR OF THE FEEDER MAKE A DIFFERENCE?

The color of a bird feeder will not make a difference as to which bird will feed from it. However, you will have better luck attracting birds with a feeder that is a neutral color.

SECRETS TO ATTRACTING BIRDS

BARN SWALLOW

These birds like an area where there is available water and mud and you must provide straw for their nests. They like a 6"X6" shelve for their nesting support and it needs to be 8-12 feet above the ground. They like eaves and well-protected areas.

Grandpa loves birds!

BLUEBIRD

These birds like a birdbath that is high enough off the ground so that cats can't get to it. They prefer mulberry, holly, blueberry, wild cherry and Virginia creeper plants to munch on. They are fussy about their birdhouses and they would prefer a 5"X5"X8" birdhouse with 1½" entry holes about 6 inches above the floor. If you place the nest 5 feet off the ground it will discourage the sparrows; they prefer nest that are higher up.

I'm helping.

CHICKADEE

They prefer a diet of peanut butter, suet, sunflower seeds and some breadcrumbs. Their birdhouse should be 4"X4"X8" with the holes 1 1/8th inches and should be 6 inches above the floor. The house needs to be 8-15 feet high.

KESTREL

Wild birdseed is their favorite and a good mix will do. Their birdhouse should be 8"X8"X12" with a 3 inch hole that is 9-12 inches above the floor. It should be at least 10 feet above the ground but not more than 30 feet.

KINGLET
It prefers to eat suet, wild birdseed, cracked nuts, and raw peanuts and likes to nest in conifers preferably near the northern gardens.

MOCKINGBIRD (from the hill)
These birds are fussy and insist on a nice birdbath and attractive surroundings. They prefer to eat crab apples, cherry, blueberries, grapes, and blackberries. However, they won't turn down a meal of dogwood, pasture rose, red cedar, elderberry, mulberry, manzanita and Virginia creeper. Mockingbirds like a nice birdbath!

OWL (old hooty)
It prefers to nest in large shade trees, oak trees or conifers. If they find a dead tree with a hollow hole they will reside there before almost any other location. They are night hunters and eat rodents and prefer a grassy area to hunt in.

OWL (barn)
They are fussy and require that you build them a nesting box 10"X18"X16" that has a 6 inch opening and about 4 inches from the floor. They dine on rodents and small animals and like an open field or pasture nearby.

OWL (saw-whet)
You will need to build a nesting box that is 6"X6"X10" that has a 2½" entry hole that is 8 inches above the floor. The house needs to be securely fastened 15-20 feet above the ground.

OWL (screecher)
Their home must be 8"X8"X14" and have a 3 inch hole. The house must be about 12-30 feet off the ground and must be in a secluded area since they like their privacy.

PHOEBE
These birds require a nesting platform that is about 6-8 inches square and 8-12 feet off the ground. They would prefer to be under an eave or in any protected area.

PURPLE MARTIN
These are apartment dwellers but don't put the apartment house up until the martins arrive or the starlings will move in. You will need 15-20 small apartments measuring 6"X6"X6" with the entry hole about 2½ inches and 1 inch from the floor. The birdhouse should be 15-20 feet off the ground. They eat wild birdseed and insects with a worm or two for dessert.

TITMOUSE

This bird will do anything for a doughnut but also loves to eat suet, nuts, sunflower seeds, peanut butter and breadcrumbs. The bird likes to be around elderberry, wild strawberry, pine, beech, mulberry, and pine. The birdhouse needs to be 4"X4"X8" and have a 1¼ inch entry hole about 6 inches off the floor. The house ideally needs to be 8-15 feet off the ground.

WARBLER

It prefers nice landscaping and pleasant surroundings (fussy bird). They will go crazy for mulberry and especially raspberries but also like wild rose, barberry, hedge, privet, grapevines, current, and elder, which provide additional nesting sites.

WREN

The birdhouse must be 4"X4"X6" with 1 inch holes for entry and the holes should be about 4 inches off the floor. The birdhouse should be 8-10 feet high.

BUILDING A BIRDHOUSE

- Don't bother with a perch since they are rarely used.
- Drill some ventilation holes just under the roofline and a few in the floor for drainage.
- The house should blend in with the scenery and not be frilly.
- The inside should be rough and even if bark is showing it is best.
- Only use screws not nails to insure the stability and quality.
- Hollowing out a small log works great as a birdhouse.
- The roof must be waterproof.
- The dimensions should be for the bird for which you are building it.
- Never use screw eyes to hang the house up since they will loosen in time.
- Hinge the bottom so that it will be easy to clean. The house needs to be cleaned after the birds leave.
- You can be creative as long as the house does not look out-of-place in its surroundings.
- If you are not handy, buy one in your garden shop.

PROBLEM BIRDS

If birds are a problem it is best to identify which bird is really causing the problem. Only four birds are really bad pests that will damage a garden enough to warrant going after them. They are crows, starlings, woodpeckers and blackbirds. However, damage that looks like birds are doing it may be from raccoons or other animals.

BUZZ AROUND, BUZZ AROUND
If you want to keep all birds away from your garden and plants, try using a piece of commercial buzzing or humming tape. This tape is stretched across an area near the garden and will make noise when the wind blows to scare away the birds.

ORDER A CAT SCARECROW
Make a cutout of a cat and decorate it to look like the real thing. If birds are a problem this works great.

THE OLD "MOVEABLE HEAD" HOOTY OWL
This really works better than almost any other means of keeping all birds away. Make sure that you purchase an owl with a movable head. When the wind blows the head moves around the body.

DOG HOUSES

GENERAL INFORMATION:
To keep fleas out of the doghouse, try sprinkling salt in all the cracks and around the corners. Also, placing fresh pine needles under the blanket or mat should solve the problem. A piece of foam rubber under the bedding will deter fleas as well as a few drops of lavender oil in the bedding.

BUILDING A DOGHOUSE

Items Needed:

Hammer	Quality plywood
Nails (roofing & misc.)	Shingles
Shingle utility knife	Circular saw
Pressure-treated lumber	Tape measure & pencil

Measure the dog and determine what size doghouse they will need. Do not make the house too big or it will be difficult for the dog to retain body heat in cold weather.

◆ Start by making a square base frame using four 2X6 boards that are nailed together at the ends. Be sure to use quality materials for this project.

◆ Next cut a piece of ½-inch plywood that will fit over the frame. Be sure that it is flush with the frame's edges.

◆ Use a quality exterior paint and paint the plywood base before going any further.

◆ To complete the floor you will need to nail the plywood to the frame along every side. Be sure it is sturdy!

◆ The wall can be framed with 2X4 studs that need to be cut to the proper size for the house then dry-fit the frames. Once you are satisfied that you have the correct size, nail the walls together. Don't forget to add center studs for the side and rear walls for added support. When placing the stud on the rear wall, the stud should be about 2-inches off center giving you easy access when securing the roof strut.

I hope he measures me right this time.

◆ Measure and cut ½-inch plywood for the outside frames and make sure that the edges are flush.

◆ Now dry-fit the finished walls then nail them into place through the bottom of the wall frame. If you toenail each corner it will provide increased stability.

◆ Be sure that the entrance is large enough for the dog to enter easily, but not too big or it will allow too much cold air to enter.

◆ When attaching the roof you will need to cut struts, ridge boards and rafters from 2X4 boards. The height of the roof struts will depend on the desired roof pitch and the size of the dog. The most common pitch is 45^0 which means that the ends of all rafters must be cut at a 45^0 angle as well.

◆ Next, you will need to center the front roof strut on the top edge of the wall frame and nail it into place from the underside of the frame. If you toenail the strut it will provide additional reinforcement.

◆ Center the rear roof strut on the top of the back wall frame then carefully nail it into place.

◆ Cut the top ridge board to the length of the doghouse including the amount you desired for the overhang.

◆ Position the ridge boards on the struts then nail it into place then cut three rafters for each side to the desired length. Be sure that the ends of the rafters are mitered to the angle that is determined by the pitch of the roof.

- Use the corner of the doghouse to mark notches on the rafters where they will meet the top of the wall frames so that they will fit snuggly over the top of each wall.
- Be sure and hold the rafters making them even with the ridge boards and then determine the angle before cutting the boards and nailing them into place.
- Attach the bottom of every rafter to the wall where the notch meets the wall frame.
- Next cut four 2X4 boards. You will need two for each side that will fit horizontally between the rafters then nail them into place. These boards will eliminate the gap between the overhang and the sidewalls.
- The fascia board will be cut from ½-inch plywood and will match the overhang on the sides of the doghouse. Nail the fascia boards to the bottom ends of the rafters.
- The overhang rafters should be cut from pressure-treated wood then painted providing some protection from the weather. The overhang rafters should now be nailed to the ends of the ridge board and side fascia.
- Use quality ½-inch plywood to cover the roof.
- The front and back of the roof openings need to be filled in with triangular plywood sheets cut exactly to fit the space.
- The shingles should now be attached to the roof. It would be best to use 12 inch gray sheet shingles. These will absorb less heat than darker shingles and keep the doghouse cooler in the summer months. Always start from the bottom and work up when installing shingles.
- To do the job efficiently, mark a horizontal chalk line 11 inches from the bottom of the roof edge. The shingles are 12 inches in length and it is best if they hang over by about 1 inch on the sides.
- Now mark a vertical chalk line 35 inches from the front edge of the roof since the shingle sheets are 36 inches giving you a hangover of 1 inch on the front.
- The next line is a vertical line that is drawn 29 inches back from the front edge. If you have two vertical lines it will help to establish two "starting points" for the shingle sheets and create offset rows. The odd numbered rows will begin at the 35 inch mark and the even numbered rows will begin at the 29 inch mark.
- The row on the bottom should be two shingles thick. Be sure and turn the first layer upside down. This will place the darker portion of the shingle sheet hanging over the edge and the second layer needs to be positioned right side up to match all subsequent rows.
- When all the shingles are nailed down in place, use a knife with a single-edge razor blade and trim the sides even with the edges of the plywood roof.

- To cover the exposed ridge board, you will need to cut shingle sheets into single shingles then place them sideways over the top making sure that they overlap. The single shingles should be tapered on the back end so that the black area doesn't peek out from under the shingles on top.

EXOTICS

TURN UP THE THERMOSTAT
Cold-blooded pets such as lizards and snakes need more than one heat source. To keep cold-blooded pets healthy, you should have two different heat sources.

BIRD FEATHERS
Birds do lose their feathers and will re-grow their feathers once a year.

FOOD DISHES

GENERAL INFORMATION:
Many of the pet's health problems are directly related to the cleanliness of their environment. If food and water dishes are not kept clean it could affect your pet's health.

SET UP A SCHEDULE
Pets should always be fed from their own dishes to avoid competition for food.

COME BACK HERE
Pet dishes tend to move easily on the floor when the pet is eating. To stop the problem, just place a rubber mat under the dishes.

ANTS ARE EATING THE PET FOOD
Place the food dish in a pan of water or sprinkle some crushed bay leaves around the bowl. The water works the best, since some pets will eat anything!

PET DOOR

HINTS FOR INSTALLING A DOGGIE DOOR

- Before getting started, be sure and measure to determine the proper sized door for your pet. The opening should be just a little wider than the widest part of your pet. The height should be 2 inches above the pet's shoulders.
- Buy a pet-door kit from PetCo™. Use a level to position the template and tape the template to the door.
- Use a hammer and nail to mark the door at the crosshairs on the template. These will be the 4 corners of the frame and will hold the screws.
- Remove the template and use a straightedge and draw a cut line between each of the corner marks. Drill through each corner with a ½" drill bit.
- Cut along the lines with a jigsaw fitted with a woodcutting blade. For metal doors use special cutting blade.
- Drill pilot holes through the door at the points that were marked for the frame screws.
- Set the door in place and attach the interior and exterior frames with screws.

PROTECTING YOUR FURNITURE

TIMBBBBER
If you have a dog that likes the taste of your furniture legs, paint the legs with oil of cloves. This will not hurt the furniture legs and will stop dogs and kids from chewing.

AYE CHIHUAHUA

To stop cats from chewing on your furniture legs, just place a small amount of crushed red pepper into a glass of water and allow it to stand overnight. Sprinkle a very small amount on the areas you are having a problem with. Best to place the liquid underneath any upholstered area so that it won't stain. It will be just as effective.

PEPE

RABBITS

PUT UP A BARRIER

A very effective method of keeping rabbits away from your vegetable garden is to build a cylindrical barrier enclosure. It should be about 3 feet high around all trees and plants and use ¼ inch hardware cloth then bury the bottom of the enclosure 3 inches below the ground. Make sure there is 1-2 feet between the barrier and the plants. You can also build a 3-foot high fence of chicken wire since rabbits are not good climbers.

SCRATCHING POSTS

GENERAL INFORMATION:

Cats rarely scratch furniture or use a scratching post to sharpen their claws. They scratch mainly for communication letting other cats or people know where they are and want attention. When they are outside they leave the marks to tell other cats *I'm tired of being ignored!* that this is their territory.

THE BORED CAT

Cats normally scratch for attention. Be sure and purchase a number of scratching posts and place them in areas that the cat frequents or scratches. Scratching posts are easy to make with a few pieces of wood and an old piece of carpeting.

Don't try and force a cat to use the post, just play with their favorite toys around or over the post.

BUILDING A CAT SCRATCHING POST

Items Needed:
Cedar post about 30 inches high and 4 inches in diameter
50 feet of non-oiled 3/8-inch sisal rope
4-inch plywood for base about 16X16 inches in diameter
Wood glue
Stain or paint and brush
Tools & circular saw
Gloves & mask

- Make sure that the wood used is dry.
- Wear gloves when you wrap the rope around the post. Nail the rope to the top of the post then use wood glue to attach the rope. Be sure that there are no spaces, so wrap the rope tight. Nail the rope to the bottom after you glue it down.
- Make sure you sand down any rough areas.
- The base must be very heavy so that the post will not tip over easily.
- Make sure you use at least 4 nails when attaching the post to the base.
- You may have to show the cat how to use the post a few times.

CAT REPAIR KIT NEEDED
To protect an area that the cat has already damaged, cover the area with plastic making it less appealing. Place a scratching post next to the area or place some oil of clove on the wood.

SNAKES

SNAKE-PROOF FENCE
It is best to use a very heavy galvanized screen about 36 inches wide and use ¼ inch mesh. You will need to bury the lower edges 2-3 inches in the ground and then slant it outward from the bottom to the top at a 30-degree angle. Your supporting stakes should be inside the fence and the gates must be tightly fitted. This is an expensive method if you have a large yard. Best to just fence in your children's play area.

WATER

GENERAL INFORMATION:
Pets should not be allowed to drink stale or dirty water. Pet's water needs to be changed every day. If you feel that the tap water is not safe for you to drink then don't give it to your pet. Buying a gallon jug of water just for your pet is inexpensive.

All driveway deicing chemicals are toxic to your pet's feet. Driveway salt will also burn their feet and if they lick their feet it may make them ill.

CHAPTER 6

LIVING ROOM

CARPETING

GENERAL INFORMATION:
Carpeting can provide both luxury and fashion, and will insulate the flooring in most climates. Choosing just the right carpet for your needs can be a chore. Carpeting is also not recommended if you have allergies to dust, mold, and pollens since they tend to be very difficult to remove even with regular cleaning.

CARPET MAGIC
If your carpet has an indentation you can remove it by laying a damp towel over the depressed area and pressing down with a warm iron. The depression should be gone by the time the towel dries fully.

I HATE BAREFOOT, GET OFF ME!
Your skin releases natural oils and walking on carpeting in bare feet can leave traces of those oils in the carpet. These oils have the tendency to attract dust. It is best to wear socks or slippers.

PATCH-EM-UP

ANSWER TO REPAIRING CARPETING

➢ If the carpet only has a small burn area or other small damage, use a small pair of manicuring scissors and cut away the damaged fibers. Be sure and feather out the side areas when you are working so that the area is not too noticeable.

➢ When you patch the area, make sure that you use a pattern. Pick something that will cover the damaged area, possibly a small block of wood. Use a very sharp utility knife to cut around the block then remove the damaged area.

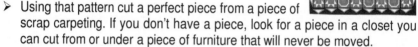

➢ Using that pattern cut a perfect piece from a piece of scrap carpeting. If you don't have a piece, look for a piece in a closet you can cut from or under a piece of furniture that will never be moved.

➢ Place the patch to the floor with a piece of double-sided carpet tape and cut it to fill the hole. Peel the backing off the tape and put into place. Be sure and match the pattern if possible. Press it firmly into place.

JUST A SHAMPOO, NO HAIRCUT

When you want the carpet shampooed, just head for the supermarket and rent a big carpet cleaner. These heavy duty machines will prevent the soaking of the carpet and reduce the possibility of shrinkage IF used as instructed. However, steam cleaning is still the preferred method.

TYPES OF CARPET WASHING

1. **Steam Cleaning** – This method is recommended by all major carpet manufacturers since it is done without the use of harsh brushes. The hot water is shot into the carpet to loosen the dirt and grime and then vacuumed out.

2. **Shampooing** – This method is commonly used by the do-it-yourselfers since the equipment is easily rented at most supermarkets or home stores. It has rotary brushes, which work the shampoo into the carpet and can be vacuumed out when it is dry. The problem is that the vacuum used may not be powerful enough to get all of the residue out of the carpet, leaving it dull and lifeless.

3. **Dry Cleaning** – This method uses a powerful granule or liquid solvent that is sprayed on then mechanically brushed into the carpet. It is then vacuumed out. However, it is not good at getting out a bad stain as well as being hard on the carpet fibers.

TOILET BRUSH YOUR CARPET

The corners of a carpeted room are the hardest places to clean and usually get permanently dirty if not cared for. The vacuum can't reach these areas but all you have to do is to purchase an extra toilet bowl brush and use it in the corners.

LEG PROTECTOR

When you are washing the carpet be sure and protect the wooden furniture legs from the chemicals and water. Just place small plastic bags over the legs and tape them. This will also make it easier to just move the furniture out of the way and return it immediately without hurting the carpet or the furniture.

STEEL WOOL TO THE RESCUE

If you have a surface burn on the carpet that is not too deep, just use a piece of steel wool to lightly scrub the burned area from the fibers.

CANDLE WAX REMOVER

Scrape off as much of the wax as you can then use a dull knife blade. Cover the area with paper towel and then iron the spot using the synthetic setting. The paper towel will show through the wax, remove it and repeat until all the wax is out of the carpet.

EENIE MEENIE MINEE MOE

Most people are not familiar with the types of carpet materials and padding, which is best for their needs.

There are four basics to carpeting that need to be considered

Fiber – This in the carpet material itself. Single carpet fibers are spun together to make two, three, or four-ply yarn, which is then attached to a woven backing.

Pile – The height of the fiber.

Density – This is the amount of fiber tufts per square inch. Carpet weight and quality will refer to ounces per square inch. The more ounces per square inch the better the carpet.

Texture – This refers to the way the fibers are looped, whether twisted or cut to provide texture.

Types of carpet fibers:

Wool – This offers a deep, rich look and has excellent resilience and durability. It is naturally stain resistant but requires a high level of maintenance.

Nylon – The most common carpet material and has the strongest fibers. Excellent for high traffic areas and is the most durable of the synthetics. It is one of the easiest carpets to clean and is soil and mildew resistant.

Olefin – Produced originally for outdoor carpeting and basements since it resists mildew, water damage and static.

Polyester – Is very wear-resistant but not as good as nylon. Tends to shred easier than most carpets but is resistant to moisture and mildew.

Acrylic – It is closer to wool than any other synthetic and mainly used for commercial offices. It is soil and mildew resistant and less likely to fade from direct sunlight.

Be sure and foot-test the padding under a piece of your carpet before choosing the padding. Remember thick padding may not be the best for your location.

BE TENDER NOW!
Carpet needs to be vacuumed regularly. Dirt in carpet acts like a piece of sandpaper.

OUT, OUT AND AWAY
Stains will set permanently if they are not removed quickly in many carpets.

GETTING A LITTLE DINGY OVER HERE

Brown areas are usually caused by over-wetting that leaches vegetable dyes from the jute backing and produces a wick effect to the surface. The carpet must be professionally acid rinsed or topically sprayed with a solution of a souring agent.

TRAFFIC LANE AHEAD
These are dark traffic lane areas, which receive the highest amount of foot traffic. The damage is in the form of scratches and abrasions to the fibers, matting, flaring, or tip compression (cut pile).

122

There is no way to repair the problem without replacing the area. If shoes are removed before coming in the home, these areas rarely show up.

GET OUT THE PAINTBRUSH
If your carpet is losing its brightness, it may be caused by a poor quality, cleaning compound that was used on the carpet. Once this problem occurs, there is no way to reverse it.

SPRINKLE, SPRINKLE
If you want to sharpen up your carpet colors, try sprinkling a small amount of salt around. The salt provides a mild abrasive cleaning action that won't hurt the fibers.

AVOIDING A SHOCKING EXPERIENCE
To eliminate getting shocked when walking across the carpet, just leave a vase with water in every carpeted room.

THROW RUG SECRET
If you want to keep your throw rugs looking great all the time, just place them into the dryer between washings on a **NO-HEAT** setting.

DON'T HAVE TO NAIL THEM DOWN
To keep throw rugs in place, just use double-sided tape under the corners of the undersurface. It can't hurt the floor and works great.

VERY UPLIFTING
An easy method of raising the nap of a carpet after a piece of furniture has matted it down is to place an ice cube on the matted down area overnight.

GENERAL INFORMATION:
A large number of furnishings now have decorative detains that are made from metal. These include substances such as ivory, brass, chromium, leather, marble, iron, etc.

Aluminum

Wash with hot, soapy water and rinse well. Never use abrasives or cleansing powders. Strong soaps and detergents will cause pitting.

Brass, Copper, Bronze Fittings

Many fittings contain a lacquered coating to protect them from corrosion. They can only be cleaned with warm, soapy water and never polished or cleaned with an abrasive cleaner. Antique brass can be cleaned with a solution of boiled linseed oil.

Chrome Fittings

Only wipe with a soft damp cloth since abrasives will wear off the plating material.

Gesso

This is a hard plaster material that is molded to resemble carved wood or used in picture frames. Vacuuming is the best method. If an area really needs cleaning, try using a small piece of sliced lemon and gently rubbing the area then rinsing the area immediately with a solution of one tablespoon of baking soda mixed in one pint of warm water.

Ivory

Ivory tends to yellow when it is stored without a light source. Piano keys should never be closed up. Clean only with a mild soap and water solution and dry immediately.

Heavily Tarnished Leaded Pewter

Prepare a paste from fine whiting and boiled linseed oil by dipping a small piece of 0000, steel wool into the paste then rubbing lightly on the pewter in one direction. This may not remove all the tarnish, but it should make it look better.

Slate

Clean with a small amount of boiled linseed oil on a clean cloth then rub briskly.

DRAPERIES

TEMPERATURE CONTROL

Draperies can be utilized to help control the temperature in the house. When the weather is cool outside you should open the drapes to allow sunlight to enter. Draw the drapes at night to keep the heat in. Be sure that the drapes do not block the heat vents.

NEED A PERMANENT ECLIPSE
Sunlight can have a negative effect on draperies. Constant exposure will damage the strength of the fibers. It is best to line the draperies with a high quality lining to protect them.

POOR DRAPERIES
Household chemicals will harm draperies especially fumes from chimneys, auto exhaust, and cooking, which may combine with oxygen and cause deterioration of the fabrics.

TURN ON THE DE-HUMIDIFIER
The level of humidity in the air in the home will cause draperies to shrink or stretch.

DRIP, DRIP CAN CAUSE A PROBLEM
Window condensation marks on draperies are almost impossible to remove and should be avoided if possible.

DUSTING

TICKLE, TICKLE
Feather dusters tend to scatter dust rather than picking it up and holding it.

SPECIAL CARE NEEDED
When dusting silk plants and flowers, the best method is to use damp cloth then use a commercial silk cleaner. The cleaner is available at craft or floral shops.

DUSTING ODDS & ENDS
Knick-knacks are easier to place in the sink and wash instead of trying to dust them. It is best to vacuum the tops of the books. Dusting is not very efficient no matter what you use.

I SMELL PRETTY………..
You can deodorize while dusting if you are using a duster, just try spraying the end with your favorite deodorizer.

TO DUST MOP OR ?
Dust mops are only effective if you vacuum the floor first. Never depend on the dust mop to do a complete job.

Same with a sock, you have to vacuum the floor first. However, grandma used an old sock on her hand and then threw it into the washing machine with the other clothes, but only to do furniture.

GONNA NEED STILTS
To reach those hard to reach locations use a long artists brush and place furniture polish on the tips.

METHODS OF CLEANING BOOKS

➢ Books get dirty and need to be cleaned. Always start at the top of the bookshelf and work down so that any dust will move to the lower books.
➢ When vacuuming dust covers, be sure and place a piece of cheesecloth over the end of the vacuum cleaner hose so that the suction will not remove any loose pieces of paper.
➢ If you have any smudges or spots, you should be able to erase them with a soft eraser called a "pink pearl." These can be obtained at any artist's supply store or stationary store.
➢ If you have a large smudge you will have to use "Opaline" from an artist's supply store.

LESS IS BETTER
To reduce the amount of dust in the house, have your ductwork and air filter cleaned regularly.

A LITTLE OF THIS & A LITTLE OF THAT
You can make your own dusting oil by mixing three parts of light mineral oil mixed with one part of corn oil then add one drop of lemon or clove oil.

MONEY SAVER
Don't bother buying fancy dust cloths that are treated to attract dust when all you have to do is to dip a piece of cheesecloth in a mixture of 2 cups of water and ¼ cup of lemon oil. Allow the cheesecloth to air dry and it will do just as good as the expensive ones.

GLASS-TOP TABLES

NO LINT MY LADY
After you clean a glass-top table, be sure and add a capful of fabric softener to a bucket of warm water then rinse the tabletop with the mixture. This will keep them lint-free and sparkling clean.

HARDWOOD FLOORING

GENERAL INFORMATION:
All hardwood flooring needs some type of protective coating to protect the surface of the wood. There are a number of chemical protectors that can be used depending on the wood floor you have in your home. Most are either oil-based varnishes or polyurethane.

PROTECTION A MUST
If you are going to try and place a protective coating on your wood floor you need to know what type of coating to put on. If possible bring a piece of the hardwood flooring to the store when purchasing the protective coating. Best describe the type of wood and the age of the wood and the coating presently on the wood to get the best protective coating. Also be sure and find out about the correct application method for the chemical chosen.

HOW DRY I AM..........
Make sure that you apply the proper number of coats or allowing a coat to dry fully before applying the next coat. Also, be sure and purchase the correct brushes, applicators, and chemicals to do the job right.

THE MOST POPULAR FLOOR PROTECTORS

Oil-Based Varnishes:
This will provide a very tough and durable sealant and is capable of lasting the life of the floor if applied properly. It is expensive and does require additional coats and adequate drying time between coats. Some older floors may not be usable for as long as 1-2 months and may need 3-4 coats. Commonly used on doors that may get wet.

Protect it or lose it!

Polyurethane:

This coating can be applied in two days and will provide a very hard water-based finish. The floor can be walked upon in about a week and needs two coats to be really durable.

BLACK HEEL MARKS

To remove black rubber marks on wood floors, try using lemon juice or 0000, steel wool very lightly with the solvent-based wax you would ordinarily use.

? DARK SPOTS

If you see dark spots from alkaline substances, just apply vinegar to the area and allow it to remain for 4 minutes before removing with a damp cloth.

SCRATCHES & WORN SPOTS

Apply a small amount of wax with very fine steel wool. Make sure you apply the wax in the direction of the wood grain. Rub until the colors blend in.

SPECIAL CARE NEEDED

Clean hardwood floors weekly with just a damp mop. However, they should also be cleaned once a month using 2 ounces of white vinegar in a bucket of cool tap water. Just mop the wood and towel dry immediately. This should improve the luster of the floor.

MARBLE TOP FURNITURE & FLOORS

MY TOP ISN'T SHINY ANYMORE

If your marble top has lost some luster it may be caused by dust. Try wetting the marble well then wash it with a mild detergent and use a soft brush. Never use an abrasive cleanser on marble. There is also a marble cleaner and polish that is available at most hardware stores.

You can also wet the marble surface and sprinkle the surface with a marble-polishing powder. Rub it in and then polish with a clean cloth. Putty powder (tin oxide) is recommended.

I'M NOT A CAR

A light coat of wax will protect the surface, but is not really necessary. Never wax white marble or it may turn yellow. A warm water bath with a mild detergent is only recommended twice a year. Make sure you wipe completely dry.

SEAL-EM-UP

Marble tops are very porous and should be sealed. If you spill a liquid on a marble surface it will need to be wiped up immediately or it may stain. If it does stain it will need a special treatment to repair the surface. The treatment may involve using a chemical and a buffer.

MARBLE RESTORATION TIPS

> Prepare a poultice of 6% hydrogen peroxide mixed with just enough flour to make it into a paste. You will need about 1 pound of the paste for every square foot of surface.
> Place the mixture on the surface of the marble and use a wooden spatula to spread it over the surface. Be sure that the thickness is about ½ inches and that the mixture extends past the dirty area.
> Tape plastic over the area and allow it to remain for 48 hours then dampen the area and remove it with a wooden spatula.
> Rinse the area with clean cool water then blot it off and let it dry.

MARBLE ENTRY HALL TIPS

MARBLE, THE TOUGHEST OF THE TOUGH, BUT BE GENTLE!

Marble is one of the toughest floor surfaces and is basically naturally compressed, crystallized limestone that can range from somewhat porous to very compact. It can be polished to a high shine and will remain that way with very little care, almost forever. The following solutions will clean and keep the marble shining with a minimum of effort. Strong detergents and abrasives should never be used on marble since they will dull the shine and may cause deterioration of the marble.

GREAT MARBLE CLEANING FORMULA

Mix together the following ingredients in a small bucket to make a paste:

6% hydrogen peroxide
White all-purpose flour

The thick paste mixture needs to be placed on the complete marble floor area, not just a soiled spot, or the balance of the marble will not have the same clean color. Place enough of the mixture to heavily coat the floor and place plastic sheeting over the mixture, taping down all around the edges. Allow the mixture to sit on the marble for 36 hours, then carefully remove it with a plastic spatula and rinse the marble thoroughly with cool water.

129

REMOVING OIL STAINS FROM MARBLE

The following ingredients will be needed:

9 ¾	Ounces of cereal flour
13 ½	Ounces of hydrochloric acid (use with care)
4	Ounces of chloride of lime
2	Teaspoons of turpentine

Wear gloves and a mask. Place all the ingredients into a glass or porcelain container and blend into a paste. Smear the paste on the stains and allow it to remain for 6-8 hours. Remove the paste with a brush or piece of soft leather. Polish the area after the stain has been removed. This formulation will remove grease from marble very easily.

A NON-RESILIENT FLOOR NEEDS TLC

This category of flooring includes ceramic tile, concrete, brick, and all types of stone flooring material. It is best to just clean stone and brick surfaces with a solution of vinegar and water (1 cup of vinegar to 1 gallon of water), whereas concrete needs to be cleaned with an all-purpose detergent or concrete cleaner. If the tile is in bad shape and needs cleaning to remove ground in dirt and residues, the following formula will be needed otherwise just use a mild soap solution.

SPANISH TILE CLEANER & CONDITIONER

The following ingredients will be needed:

21/3	Cups of oleic acid
1	Tablespoon of triethanolamine (from drug store)
3	Cups of cool tap water

Place the ingredients into a double boiler and just heat - do not allow boiling. Remove from heat and beat with an electric mixer until the mixture becomes milky. Apply the mixture to the tile floors with a sponge and allow it to dry for 8-10 hours before rubbing off with a dry bath towel.

SILVERWARE

SLOWING DOWN TARNISH

If you place a small piece of chalk in a silver chest it will absorb moisture and slow tarnishing. Calcium carbonate (chalk) absorbs moisture very slowly from the air. If you break the chalk up and expose the rough surface it will be more efficient.

RUST PREVENTION

If you place a few mothballs, a piece of chalk, or a piece of charcoal in your toolbox you will never have any rust on the tools. If you don't use certain tools very often and they get rusty, just clean them with steel wool and then coat them with a thin coating of petroleum jelly.

DARK STAINS ON STAINLESS

The high mineral content of hard water and certain detergents or foods with a high salt content may cause stainless steel flatware to develop dark areas. To

It will ruin the silver.

remove these dark spots, just use stainless polish. Remove the cleaner immediately to avoid damaging the flatware.

DISHWASHER ALERT

Keep your good sterling silverware out of the dishwasher since many of the detergents use chemicals that may harm the surface of the silverware.

SERIOUS TARNISH

If silver is too badly tarnished and silver polish won't remove it, you will have to try another method. If the following method does not work it would be best to have the silver re-plated. Try sprinkling the silver with salt then rub it with a sponge that has been lightly dampened with white vinegar. The reaction should remove the tough tarnish without a problem.

UPHOLSTERED FURNITURE

LEATHER

LEATHER LOCATION, LEATHER LOCATION

Make sure that you maintain at least two feet between the furniture and any heat source. Radiators, vents and fireplaces will cause the leather to dry out and crack. Direct sunlight will cause leather to fade over time.

YOU SPILLED OIL ON MY LEATHER

This is a serious problem since oil will eat the leather. Blot up as much of the oil before it has a chance to seep into the leather and keep dabbing it until all the oil is gone. The small amount that escapes should not be a problem and will seep into the leather.

HOW CLEAN I FEEL

There are only certain chemicals or cleaning solutions that can be used on leather. Use a mild solution of Ivory Liquid Soap on a clean wet sponge. Wash and rinse immediately and dry thoroughly. This should be done monthly. Never use saddle soap, oils, abrasive cleaners, furniture polish, soaps, varnish or ammonia-based products. When cleaning leather, check for the direction of the grain (if it's real leather) and clean in that direction.

LEATHER REVIVAL
If you want to revive the beauty of leather try beating two egg whites lightly, then applying the mixture to the leather with a soft sponge. Allow it to remain on for 3-5 minutes before cleaning off with a soft cloth, just dampened with clear warm water. Dry immediately and buff off any residues.

FABRIC

BAD STAIN, BAD STAIN
Stains on upholstered fabrics are difficult to remove. Mix ½ teaspoon of a mild liquid detergent in a quart of warm water then beat with a hand mixer. Clean the area using only the suds and work on one small area at a time. Overlap areas to avoid spotting. Rinse with clean damp cloth and dry with a fan or hair dryer.

EL STINKO!
If the fabric gets an odor just sprinkle baking soda on the area and allow it to remain for 3-4 hours before vacuuming it off.

WOOD FURNITURE

FIX DENTS AND DINGS ON WOOD FURNITURE
To fix small dents on wood furniture, poke several holes in the wood with a pin then lay a slightly damp cloth over it and hold a steam iron just above the area. This allows enough moisture to swell the wood back to its original size.

RETURN IT TO THE STORE
If you a table with one leg shorter than the other and the table wobbles just build up the short leg with layers of plastic wood. If you get it too tall, just sand it down to the right height.

A BAD JOINT (on a chair)
If a joint has become loose on a chair it may cause the piece of furniture to eventually fail. If possible, try and insert some glue (you don't need a lot) into the space and clamp it to hold it together. If possible, scrape out any old glue and clean as best as possible before applying the new glue.

PAIN IN THE GROOVE

To remove old paint from the grooves in turned wood, just use a string that has been saturated with a paint remover solvent. Try working the string back and forth until the paint loosens.

GETTING MESSY ON HERE
To remove the dried paint from a surface that has a varnish finish and has been waxed, just use a hair dryer on low heat and move it back and forth for a few seconds until it loosens up. Peel it off gently with a dull knife.

NEED SUNGLASSES
Direct sunlight will dry the wood out and may cause the color to bleach out.

HUMIDITY IS GETTING HIGH
Very moist air will damage the wood furniture.

GET THAT YUCKY STUFF OFF ME
To remove candle wax or chewing gum from wood furniture, just hold an ice cube over the wax or gum for a few seconds until it hardens. Remove with fingernails or a dull knife trying not to go into the surface.

DON'T BRING ME TO A BODY SHOP
A small dent or depression in wood can be repaired and raised back to their original level. Place several layers of clean damp fabric over the dent. Touch the fabric with a warm steam iron, which should cause the wood fibers to swell up and go back into place. It should go back to the same level as the area around it. If the wood fibers have been split, this will not work.

FILLER UP
If you need to repair a hole in a piece of wood, try adding a small amount of instant coffee to the spackling or a thick paste made from a laundry starch and warm, water.

A SALAD SOLUTION
If you run out of wood oil, try using mayonnaise. A very light coating rubbed into the wood will help protect the finish. It should be rubbed in well and be sure not to leave a residue.

Leftover tea is a beverage that can be used on wood furniture and also to clean varnished furniture.

CHAPTER 7

GARAGE

CARS

REMOVING TAR
The easiest and least expensive method is to use some sodium bicarbonate on a damp cloth. However, you can also use kerosene or a special tar remover from an auto supply store.

FROZEN LOX
If your car locks become frozen in the winter just use a hairdryer on them for a few seconds.

BABY, IT'S COLD OUTSIDE...............
If you have trouble starting your car on cold mornings, the problem usually has nothing to do with the battery but with the oil. Freezing temperatures tend to turn your oil into thick syrup, making your battery work harder to turn the engine over. Manufacturers make higher amp batteries that may help alleviate this problem or you may want to consider a heated blanket to keep the motor oil from becoming a semi-solid.

GIVE EM A SHOT
If your windshield wipers are smearing the windows, try wiping them with rubbing alcohol.

PAINT REMOVER
Paint can be removed from a car finish by using Benzol™.

MORE MILES, LESS GALLONS
Add 4 ounces of Benzol™ to every 10 gallons of gas.

AUTO RESUSCITATION
To revive a dead battery, just dissolve 1-ounce of Epsom salts in warm water and add it to each cell.

AN EASY SOLUTION
If you want to keep your windshield free from frost just mix up a solution of 1-part white vinegar to 3 parts of water and apply to windshield. You can also just cut an onion in half and rub the fleshy area on the windshield.

I USED TO BE SHINY
To remove rust from a chrome surface, just rub the area with a piece of aluminum foil.

GETTING BACK ON SOLID GROUND
If you get stuck in snow or mud, try using your car floor mat or a blanket kept in the trunk for traction.

HOW DOES ANTIFREEZE WORK?
Antifreeze is composed mainly of propylene alcohol which when added to water lowers the freezing point and also increases the boiling point. Therefore water can't freeze at 32^0F and it will not boil at 212^0F. The coolant is circulated through the engine by the water pump and the engine heat is transferred to the coolant, which returns to the radiator. The radiator is cooled by the outside air, which cools the antifreeze, preventing boil-over.

WHAT IS THE DIFFERENCE BETWEEN A CAR POLISH AND A WAX?

A car polish is only meant to enhance and restore the luster to a wax coating. They remove dirt and debris trapped in the wax and restores a smooth finish to the surface. The polish will not provide any protection, it will just keep the wax clean.

LET THERE BE LIGHT
Used milk containers can be filled with old candle wax and kept in the car for emergencies. Place a long candle in the center for the wick. It will burn for hours.

RUB-A-DUB-DUB
To prevent the rubber around your car doors from freezing try rubbing the rubber moldings with vegetable oil.

BE GENTLE
Steel wool pads make an excellent white wall cleaner. Best to use as fine a steel wool pad as you can find.

TO THE SEAT OF THE PROBLEM
If you place a sheet of fabric softener under your car seat it will keep your car smelling fresh. Cleaning it out will help, too.

BIGGER IS BETTER, WHEN IT COMES TO TIRES
Next time you buy tires, consider replacing the old tires with a larger tire. Check your manual and put on the largest tire that is acceptable on your car. Larger tires will last longer, the engine will operate slower at any given highway speed, it will increase mileage, and even reduce engine wear. Most cars come with undersized tires since they cost less.

BUG SLIDE
Oven Guard or spraying vegetable oil on a clean car bumper before a trip will make it easy to remove the bugs when you return.

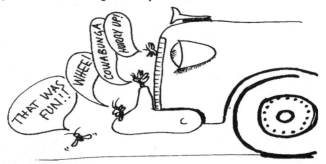

REMOVE CIGARETTE ASHTRAY SMELL
To really clean and deodorize car ashtrays, use baking soda and leave some in there after you clean it. It will keep the smell from getting into the car upholstery in most cars.

OIL AND WATER DON'T MIX
Oil is easily contaminated from moisture. To get rid of the water in your crankcase, you need to drive the car at least 7 miles in a warm climate and at least 10 miles in a cold climate each time you use the car. If you don't, the engine does not get hot enough to evaporate the water. Most people don't drive that far so be sure and change your oil every 3,000 miles at the most.

YOUR BRAKE OIL NEEDS A BRAKE
Because of the newer disc-brake systems on today's cars, you should change the brake oil every 2 years to be on the safe side. Brake fluid has an affinity for moisture, which may corrode the brake parts.

ALUMINUM CHROME CLEANER
Try using a piece of aluminum foil to shine the chrome on your car. Just turn the shiny side out, dampen the chrome and polish the chrome with the aluminum foil.

DRIVEWAYS

CONCRETE

HAVING A CRACK-UP
Driveways will sometimes develop cracks in the concrete. This is usually due to shrinkage or settling. Most cracks can be sealed with a concrete sealant.

I CAN SEE A RAINBOW
Sometimes a white/gray or rainbow discoloration may occur on a newly paved driveway, it will usually disappear naturally over time.

HERE KITTY, KITTY
If you have a driveway that has oil residue that is hard to remove, just cover the area with sand or cat litter and allow it to remain for 2-3 days before sweeping it off.

I PROMISE I'LL BUY YOU MORE

Hisssss!!

DON'T NEED AN ARTIST
You need to use the right paint for the job if you are going to paint concrete. Never use a latex paint since it will react with the rubber car and bicycle tires, even lawnmower tires. The latex will end up peeling. Use alkyd floor enamel, which are more moisture-resistant, will hold up better, but are more slippery when wet. To clean the floor use TSP and water.

RUB-A-DUB-DUB

To remove grease and rust stains from a concrete floor sprinkle dry TSP on a wet or oily surface and allow it to remain for at least 30 minutes before washing

off. You can also mix 1 part of sodium citrate in 6 parts of water and add enough Fuller's Earth to prepare a thick paste. Spread the paste on the area that needs cleaning and allow it to remain for 5-7 days before scraping it off. Keep adding new paste if it dries out.

PRE-PAINTING PREP

Before painting a concrete slab the surface must be sealed. If you are just pouring the slab you will have to wait 3 weeks before applying a sealant with a brush. Allow 1 day for it to dry and the lime to work its way out. Vacuum up the white powder then use a stiff brush and water to clean the concrete before paining it.

WATERPROOF YOUR CONCRETE

The following ingredients will be need:

1¼   **Pound of ammonium stearate (from pharmacy)**
1   **Gallons of hot tap water**

Place the ingredients in a large pain and mix thoroughly. Apply immediately to concrete walks, driveways or cement walls.

CLEANER FOR CONCRETE

The following ingredients will be needed:

3   **Pounds of metasilicate**
1   **Gallon of hot tap water**

Place the ingredients in a bucket and mix well. Use a broom to scrub when applying. For stubborn areas, allow the mixture to sit for 15-20 minutes before scrubbing. Sometimes a more concentrated solution may be needed in bad areas.

ASPHALT

GENERAL INFORMATION:

Materials that will be needed include emulsified liquids, plastic fillers, and solid cold patches. If there are impressions left by car tires, this is an indication of a poor construction job. Buckling or cracking in cold weather are signs of poor drainage. Both these conditions will require a new driveway and cannot be repaired.

BLACKTOP CRACKS

It would be best to fill any crack as soon as you spot it to keep water from getting under the slab. If the cracks are ½" or wider they should be filled with cold patch! If the crack is narrow, fill it with crack filler. Make sure you clean out any small pieces of material before you patch. Clean off any dust with a power washer or garden hose.

WHERE'S MY CAR?

If you are going to repair a chuckhole, make sure that you remove any loose material and dig out the dirt down to a solid base. Make sure the edges are solid and remove any dust from around the edges. Place fluid cold patch in the hole and work in with a trowel to be sure there are no air pockets.

Compact the area to within 1-inch from the top and allow setting for a short period time before adding the balance of the patch material to just above the surface. After 12 hours, place a board on top and drive your car over the top a few times. Seal coat the entire driveway.

METHOD OF SEALING A DRIVEWAY

Good preparation is really needed if you want the job to come out right and last for a while. The following are the steps you need to follow:

- ✓ Sweep the driveway well to remove any loose stones and debris and be sure to trim back any weeds or grass that has crept over the edges.
- ✓ If you have oil or gas stains they should be treated with a driveway degreaser and sealed with a spot sealer. If this is not done they will bleed through the asphalt.
- ✓ Use a driveway applicator brush and apply a driveway cleaner working it in good. Allow it to dry before filling in any holes or cracks.
- ✓ Fill small cracks or holes with a flexible crack filler. Anything more than ½ inch in diameter will need blacktop patch applied with a trowel.
- ✓ Pour out a small amount of sealer at a time and spread evenly with the squeegee side of the driveway applicator. Only work a four-foot area at a time.

- ❖ Make sure that the material you are using does not come into contact with your skin.
- ❖ Try not to breathe in the fumes for too long a period without wearing a mask.
- ❖ Wear gloves and old shoes you can discard when you're done.
- ❖ Wear eye protection when chipping away the old asphalt.

GARAGE ROLL-UP DOORS

ROLL-UP MAINTENANCE TIPS

Sluggish Operation

Make sure the rollers are lubricated as well as the hinges and pulleys. This maintenance should be done about twice a year. Never oil or grease the tracks. They should still be wiped down and sprayed with a silicon spray or penetrating lubricant.

Rollers do not operate smoothly

Make sure that the rollers are not damaged. If they are then replace them. If they are clogged with grease and grit, they should be removed and cleaned in a solvent solution such as mineral spirits, then reinstalled. If you see that the rollers are OK then check the alignment of the tracks with a level. Adjust the brackets until the vertical parts of the tracks are plumb. If you find any bent tracks they will need to be replaced. It is best to tighten all screws on loose hinges.

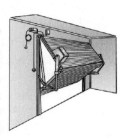

The cable is frayed

Make sure that the door is locked open when replacing cables. Be sure that the cables are of equal length or the door will not move smoothly.

Door is opening too fast

While the door is raised, loosen the tension by repositioning the hook ends of each cable, making them closer to the springs on the cable anchors.

Door is getting hard to open

While the door is raised, just tighten the tension by repositioning the hook ends of each cable closer to the springs on the cable anchors. The tension needs to be equalized on the springs and make sure that the tracks are not too far apart.

The door lock is sticking
Try lubricating the latch mechanism with powdered graphite. Check the fit of the lock bars into the slots on the strike plate. Adjust the brackets up or down until they will support the lock bar in the correct position.

WHOOPS, IT WENT THROUGH THE WALL
The torsion springs are very dangerous and should only be adjusted by a garage door professional.

KEEP CROOKS OUT OF THE HOUSE
When you go away for an extended period, be sure and reinforce the overhead door with a long shackle padlock. Place the padlock through the door track, just above one of the door rollers to prevent entry.

GARAGE DOOR OPENERS

PREVENTION A MUST
Regular servicing is needed for garage doors. The springs should be lightly lubricated. The chain should be greased and you should make sure that you check for loose screws.

THE MOST COMMON PROBLEM
The most common problem results from dirty tracks.

STRANGE NOISES
If you hear grinding and scraping noises, the problem is with the gears in the motor or the sliding mechanism is going bad.

SPRINGING INTO ACTION
The springs can be very dangerous if they break and need to be secured with safety cables, which can easily be purchased in any hardware store.

SAFETY TEST FOR GARAGE DOOR OPENERS

- ♦ To test for the downward force of the door, place a piece of 2X4 on the garage floor in the center of the doorway and trigger the door to close. When the door comes into contact with the 2X4, it should strain slightly and then open. If you see that the pressure is too great or too slight, you can make the proper adjustment.

- There are 2 screws on the front of most units that control the down force of the door. Unplug the power unit and adjust the down force screws.
- To test the door then stand in the center outside the door and place your hands so that the door will hit them. See how much force is exerted that stops the door and reverses it. Think of a child under the door and how much pressure should be allowed before the door reverses.
- If you have safety reversing sensors, they should be checked to be sure they would stop and reverse the door if the beam of light is broken.

GARAGE FLOORS

HINTS FOR PREPARING A GARAGE DOOR FOR PAINTING

- To prepare a garage floor for painting you will need to clean it thoroughly.
- Use a stiff broom to sweep it first then remove any oil spills with cat litter.
- Wash the floor with a concentrated garage floor cleaner using a stiff brush.
- If any stains remain you will need to clean them off with muriatic acid wearing a respirator approved for chemicals.
- Wear gloves, eye protection and old clothes and shoes.
- Rinse well and clean twice. Purchase paint that resists flaking from hot tires.

HOT WATER HEATER

GENERAL INFORMATION:
If you go on vacation be sure and turn the hot water heater to its lowest setting to save energy.

DRAIN ME, DRAIN ME
The hot water heater may need to be drained depending on the type of water in your area. If you are in an area that has high mineral content water, the hot water heater should be drained according to the instruction booklet that came with the heater. If you can't find the booklet, try and drain the heater about every 2-3 months until the water runs clear.

IS YOUR HEATER HOT?
If you feel the heater and it feels warm, you are losing heat and should purchase an insulated blanket. This will help retain the heat and save you about $15-$20 a year.

BRRRRRRRRRRRRRR
If the water is not hot enough it is usually one of two problems. Either the thermo-coupler or the thermostat is bad.

BUY QUALITY
The recommended water heater is the Rheem™ brand found in plumbing supply houses. Be sure that the heater you choose has the same wattage and holds the same amount of water as the one you are replacing. Also, be sure and purchase a new relief valve, which should be replaced every time you replace the heater.

PERMIT ME?
Check with the local building department since some areas of the country do require a permit when you change the water heater.

WHERE'S MY HEAT?
If the water heater will not light up or stay lit, it is probably a bad gas valve or thermo-coupler or both.

DRIP, DRIP, DRIP
When the heater leaks from both the top and bottom or from the temperature control, the glass liner is probably cracked and it is best to drain it as soon as possible and buy a new one.

PLEASE, PRESS MY BUTTONS
Having to continually press the reset button means that the heating element housings are corroded and allowing water to drip on the element and cause a short. It would be cheaper to just replace the element instead of buying a new heater unless it is an old one.

POP, POP, POP
If the electric heater keeps popping the overload reset button, it is probably the element, which should be replaced or if you have hard water, you can wait until it builds up enough to stop the leak. It is best to replace the element.

WHERE'S MY HOT WATER?

If the water is not heating enough, the problem is usually due to a bad heating element or thermostat.

DIRTY THERMOSTAT CONTACTS

It is not unusual for the contacts in the thermostat to become dirty and cause a problem. This is an easy fix and all you have to do is run a new dollar bill or other clean sheet of thin, stiff paper between them to clean off any dirt that may have accumulated.

THERE'S A GHOST IN MY WATER HEATER

The strange rumbling noise when the water is heating up is probably heavy sediment moving about in the tank. The only way to solve the problem is with a new water heater.

THE SECRET ANODE ROD

The rod is inside almost every water heater; there is a magnesium bar called an "anode rod." This metal rod protects the water heater tank from rust by corroding before the tank does. However, when the rod disintegrates and rusts away, the tank will start rusting. You can double the life of your water heater if you replace the rod before it has a chance to dissolve completely. The rod should be replaced about every 4 years depending on the quality of the water.

HOW TO REPLACE THE ANODE ROD

- ❖ First you will need to shut off the cold water supply line to the heater then you need to turn off the gas supply and the circuit breaker.
- ❖ Next attach a garden hose to the drain cock and slowly drain off several gallons of water.
- ❖ To remove the old rod you will need to loosen the hexagonal fitting located on top of the heater with a long-handled ratchet wrench.
- ❖ Lift out the rod and before installing the new rod, wrap its threads with Teflon tape so that it will seal better.
- ❖ Insert the new rod back into the heater and tighten the fitting.
- ❖ Bendable rods are available if there is not the room to put in a straight, solid rod.

I'M NOT RECOVERING WELL
You probably have a bad heating element that is slowing down the recovery time and needs replacement. Call a plumber!

ENERGY DRAINER
Heating water for taking a bath, washing the dishes and clothes, preparing food and general housecleaning uses about 20% of all the energy used in the average home. Your water heater should be turned to 120^0F instead of the average 140^0F that the heater is set at in most homes. However, if you have a real old model dishwasher it may require the 140^0F water so that the detergent will work properly.

A LITTLE HERE, A LITTLE THERE, WATER EVERYWHERE
Water on the floor around the hot water heater usually means that the tank is rusting away and you need a new hot water heater. If you only see water occasionally then it is probably the thermostat or pressure release valve that has gone bad.

STORAGE SPACE

GENERAL INFORMATION:
Garages can be a storage nightmare, especially if you have a small garage and no storage shed. Some garages do have a storage area above the car parking in an attic, which is helpful; however, many garages do not have an easily accessible one.

SOLVING STORAGE SPACE PROBLEMS

Develop storage space in a minimal space area that can accommodate items that cannot be stored in the house and allowing the cars to still be parked in the garage.

1. Install a collapsible ladder or a bunk-bed style ladder with a hook in the overhead storage area to make the area more easily accessible. Place floorboards on top of the studs to create storage space without disturbing the insulation.
2. Utilize the back wall and build cabinets that overhang the front of the car allowing the front to go underneath the cabinets.
3. Make a workbench with collapsible legs so that it can be placed in the down position when not being used.
4. Utilize a grid and modular storage system that is configured to hold all garden tools and ladders.

5. Utilize bicycle flush wall mounts to keep bikes out of the way.
6. Use ropes and pulley systems to store larger light items (canoe, etc.) next to the ceiling.
7. Electrical cords should be stored in cardboard tubes from rolls of paper towels. Then label them as to which appliance they go to.

STORING CHEMICALS

HOME PROTECTION A MUST
If you store chemicals in the garage and there is a door that opens from the house to the garage, the door from the house to the garage should be fire-rated and should be able to withstand fire for 20 minutes.

SAFE STORAGE
Chemicals that are sold in their original containers are safe to store in the garage as long as there is no damage to the containers. Make sure that they are in a cool, dry location.

KA-BOOM
Gasoline containers should only be filled 95% full. Place the cap on securely. Store the containers out of direct sunlight and be sure that the temperature is below 80^0F. Use a fuel stabilizer like Sta-Bil™ or Pri-G™.

MISCELLANEOUS

This one's a winner.

DE-KNOTER UPPER
To stop cords from separating when you are working in the garage, just tie a knot with the two cords you are using then plug then two cords together. The strain will only be on the knot not the electrical connection.

TRY SODIUM PHOSPHATE
TSP will remove grease stains from concrete after you scrape off the excess.

TRY IT, YOU WILL BECOME A BELIEVER
If you want to remove glue residue on almost any surface, try using vegetable oil on a rag. Residue from sticky labels, are also a breeze to remove. The vegetable oil tends to neutralize the glue's bonds.

PREVENT WOOD FROM SPLINTERING

Driving nails into wood that splits easily is a problem that can easily be solved. Just barely blunt the tip of the nail with your hammer. The flattened out tip is less likely to split the wood. You can also try placing the nail into a block of soap before nailing it.

A GIRL'S BEST FRIEND: Jewelry Cleaning

All diamonds and gold jewelry can easily be cleaned by mixing a solution of 50/50 white vinegar and warm water. Dip a soft toothbrush into the solution and brush gently. Opals, emeralds, and pearls are too delicate for this type of treatment. Costume jewelry should only be cleaned with a weak solution of baking soda and water to avoid damaging the glue bonds.

Polish gold – Wet a piece of cloth with some beer and start rubbing your gold (no stones) to get the shine back. Use a second cloth to dry it.

Diamonds

- Diamonds can be chipped and should never be worn when doing rough jobs.
- Chlorine bleach will discolor the setting.
- Have the prongs holding the stone checked annually.
- When storing your jewelry, make sure they don't touch each other.
- Diamonds will scratch other pieces of jewelry very easily.
- Clean your diamonds regularly with a mild detergent and warm water.

Colored Gemstones

- Never expose the gemstones to salt water or harsh chemical solutions.
- Check with your jeweler for cleaning methods for colored stones.
- Emeralds need special care, check with your jeweler.
- Hairspray will dull gemstones.
- Wipe gemstones with a soft cloth after each wearing.

10-24 Karat Gold Jewelry

- Gold scratches easily, keep pieces away from other jewelry.
- Do not bathe or shower using soaps and shampoos.
- Use a soft bristle brush.
- Grease is easily removed with rubbing alcohol.
- Try not to get makeup and powders on the gold.

Silver

- Store silver in a cool, dry location.
- Only rub silver with a soft cloth. Paper towel and tissues will scratch it.
- Never wear silver into a swimming pool that is chlorinated.

Pearls

- Put on pearls after applying cosmetics, perfume, and hair spray.
- Quality pearls should be re-strung annually with knots between each pearl if worn regularly.
- Store pearls in a chamois bag or wrap in tissue to store.
- Never use harsh chemicals to clean pearls.
- Special pearl formulas or mild soap and warm water can be used to clean them.

MAKING JEWELRY CLEANER

The following ingredients will be needed:

1	Tablespoon of household ammonia
1	Tablespoon of washing soda (from supermarket)
1	Tablespoon of liquid dishwashing detergent
3	Cups of very warm tap water

Place all the ingredients in a medium bowl and mix thoroughly. The solution should be stored in a sealed glass jar. When you want to clean your jewelry, just soak the pieces in the solution for 5-7 minutes and brush with a soft-bristled toothbrush. Rinse the jewelry in warm water and dry well.

CAUTION: Do not place pearls or emeralds in this solution and never add chlorine bleach to these chemicals. Keep out of the reach of children.

SILVER JEWELRY CLEANER

The following ingredients will be needed:

½	Cup of white vinegar
2	Tablespoons of baking soda

Place the ingredients in a small bowl and mix well.
Place the jewelry in the bowl and allow it to stand for 2 hours before rinsing with cold water and drying with a soft dry cloth.

DE-KNOTTING A CHAIN
If you get a knot in a chain, just place a drop of vegetable oil on the knot and work it out with a straight pin.

JEWELRY POLISH
The following ingredients will be needed:

2	**Tablespoons of ferric oxide**
2	**Tablespoons of calcium carbonate**
	Cool tap water

Place the ingredients into a small bowl and mix well using just enough water to produce paste. Rub on the jewelry with a soft cloth and buff with another clean, soft cloth.

A POPPER OUTER
Tough nut and bolts are easy to remove after you pour some cola or other carbonated water on them and allow them to sit for about 20 minutes. The mild acidic action of either citric or phosphoric acid will usually do the job.

CLOGGED SPRAY CAN NOZZLE
If you turn a spray can upside down after you use it and spray until it comes out clear, it will not clog up. If it does clog up, just soak the nozzle in paint thinner for a few minutes. You can also try placing the nozzle on a can of WD-40 to clear the nozzle very quickly.

NEUTRALIZE ME
The acid around a battery post can easily be cleaned with a thick solution of baking soda and water. Allow it to soak for 10-15 minutes before washing it off. Baking soda is a mild base and will neutralize the weak acid.

DON'T HAVE A SCREW LOOSE?
Trying to remove a screw can be a difficult task and may take a lot of patience. Here are few suggestions that may make the task easier:

- ✓ If you heat-up the tip of your screwdriver you may be able to loosen a stubborn screw.
- ✓ If the slot is filled with garbage, you must clean it out before you try and remove it.
- ✓ Be sure that the blade of the screwdriver fits the slot.
- ✓ Place the screwdriver into the slot and tap it gently since the vibration may loosen the screw.

✓ If you only get the screw partially out, try squirting a little penetrating oil on the part you can see and then screwing it back in before trying to remove it again.

SUPER HAND CLEANSER
The following ingredients will be needed:

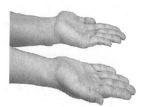

4	**Quarts of cold tap water**
1	**Box borax soap chips or powder**
1	**Box of Lux™**
1	**Pint of corn meal**

Place all the ingredients together in a medium bucket and mix thoroughly into a paste. Place the paste into jars with lids and label as a super hand cleaner.

MASKING TAPE DRIED OUT?
Masking tape should be stored in an empty coffee can with a lid to stop it from drying out.

BEGONE STINKY HANDS
Often when you pump gasoline, you get gas or the smell of gasoline on your hands. After pumping gas use some baking soda on your hands to remove the smell then wipe them clean with a piece of damp paper towel or keep a box of damp handy-wipes in the car.

CIGARETTE FIRE
Keep a box of baking soda in the glove box for a small fire emergency. Just sprinkle it on to put out the fire.

REVIVING A DULL RAZOR BLADE
You can bring a dull razor blade back to life and make it sharp again by sharpening it on the striking edge of a matchbook cover.

CHAPTER 8

GARDEN SHED

CARING FOR GARDEN TOOLS

YUMMY, MOTOR OIL & SAND

If you want to keep your garden tools clean and always ready to use, try mixing ½ quart of motor oil in a 5 gallon bucket of sand. Leave enough room to place some tools in and stick your shovel, small rakes, and garden tools in the sand. It will clean and condition them.

NASTY, RUSTY

When your garden tools get rusty just sand off the rust with medium sandpaper and place the tools in the bucket of sand and oil. Make you sure you move them in and out a few times to clean them off. Rust can also be cleaned off using white vinegar. Just soak the metal end of the tools for a few days or until the rust disappears.

BE SHARP!

Always have a whetstone or a file handy to sharpen the blades on your garden tools as they need it.

WINTER STORAGE

To keep your garden tools in great shape and ready for the spring, just store them all winter with the end in the bucket of sand and oil.

DARN SOCK?

Use an old sock that you would not miss to clean your yard tools. Just place some WD-40™ on the sock and clean them after removing any debris that has accumulated on them.

IT'S A STICKY WICKET

When the joints of your garden shears become sticky, just clean them with rubbing alcohol then spray them with WD-40™.

GARDENING HAND TOOLS

SHARPENING HEDGE TRIMMERS

Secure the hedge trimmers in a D-vise with the cutting edge up and the bevel toward you. Work the Dremel (#932) at the angle of the trimmer edge's bevel (don't alter the original bevel). Always start the pass at the edge and move left to right.

A file can also be used to sharpen the blade by moving the file away from and diagonally across the sharp edge (maintain the factory bevel). Then you need to decrease the angle slightly and hone just the last $1/16^{th}$ of the blade with a sharpening stone.

SHARPENING A WEED CUTTER

First disassemble the weed cutter and screw the blade to a wood block and be sure that the blade overhangs one side. Place the block in a vise and use a double-cut flat file. Push the file toward and diagonally across the sharp edge and be sure and maintain a factory bevel $(45^{0}\text{-}60^{0})$. Reverse the blade and repeat.

SHARPENING A PRUNER

Maintain a sharp cutting edge with a medium-grit sharpening stone. Be sure and wet the stone with water or lubricate it with honing oil, depending on the type of stone you are using.

SHARPENING DIGGING TOOLS

The majority of digging tools are not sold sharpened. You will need to sharpen them with a coarse file working to a 45^{0} bevel.

SHARPENING A GARDEN SAW

Place the saw in a vise and use a triangular file to sharpen the blade. Sharpen each side of every bow saw tooth to 45^0-60^0 bevel of any saw that cuts in both directions.

BAD CORROSION

Since garden tools get wet, they must be protected against corrosion. Be sure and clean the tools after every use with a wire brush and wipe down the metal with light oil.

REPAIR A WOOD HANDLE

When the wooden handle becomes rough, try smoothing it out with medium-grade grit emery cloth. Sandpaper will work but tends to tear too easily. Wipe the handle down with a heavy coat of boiled linseed oil and dry well.

REPAIRING YOUR HEAD

When a tool head becomes loose the best way to repair it is to mix equal amounts of 2-part epoxy resin and a hardener on a piece of scrap wood. Coat the end of the tool that goes back into the ferule and drive the end back in with a block of wood and a hammer.

REPLACING A WOODEN HANDLE

Lock the tool in a vise and remove the broken handle by drilling ¼-inch holes in the end and cracking it apart. Slip the new head over the new handle and hit the butt end of the handle down hard on a wooden block to draw the head tight. Then drive a small hammer wedge to expand the wood, which will secure the head.

POWER MOWERS

WALK-A-BOUT MOWERS

There are three categories of these mowers: Side discharge, rear discharge, and mulching mowers. Best to have two blades and always keep one sharpened.

I prefer the mulching type.

Side-Discharge Mower – The discharge chute is located on the right side of the mower. Best for smaller lawns and can be purchased as an electric or gas-powered mower.

Rear-Discharge Mower – The grass clippings are thrown out the back into a catcher. Many models have a door that can be opened or closed if a bag is not used.

Mulching Mower – Cuts the grass into very fine particles that can be absorbed back into the turf. The clippings can then provide moisture and nutrients back to the lawn.

PUT, PUT, SPUT, SPUT

The motor will start but will shut off after a few seconds. Best to remove the tank and engine covers to expose the carburetor and governor linkage. Clean everything well with a stiff brush. Remove the air cleaner and carburetor and dismantle the carburetor. Wash all the parts with a spray can of carburetor cleaner and replace the air filter element. Oil the governor and throttle linkage and wash out the tank with clean gas. Change the oil and replace the spark plug.

VERY DISENGAGING

If the cutting deck will not disengage, the "A" spring or lever may be gone or bent and needs replacement.

REPLACING A STRETCHED BELT

Cut the belt off and take it to your dealer for an exact size replacement. When you are there be sure and get a threading diagram and procedure.

GETTING MIXED UP

Be sure and prepare the right mixture of oil and gas. Check your instruction book. Many new 4-cycle engines do not require oil to be mixed with the gas. If you have an older 2-cylcle engine, the mixture is 16 to 1 pint or 16 to ½ pint of oil per gallon of gasoline. Some books recommend 32 to one, but 16 to one seems to work better.

SPUTTER, SPUTTER

If your power mower is losing power, just remove the air filter and see if the power comes back. If it does, wash the sponge filter in gasoline and replace or remove the tank and upper cover and check the governor spring. The spring should be opening the throttle wide under spring tension when the engine is shut down. This spring is probably the problem. Other problems that cause this are a dirty carburetor or a partially plugged gas line.

WHOOOOPS

If the lawnmower keeps stalling be sure that you have changed the oil twice a season and replaced the filter and spark plug.

The engine compartment may be plugged up with old grass or dirt. Remove the spark plug and add a small amount of starting fluid then replace the spark plug and start the engine.

HELP! I'M HALF CHOKING
The carburetor needs to be disassembled and cleaned thoroughly.

OIL, OIL, EVERYWHERE
If you have oil going into the filter and oil is coming out of the exhaust it would be best to purchase a new motor.

BAD COIL, BAD COIL
If the motor runs fine and then decides to stop and not restart until it cools down, you probably have a bad coil in the electrical circuit or clogged cooling air passages. First, try removing the engine coil and clean the cooling fans. Second, degrease the engine, then replace the air filter and spark plugs, and finally change the oil.

EASY DOES IT!
Remember to always mow across a slope if you are using a walk-behind mower. This will keep you safe from a slip or fall and never attempt mowing on a steep hill with this type of mower.

If you are using a riding mower on a hillside or slope, be sure and mow up and down instead of across the hill to prevent the mower from tipping.

POWER YARD EQUIPMENT

CHAIN SAWS

IS BIGGER BETTER?
For around the home use it is best to purchase one with a 12-14-inch bar. The bar is the portion of the saw that the chain attaches to. These are usually lightweight and easy to use.

SAW WEAR, THE LATEST STYLE
You should wear certain protective clothing when using a chain saw. Invest in a pair of cut-retardant chaps. The fabric is made to jam the chainsaw blade if it comes into contact with the fabric. An eye, face and ear guard is also recommended.

HEAVE HO
Always carry a chain saw with the blade to the rear and be sure that the scabbard is on.

CALL 911
The most serious injuries occur from "kickback." This happens when the chain bar kicks back in the direction of the operator. This may occur when the saw hits an object such as a nail or screw in a piece of wood.

CHIPPER/SHREDDER

MULCH, MULCH, MULCH
Whether you need to purchase a chipper/shredder depends on your yard. These machines will turn leaves, garden refuse, and tree trimmings into raw material for a compost pile or provide mulch for your garden. The size of the unit will depend on your needs. It is really two machines in one. The chipper will turn tree limbs and branches into small chips and the shredder converts plants and leaves into usable material for a compost pile.

FRESH CHIP ALERT
It is best not to place fresh wood chips on the garden soil. They tend to rob the soil of nitrogen and should be composted for a year before using them.

I'M ALL CLOGGED, MUST BE SPRING
Shredders tend to clog easily and this is the nature of this piece of equipment. Be sure and purchase one with a shredding chamber that is easily accessible.

If the shredder has a discharge screen, it will be more likely to clog than one without a screen. However, it is recommended that the shredder have a screen, which will improve the quality of the shredded material by being pushed through the screen first. It will just need regular cleaning.

SHREDDER SAFETY
Be sure that children and pets are kept away from the machine. Never wear loose-fitting clothing. Wear gloves, ear protection and safety goggles. When filling the shredder chute always use the plunger to push material into the unit. Always disconnect the spark plug if the unit becomes jammed and wait for all parts to stop before clearing the jam.

GARDEN TILLER

AVOIDING WARPING
Always idle your tiller on a level surface for 1-2 minutes before you shut it down. If the engine cools evenly it will reduce the chance of warping and allow oil to lubricate all parts.

OIL CHANGING TIME
Change the oil shortly after you use the tiller while the oil is still warm and any dirt or residues are still in suspension. Residues will settle out after the engine cools down.

STORE THAT TILLER
When you store the tiller, make sure you close the fuel shutoff valve all the way to stop gas from seeping into the engine or leak on the floor.

DO I NEED A ROTOTILLER?
This is the most efficient method of turning the soil, weeding, and aerating. When aerating the soil, oxygen is put back into the soil causing an increase of microbial activity, which feeds on organic matter and speeds up decomposition.

HOW OFTEN DO I TILL
Usually you only need to till just once a year. Anymore and you may damage the soil. Never till the soil if the soil is wet.

WHAT TYPE OF TILLER IS BEST
Front-tine tillers are very hard to handle because of lack of weight over the tines. They may bounce around and you are forced to walk behind the tiller, compacting the soil as you go. Rear-tine tillers are recommended since the engine is in front of the tines, the machine is more stable and you can walk to the side and not compact the soil.

IS THERE A LOOSE NUT AROUND HERE?
Make sure you always check the tiller for loose nuts and bolts every time you store it.

A CLEAN TILLER IS A HEALTHY TILLER
Cleaning any residue when putting the tiller away will increase the life of the tiller and reduce the chances of overheating the gear housing and shaft.

HEDGE TRIMMERS

GENERAL INFORMATION:
These are sold as gasoline powered, electric or rechargeable battery-powered tools. The new designs are lighter and reduce vibration with special holes in the units. The newer machines will stop in ½ second when the trigger is released for safer operation.

LAWN VACUUMS

GENERAL INFORMATION:
Most have a large capacity bag on walk-behind machines and can clear leaves and twigs from large areas quickly. Most bags have a 6-bushel capacity and some models can easily be converted into a blower. Engine size varies from 5hp to 8hp and it is best to get one with a hose attachment for hard-to-reach places.

LEAF BLOWERS

GENERAL INFORMATION:
Leaf blowers are a very noisy method of clearing large areas. It is best to check on the ordinances in your area before purchasing one. Local laws sometimes only permit their use during certain hours of the day. However, some cities ban them altogether.

LOG SPLITTERS

GENERAL INFORMATION:
These are hydraulic-powered rams that drive wooden logs against a solid steel wedge to make firewood. Be sure and purchase one with a forward ram control that must be engaged before the log splitter will operate. Make sure it also has a jack stand to keep the log splitter level while it is in operation.

SNOW THROWERS

WHAT HORSEPOWER IS BEST?
There are several sizes of snow throwers and it depends on the area that you need to clear. The smaller ones are only 3hp and will do a short walkway, patio or steps. The medium ones are 5hp to 8hp and can handle snow up to a foot deep. If you live in an area that gets a lot of snow you will need one with 8hp to 12hp engine. These are great for long driveways and small retain parking areas.

158

There are single-stage throwers that are powered by 2-cycle or 4-cycle engines and use a single auger to clear a 24" path of snow and throw it 5-55 feet away. The double-stage throwers use a large front auger and a secondary impeller to throw even farther.

STRING EDGER/TRIMMER

TO PURCHASE A GAS OR ELECTRIC TRIMMER

Electric edger/trimmers do not really have the power to do a good job. Gas trimmers do a much better job and have the power. String trimmers are not really recommended since they are very noisy and tend to spew out a large amount of pollutants. If you do purchase a string trimmer, purchase one that has a 4-cycle engine rather than a 2-cycle engine since the 4-cycle uses just gas and not a gas and oil combination.

PROTECT THYSELF

It is recommended to wear long pants and closed-toe shoes. Also, protective goggles, earplugs and a dust mask. If you have anti-vibration gloves, it would be best to wear them. Injuries occur from the constant vibration to the hands and wrists.

RIGHT OR LEFT?

All trimmers are designed for right-handed people with the hot part of the engine and muffler away from the body.

CHAPTER 9

HOME OFFICE

COMPUTER

CAMCORDER CONFUSION SOLVED
In order to connect a camcorder video output to your computer you will need to purchase a special USB to video or S-video adapter.

NEED A USB PORT?
To add a USB port to a MAC or PC you need to install a USB controller card to your MAC or PC. Make sure you know what you are doing or call a professional to put it in.

CALL RESCUE
If your computer dies first make sure that it is turned on and that a circuit breaker has not tripped. Be sure that there is no disk in any of the slots when you first turn it on.

MY COMPUTER CAN'T READ
If your computer won't read files from a floppy disc the disk has been mishandled and some of the files may be corrupted. Very common: when children are present or someone using the computer who is not familiar enough with it. You may have lost the files, but have a professional check and see if they are on the hard drive before you panic.

BETTER INTRODUCE THEM
When your computer fails to recognize your mouse, just hold the mouse in front of the screen and introduce them properly or check the connection in the rear of the hard drive (more than likely to be the problem).

TWO PRINTERS ARE BETTER THAN ONE

If you want to hook up two printers to your computer you will need to purchase a switchbox and cables to connect it to the printer.

SHARING PRINTERS

To share two printers with two computers, you need to purchase an auto switchbox, two normal printer cables and two DB25 male to DB25 male cables.

COPIERS

DAMN JAM
Non-Machine Causes

The majority of all paper jams are caused by using the wrong paper. If you are getting jams frequently, try switching to a higher quality paper and you will see the difference. Purchasing the cheapest paper is a mistake. Humidity can also cause paper jams and be checked by looking at the paper. If the paper has small bumps or appears uneven it is probably high humidity.

Machine Caused Jams

Dirty or worn rollers or separator belt damaged. Timing switches are malfunctioning. Clutches may not be working right. When clearing a jam, avoid tearing the paper at all costs.

IS QUALITY A PROBLEM?
Light or Dark Copies

Due to improper exposure adjustment or poor quality paper! Adjust the light/dark setting and replace present paper with better quality. Also light copies may be caused by low toner concentration and you may need toner.

CAN'T SEE MY COPY
Blank Copies
You may have a broken or missing corona wire or faulty corona block contacts. Need to call service tech for repair.

AWFULLY DARK DOWN HERE
Black Copies
It may be caused by a blown exposure lamp, faulty exposure lamp thermo fuse, contaminated lamp contacts or a light path/optics obstruction. The lamp or fuse can be replaced and the lamp contacts can be cleaned. If there is an obstruction in the optics path it needs to be cleared.

THERE ARE STRANGE LINES EVERYWHERE
Vertical Line Problem
Usually caused by a scratched drum, faulty drum or scratched upper fuse roller. This problem needs the attention of a service tech.

Horizontal Line Problem
Usually caused by scratched upper fuse roller or scratched drum. It is best to call a service tech.

I'M SEEING WHITE & BLACK SPOTS
White Spots
The drum may have a pinhole or you have a bad photoreceptor. Replace the bad item or call service tech.
Black Spots
This is usually the result of a dirty copy board glass or pin-holed drum. Cleaning the glass usually resolves this problem. The other possible problems may be a contaminated drum cleaning roller, or contaminated toner.

BAD COPY, BAD COPY
Print Smearing or Coming Off
This is usually caused by depleted fuser oil and oil needs to be added.

ELECTRICAL

GENERAL INFORMATION:
When you set up a home office be sure to purchase a high quality surge protector. One of the easiest ways to damage office equipment is a power surge. It is also best to keep cords from touching each other with a spiral plastic wrap.

FAX MACHINES

CLEAR OUT THAT JAM
The following steps will help you to clear a paper jam:
> * First unplug the machine
> * Open the cover and remove the thermal paper roll
> * Hold down the start and stop keys at the same time and then plug the machine back in.
> * Release the two keys and the display should read *"OUT OF PAPER"*
> * Open the cover and replace the thermal paper roll then close the cover
> * The display should return to the date and time

NOT RECEIVING, BUT SENDING OK
Set the fax machine to *AUTO* reception.

WHERE OH WHERE HAS MY LITTLE FAX GONE
If your fax machine will not receive an incoming fax when it is connected to your answering machine, make sure that the phone line of the fax machine is plugged into the *TEL LINE* of the fax machine. The phone line that comes from the answering machine should be plugged into the *TEL SET* position of the fax machine.

TELEPHONES

WHERE IS MY RINGI-DINGI?
If your phone won't ring, first, be sure that the ringer volume is up and that the set is plugged in. Also be sure that the receiver is not off the hook, even the slightest.

I'M SUPPOSED TO HAVE A DIAL TONE
When there is no dial tone, make sure that the phone is plugged properly. Try replacing the phone cord with another phone cord. Try another phone in the same jack to eliminate the possibility of the phone being bad.

HUMMMMMMMMMMMMMMMM
If you encounter a strange hum on the line, it is usually caused by one of the dialing buttons sticking down. Just drag your finger across the buttons to release it.

WHY STATIC?

Static on the line is usually a problem with too many phones on the same line. It can also be moisture in the jack or a faulty cord. To check if there are too many lines, just unplug all the lines in the home and then plug back in the one that you were getting static on. If there's no static, keep plugging phones in one at a time until you get static. Try another phone on the static jack phone to see if it is a phone problem and then switch cords around.

CHAPTER 10

ATTIC

ATTIC FANS

GENERAL INFORMATION:
In the winter be sure and cover the attic fan with a plastic bag covered in fiberglass insulation to keep the cold air out of the attic.

THE LOWER, THE BETTER
It will reduce energy costs by exhausting super-heated air trapped in the attic and replacing it with cooler air from the outside. The fan can reduce the temperature in the attic by as much as 55^{0}F. An **The roof will last longer!** attic fan can lower utility bills by as much as 25%.

FAN TO THE RESCUE
An attic fan can have a positive effect on the life of your roof. Hot air trapped in an attic can cause heat damage to roof sheathing, felt and composition shingles. Many shingle manufactures will not honor warrantees unless an attic fan is installed.

FAN CREATES MORE COMFORT
By lowering the attic temperature, the heat is prevented from getting into the living areas.

GOOD PLACEMENT, A MUST
The fan should be placed as close to and above the roof peak as possible. If two or more fans are installed, be sure that they are at the same height.

It will be important to choose the right size fan for the job. Multiply the square footage of the living area by 3. This number should be less than the CFM fan rating at high speed.

One air change per minute is what you are looking for.

INSULATION

WHAT DOES "R" VALUE MEAN?
The "R" value is a measure of how a material resists the passage of heat. The higher the value, the more effective the material will be.

INSULATION TIPS

Mild Climates
R-11 Used in floors and walls
R-19 Used in ceilings below ventilated attics

Moderate Climates
R-19 Used in walls and floors
R-30 Used in ceilings below ventilated attics

Cold Climates
R-19 Used in walls and under floors
R-38 to R-49 Used in ceilings below ventilated attics

PROTECTION, A MUST!
Be sure and always wear protective goggles, dust mask, or respirator and gloves as well as long sleeves and long pants. For added protection wear a hat, tuck your sleeves into your gloves, and be sure and tuck your pant legs into your socks.

AIR LEAK, GET A CORK
It is best to avoid disturbing the existing insulation especially if it is a loose fill. Moving it may create gaps where air can leak through.

NEED MY SPACE
Never place insulation over recessed lighting fixtures, ceiling fans, or ventilation fans. When using loose-fill insulation use sheet metal to create a barrier around the openings. Be sure and also keep insulation at least 3-inches away from chimneys and gas flue pipes.

I NEED BREATHING SPACE
Be sure and allow for adequate ventilation. Never cover an attic vent and leave about 1-inch of airflow between the insulation and the roof. However, don't forget to insulate and weather-strip the attic opening.

HOW MUCH IS TOO MUCH?

If you live in the Midwest, you will need to insulate at R-38. However, check your local building codes for the appropriate "R" value in your area.

DANGER IS LURKING EVERYWHERE

Moving around your attic can be dangerous so watch out for overhead rafters and be sure and only walk on ceiling joists. If there is room, it is best to lay a plywood panel across the ceiling joists to walk or kneel on.

THE RIGHT ANGLE MAKES A DIFFERENCE

When you add insulation batts or blankets be sure and install them at right angles to the first layer.

WHAT INSULATION IS BEST?

The easiest to use is batt insulation, and always use unfaced batt since the paper or foil vapor retarder will trap water vapor, causing a mold problem. It should also be installed perpendicular to the attic floor joists, which will reduce heat loss through the joists. You can also use loose fiberglass or cellulose.

SCRATCH, SCRATCH

If you are going to use fiberglass insulation, be sure and purchase the "no-itch" products. They are worth the extra money, are much easier to handle, and safer to work with.

SHOULD THE ATTIC FLOOR BE INSULATED?

The attic floor can be insulated if you are not using the floor for a living space.

FLOORING

PLYWOOD FLOORING AND INSULATION

How should the plywood floor be placed if we have blown-in insulation? Move the insulation aside and don't place the plywood on top of any insulation that is on the joists. Place the plywood on top of the joists.

CHAPTER 11

BASEMENT

FLOORS

PEEL ME A FLOOR
Painted cement basement floors are notorious for peeling after they are only a few months old. To avoid the floor-peeling problem just place white vinegar into a bucket and paint the floor with the vinegar first. After the vinegar dries, apply the coat of floor paint.

FUEL STORAGE

TANKS-A-LOT
The oil heat tank lines should be checked by fuel company delivery personnel at least once a year. It is usually before you put in the oil for the winter.

SECURITY OF ABOVE GROUND TANKS
They should be 100% level, on a secure cement slab and preferably anchored to the slab. The tank must definitely be anchored if you are not in a flood zone.

COPPER LINE INFO

If the tank has copper lines that run from the tank to the furnace, be sure that there is no direct contact between the line and any concrete in walls or floors. The chemicals in concrete tend to react with copper and may cause excessive corrosion of the line.

BRRRRRRRRRRR

Ice and/or snow may affect the fuel lines. The outside lines should be protected against ice or snow that may fall from a roof or tree.

FILL-ER-UP

Be sure and install a vent alarm, which will tell the delivery person when the tank is full.

FURNACES

GENERAL INFORMATION:

Your furnace does need to be serviced every year for optimal efficiency. Have the servicing done in the late summer or early fall, which should include a cleaning and general tune-up. If you use oil, the tank should be filled in late summer to avoid the winter costs of heating oil. Having the furnace cleaned can increase the furnace efficiency by as much as 25%.

The heat is created in a furnace by burning gas or oil inside the furnace. The hot gasses then pass through the curved metal tubing called a heat exchanger then out of your home through a plastic or metal vent pipe. While this is occurring, the air circulates through your home passing over the outside of a "heat exchanger" and takes on the heat from the hot metal. This warm air is then circulated through your home.

WHERE OH WHERE DID MY OIL PIPE GO?????

If the snow gets too deep, you may have a problem finding your oil pipe for a delivery. Just place a colored flag on a stick that is anchored next to the oil delivery pipe so that the deliveryman can easily find the pipe.

Can't fill it, can't find it!

FURNACE DIFFERENCES

Two-Speed Furnace – These furnaces can run on low speed up to 90% of the time and operate more quietly and will run for longer periods of time than single-speed furnaces. This means fewer drafts caused by frequent on and off cycles. The temperature tends to remain more constant.

Variable-Speed Furnace – These provide the ultimate combination of comfort, efficiency, and they are quiet. They are one-step above the two-speed furnace since they offer "smart" motors that monitor your home and adjust the volume &

speed of the air providing the most efficient heating and cooling. They also provide significant energy savings.

DOES MY FURNACE HAVE A FILTER?
This depends on the type of furnace you have. If you have a warm air furnace, you have an air filter. If you have a boiler with radiators then you probably don't have a filter.

Most furnace manufacturers place inexpensive fiberglass filters in their furnaces, which remove most airborne particles that might damage the fan and heating coil. However, it is better to have the more expensive filters, which can improve the air quality in the home and remove pollens, mold spores, and bacteria.

Pleated filters last from 3-9 months. Disposable fiberglass panel or electrostatic filters should be changed every 1 to 3 months. If you don't change the filters regularly, you will cause the furnace to work harder.

DIRTY FILTER = DIRTY HOME
You can spend less time cleaning and dusting if you change your filters regularly. Duct cleaning is also important and should be done by a professional. The cost is usually from $75-$300 depending on the size of the home. It is a must if someone has allergies.

TROUBLESHOOTING AN ELECTRIC FURNACE

I'll find the problem.

Not getting heat
The furnace switch or the main breaker may be open or the thermostat is set too low for it to turn on. Be sure and check the switch and fuse or breakers and the setting on the thermostat.

Cycling on & off too often
The furnace may have a clogged filter or the blower may be going bad causing the unit to overheat. Try replacing the filter and lubricate the blower.

Not getting enough heat
The thermostat setting is not set right, defective heating element or you have a clogged filter or duct. First, check the thermostat setting then check the fuse or breaker. If the fuse or breaker trips when re-set, call a serviceman.

TROUBLESHOOT A GAS FURNACE

No heat
The thermostat may be set too low or the switch, fuse, or circuit breaker may be open. The gas might be shut off or the pilot is out.

170

The furnace is cycling too often
This is usually caused by a clogged filter or there is something wrong with the blower. Try replacing the filter and adjust the blower.

Not getting enough heat
Either a clogged filter or the burners need to be cleaned. Replace the filters and have the burners cleaned by a professional.

The blower will not shut off
The fan switch is probably set for continuous circulation or the limit control is out of adjustment. Re-set the fan switch on the furnace or wall or adjust the limit control.

The furnace is squeaking and rumbling
The squealing noise may be from the blower belt slipping or the bearing may need lubrication. If there is rumbling with the burners off it is usually a misadjusted pilot. If there is rumbling with the burners on it usually means that the burners are dirty. Just oil the blower and adjust the belt. Adjust the pilot if the burners need cleaning. This should be done by a professional.

Pilot light out at end of season
Be sure and put out the pilot light at the end of the season. It will save you energy and actually prevent rust. Water vapor has the tendency to condense on the surface of the heat exchanger and promote rust.

TROUBLESHOOTING AN OIL FURNACE

It's usually the burner.

Burners don't run
The thermostat setting may be too low or the main switch, circuit breaker, or fuse is open. The motor may be overheated. Try setting the thermostat 5^0F higher than your normal setting. Check the switches, breakers and fuses or possibly the motor needs oiling. Check for any reset switches.

Burners are running but won't fire up
Possibly either the oil or the spark is not getting to the unit or the safeties may be sooty. Be sure all oil valves are open and that there is oil in the tank, best not to trust the gauge. Dip a rod into the tank and check it. Clean the safeties!

Burners are cycling too frequently
You may have a clogged air blower motor or it needs oiling. Replace the filter and oil and adjust limit control.

Burner is squealing & smoking

The combustion air blower motor probably needs oiling. Be sure and shut off unit and allow it to cool then fill the oil cups and check them again after the motor has run for about an hour.

The chimney is smoking

A cold flue may cause this problem when the burner is first fired. If the smoking persists, it's a sign of incomplete combustion, i.e. fuel being wasted in the unit.

TROUBLESHOOTING A HEAT PUMP

Heat pump is not running

Either there is no power getting to the unit or the thermostat is not asking for heat.

First, check the thermostat setting. Follow this by then checking the electrical disconnect switch and the fuses or breakers in the circuit panel. It is best to also check the reset switch in the outdoor cabinet.

Short cycles are occurring

There may be an obstruction blocking the outdoor coil or possibly the blower unit is not working properly. A clogged filter will also cause the problem. Clear the outdoor coil and check the filter and the blower unit.

Having long or frequent defrost cycles

If the outdoor coil is blocked, it could cause the problem of defrosting that lasts longer than 15 minutes or occurring more than twice an hour. See previous answer.

Getting uneven heating

The heat pump is putting out a cooler flow of air than you are used to. Also, the indoor temperature will normally drop 2^0F to 3^0F when the outside temperature reaches the system's balance point differential. This is the point when the backup heating should kick in. You can minimize the airflow discomfort by balancing the duct system to offset the balance point differential. However, you may have to raise the thermostat setting during cold weather.

NOT OPERATING PROPERLY

If it is an outside unit, it may be obstructed by bushes or trash.

EXCESS WATER DRIPPING FROM HEAT PUMP

The unit is probably iced up and is in the process of defrosting. This is normal.

WATER ON WINDOWPANES

Too much humidity in the home! Turn on an exhaust fan if you have one or possibly too much plant watering or steam ironing.

TROUBLESHOOTING A STEAM BOILER

Where's the heat?

There is probably no power to the unit, no water or you have a burner problem. First, check the thermostat, switches, breakers, or fuses then the water level and make sure that the burners are working properly.

Not enough heat

You may have rust and scale in the boiler and it needs to be flushed. This will constrict the passages and will lower the efficiency. There may also be a buildup on the heating surfaces of soot from combustion. This job is for a professional.

Water level keeps getting too low

You may have a leaky return line. Call a plumber. If there is a leak within the boiler it will require a major repair.

Glass gauges are getting cloudy

The glass may just need cleaning or the boiler needs to be flushed. To clean the gauges turn off the boiler and close all the valves. Then loosen the nuts above and below the glass. Lift up the glass and remove it, clean it, and replace it.

There are ghosts in my pipes

If you have a problem with noisy pipes, it is probably water trapped in the return lines or in the return main. First check the pitch of all returns and make sure that they slope back toward the boiler. You may need to adjust the slant with new pipe hangers.

INSULATION

GENERAL INFORMATION:

Basement insulation is lacking in most homes and the average well insulated home in the United States and Canada loses about $1/5^{th}$ of its total heating bill to the basement walls and the air surrounding the basement.

The average homeowner can save $120-150 per year on their heating cost if they insulate the basement.

HEAT LOSS IN THE BASEMENT

Insulating the basement is fairly easy and should cost about $150. Best to talk to a professional at a store that sells insulation for their recommendations and materials.

MOISTURE HAZARDS

DIY, NOT A GOOD IDEA
When it comes to waterproofing your basement, don't try it unless it's a minor problem. Call a professional.

BASEMENT WALLS
The best method of testing a basement wall for moisture or condensation is to tape a 1-foot square piece of aluminum foil to the wall with duct tape and after two days, inspect the foil. If the foil side that was facing the wall feels moist, you probably have a water seepage problem. It is best to use a good masonry sealer and waterproof the walls.

BASEMENT SWIMMING POOL
The most common cause of water in a basement when it rains is from either a poor grade around the property that does not allow water to drain away from the house or poor gutters that do not drain at least 10 feet from the house.

LEAKAGE MAY BE A PROBLEM

A small amount of leakage may not cause a foundation problem; however, it may become a bigger problem over time. You should have the drainage checked around your home and consider waterproofing the basement. If the hydrostatic pressure gets too great it may cause foundation problems, and even cause a wall to collapse. A water leakage problem will affect the value of your home.

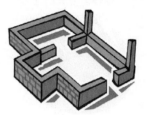

WATERPROOFING IS WORTH IT

If your home has been professionally graded, drain tiles installed, and you still have leaks, it may depend on the water table in your area. Consult a waterproofing professional to assist with this problem. Waterproofing will increase a home's value.

ARE YOUR PIPES PRESPIRING?

If you have exposed cold water pipes in the basement, they can drip and create puddles. This will probably be worse in the summertime when the pipes collect water from the air and form condensation. The pipes need to be wrapped with an insulating material that is waterproof. The material can be found in any hardware store and you can easily do the installation.

BASEMENT MOISTURE SEALING TRICKS

♦ The first step is to wire brush the surface of the cement wall to remove any loose or broken mortar or other extraneous material that has adhered to the wall. Old paint needs to be removed using the wire brush or sandblasting.

♦ Look for any multi-colored stains, which will affect a good bond between the cement wall and the waterproofing material. If there are any of these stains they will have to be cleaned with muriatic acid. Make sure when using an acid you wear protective gloves, clothing and a mask.

♦ Any cracks or holes should be patched with fast-drying hydraulic cement that sets even if it is wet. This can be purchased from a paint dealer.

♦ Be sure and seal the joint between the floor and the wall first. In most instances this area is the first area to shrink and pull away from the wall. If there is even the slightest space, water will enter. Fill the areas with a sealer such as Drylok Fast Plug™.

♦ The first coat of waterproofing should be applied with a brush so that it can be worked into the pores of the cement wall.

♦ Additional coats can be put on with a masonry roller. Be sure that you have good ventilation when working with these products so leave a window open if possible.

- One gallon of waterproofing should cover about 75-100 square feet.
- Best not to spread the waterproofing on the floor since these products will not take the abuse of walking on them. These products are made for walls. Be sure and spread it on thick, however, a second coat may be necessary if the seepage is bad. Especially if the seepage continues for several days.

CHAPTER 12

THE PATIO

BARBECUES

DIFFERENT TYPES TO CHOOSE FROM

Briquette Barbecue – These can only be used outdoors and takes about one hour to heat up. The temperature is impossible to control, but some chefs say that it does enhance the flavor of some foods.

Gas Barbecue – Very fast and the temperature can be controlled. It is produced for outdoor use only and may be banned in apartment and condo developments.

Wood-Burning Barbecue – These will heat rapidly and can only be used outdoors. Depending on the type of wood used, it may impart some excellent flavors to meats.

Electric Barbecue – Takes more time to heat up and cooks more slowly. However, it can be used indoors as well as outdoors.

WHAT BTU LEVEL?

This relates to cooking heat intensity. The BTU (British Thermal Units) of a barbecue should be 35,000 BTU if you are only cooking for two people and 40,000 BTU for a family unit.

SHAPE MATTERS
The burners should be in the shape of an H, an 8, butterfly or serpentine. These will do a better job of spreading the heat evenly than a burner in the form of a horizontal bar.

BARBECUE SURFACES
Barbecue surfaces range from 273 to 611 square inches. Select a barbecue with a surface that will be adequate for the number of people you will be serving on a regular basis.

CERAMIC OR LAVA ROCK, THAT IS THE QUESTION
These briquettes serve an important purpose in the barbecue. They prevent grease from falling down directly onto the burners and absorb some of the smoke. The ceramic briquettes hold and distribute heat more efficiently but need to be replaced every three years. Lava rock must be replaced every year.

WHICH COOKING GRATE IS BEST?
Cast iron and stainless steel will conserve heat longer but they are a little more expensive than the porcelain ones. The porcelain is easier to clean.

BURNER MAINTENANCE A MUST
The feeder tubes that enter the control valves located ahead of the burner should be cleaned at the beginning of every season. Spider webs and small dirt particles will clog these very easily and hamper the gas flow to the burners. It can even be a potential fire hazard. If the flames are yellowish and flow slowly, there may be a problem and a clog.

DECKING

WOOD DECKING

GETTING LOOSE ON DECK
Wood has the tendency to expand when it gets wet and shrinks when it dries out. The deck will get elastic and tends to move more when you walk on it. The nails and screws get loose and the problem must be fixed immediately.

SWAYING BEAMS & POSTS
Beams and posts will lose their stiffness over the years and become more elastic and bouncy. To repair this problem just install cross braces between the posts and beams.

178

Cut 4 X 4's or 6 X 6's (the longer, the better) with 45^0 angles on each end. Use 6-inch or longer lag bolts and secure the ends to the posts and beams.

LOOSE GUARDRAILS, POSTS & PICKETS

You will need to install lag bolts and washers to firm up the guardrail posts and pickets. Drill holes, then install one or more lag bolts to hold the pickets and posts in place to the deck rim.

BOUNCY, BOUNCY DECK SURFACE

You will need to add blocking between joists to reduce the bounciness. This will unify the joists so that when weight is applied to one joist it is partly distributed to those on either side. Never install blocking directly under gaps between the deck boards since this may cause areas that will hold water.

ARE YOUR STAIRS GETTING LOOSE?

You will have to temporarily remove the stairs and add solid stringers to the two outside stringers. You may also have to add 2 X 4's to both sides of the middle stringer, which will increase the strength.

BAD JOIST HANGERS

The joists may shrink so that the bottoms can no longer rest on existing hangers. To repair the problem you will need to install wedges and drive them into the gap until they are good and snug. If your deck is constructed without joist hangers, you will need to install them using 16d galvanized nails and secure them to the ledger strips and beams. For the joists you need to use galvanized stubby nails.

IS YOUR WOOD CHANGING COLOR?

You will need to apply a wood conditioner then pressure-wash the wood to

remove the old coatings. Prepare the clean surface by allowing the deck to dry before sanding and repairing any flaws. Be sure and use an oil base, naturally pigmented, penetrating finish for natural wood surfaces that will protect the deck from rain and sun. Be sure it will still show the grain of the wood.

SCRUB-A-DUB-DUB

If you want to clean your wood decking use a mixture of 2-cups of baking soda in 1-gallon of water. It will give the deck a weathered look, but be sure to test an area first to be sure that it won't affect the finish or affect the present stain.

FURNITURE

ALUMINUM

GIVE 'EM A WAX JOB
To keep aluminum lawn furniture in tip-top condition and looking great, just coat the aluminum with auto paste wax at the beginning of every season.

CANE, WICKER & RATTAN

GENERAL INFORMATION:
Reed furniture may need to be protected from too much moisture. It can withstand a certain amount of moisture but it is always best to protect it with a plastic bag if possible. When cleaning cane furniture use as little water as possible.

IT'S STARTING TO SAG AND GET LIMP
If the furniture has become wet and is limp, loose and sags, just allow it to dry and it will tighten up and retain its original shape and size. If it is dry and there is a separation, just wet it well and allow it to dry in the sunlight. If you have a cane-bottomed chair that has loosened, try applying very hot water to the underside and allowing the chair to stand in direct sunlight until it dries.

CLEANING WICKER
To clean wicker, you will need a toothbrush or other type of stiff bristle brush. Use vegetable-based oil soap like Murphy's Oil Soap to clean the furniture. Always tip the furniture when using any liquid to clean it so that the excess liquid will fall off. Another method is to use an old paintbrush and spray it with furniture polish to get into those hard-to-reach areas.

CANE PRESERVATION
Apply two coats of equal parts white shellac and denatured alcohol. The shellac will soak into the cane and preserve it. Then brush on a coat of clear varnish to keep the cane clean and tight. Coat the underneath side as well or it will absorb moisture and stretch out of shape.

DISCOLORED WICKER, YUCH
To lighten the wicker, use a paintbrush to apply a solution of ¼ cup of household bleach mixed into 1 quart of water. Be sure and wear rubber gloves. You can also use ¼ cup borax mixed into 1 quart of water.

180

If you want a finish then spray the wicker with clear satin urethane varnish or lacquer after it is fully dry.

VINYL FURNITURE

WARM THAT VINYL
After you remove the vinyl strapping, how can you get it taut again when re-weaving it? Use a hair dryer to warm the vinyl that you are working with and it will cool and be taught.

BUYING VINYL STRAPPING
If you can't find a location to purchase vinyl strapping, try the following Internet site. www.umbrellasusa.com.

RUB-A-DUB-VINYL
Cleaning vinyl straps can be a problem. If regular liquid soap and water will not do the job, start adding a small amount of liquid bleach to the water. Try using about 20% bleach to 80% soapy water to start and then keep adding more bleach until it does the job. If a 50/50 bleach/soap solution does not clean them then replace them.

POOL VINYL
Vinyl will only last 2-3 years when used near a pool. Chlorine, bleach, the sun and solvents will damage the finish and eventually lead to failure of the vinyl. If the vinyl is subjected to suntan lotions the pores will clog and the vinyl will not last very long.

WATER BEWARE
Avoid using unfiltered water from wells or ground water to clean vinyl. Unfiltered water will cause staining of outdoor furniture due to the high sulfur content of the water. This is especially true in Florida.

LIFE EXTENSION
Placing a towel that has been draped on the vinyl furniture will extend the life of the vinyl.

POWER WASHING
Power washing using plain filtered water is one of the best methods of cleaning vinyl furniture.

WINTER STORAGE

Be sure and wipe down any furniture that has plastic strapping with a solution of baking soda and water before putting them away. Sprinkle it directly on hammocks and canvas chairs as well.

OH MY! MY METAL IS EXPOSED

If you are going to leave metal furniture out during the rain or in the winter, be sure and put a coat of automobile wax on all metal surfaces to protect it from rust.

WAX ON, WAX OFF

A coating of car wax on the painted metal surfaces of vinyl furniture will help to protect it.

WROUGHT IRON FURNITURE

A DAB HERE AND A DAB THERE

This is very difficult furniture to paint and it is much easier to use a sponge and just dab it on.

CHAPTER 13

SPAS & HOT TUBS

CHEMICALS

GENERAL INFORMATION:

Chemicals are used in swimming pools, hot tubs, and spas to control the growth of algae and bacteria. The chemicals that are available on the market are safe when used as directed and most contain chlorine. The most common is calcium hypochlorite and is used every few days. If the chemical is used in sunlight, a large percentage of the active hypochlorite is lost to the air as chlorine gas.

The buildup of chlorine gas is only of concern if you have an indoor pool. Since most chemicals are strong oxidizers and corrosives, they are toxic if ingested. Never drink pool water or you may become sick or develop a skin rash.

HOT TUBS

WOODEN TUB WAS EMPTY FOR A YEAR AND NOW LEAKS

Never allow wooden tubs to dry out, the staves shrink. The wood may reabsorb water after a while. If not get a leak sealer from a spa shop!

YUCH, CLOUDY TUB WATER

The water may be out of balance, you may have a clogged filter or the sanitizer level is low. Adjust pH and change water if over 90 days old. Have children shower before using spa.

I'M NOT BALANCED

If the water turns milky white from small bubbles when jets are running then the water is out of balance. Adjust pH level or possibly just replace filter.

FOAMING AT THE MOUTH
It is usually caused by high contamination or soap residue.

I'M GETTING IRRITATED
If you are getting a skin irritation, rash or burning eyes then problem is probably too much chlorine and the water is out of balance. Open spa cover and allow spa to aerate for 10-15 minutes before using it.

RING AROUND THE TUB............
Maybe from body oils or cosmetics and filter is too old to handle the contaminants.

WHAT'S THAT GREEN STUFF?
You may have hot tub algae forming. The sanitizer level is too low and there may also be contaminants in the water. Need to add an ozonator and shock the hot tub.

IS THE WATER TURNING BROWN, BLACK OR GREEN?
This is usually due to excessive mineral content. Metal parts in tub may be eroding. Filter needs to be run more.

BAD ODOR IN THERE!
The sanitizer level may be low. You may have mold forming or have contaminants in the water.

I'VE GOT SCALES ON MY SURFACE
It is caused by high mineral content in water. Use a surface stain remover.

WHY IS MY HEATER SO NOISY?
The heating element is rarely at fault. The element may need to be re-aligned to reduce the vibration or tying down the noisy part with a clip or piece of wire.

UH OH, pH GETTING TOO LOW
Low pH results in the water becoming too acidic. This problem can cause erosion of parts and ruin the spa.

GETTING COLD, COVER ME UP
Purchase a winter cover that will not allow any water to leak in from rain or snow. If you have a hard cover with a hinged center, you will need to place a vinyl cover over it.

NOT GETTING HOT ENOUGH
In 80% of all cases, you will need to replace the filter. If that doesn't fix it, you need to call a professional.

I NEED MY THERMAL BLANKIE
Great investment to keep the heat in the tub if the tub is outside! They also work great for indoor tubs.

KID'S POOL SAFETY

GENERAL INFORMATION:
The following are safety tips and recommendations to protect children around swimming pools:

❖ Children older than 4 should learn to swim from a qualified instructor.
❖ Never allow children to swim alone. They may accidentally hit their head.
❖ Don't allow horseplay since it is too easy to get injured.
❖ Be careful about diving and the depth of the water.
❖ Never allow your child to rely on an air mattress, inner tube or inflatable toys as a life preserver.
❖ Keep a safety ring with a rope beside the pool.
❖ Keep a phone around the pool.
❖ Children should always wear a life preserver even if an adult is present if they are unable to swim.
❖ Never allow anyone to swim during a lightning storm.
❖ Someone in the home should know CPR.

SPAS

HOW OFTEN DO I DRAIN MY HOT TUB OR SPA?
It will depend on the size of the spa. Every 2-4 months should be sufficient as long as it is treated with non-chlorine shock.

REPLACING THE FILTER
Filters are only good for about one year.

HOW CAN I GET RID OF A SCRATCH?
The only product that will do this is Novus™ Scratch remover.

PLASTIC FITTING ARE GETTING BLACK STAINS
Metals in hard water will cause this problem. They can be removed with a spa stain and scale remover.

TREAT ME TENDER
Best to treat the wood with a good quality water repellant sealer. The wood will resist cracking better.

LIGHTS OUT
If the bulb goes out in the ozonator it can be replaced. It should not be a problem obtaining a new one from a spa or pool supply store.

I THINK WE HAVE A LEAK
The leak is usually from the pump seal. If you can't find the leak, try adding some food dye to the water and watch for the leak.

PUMP IS JUST HUMMING AND NOT PUMPING
You probably have a jammed or broken impeller or the bearings have seized up. If the motor shaft can be rotated by hand then it may just be a dirty pump switch, defective starter capacitor, burnt motor winding, or electrical problem with the motor.

MOTOR RUNNING BUT NO HEAT
It is usually caused by a clogged filter, which will restrict water flow and affect the heat. Try and run the spa with the filter out. If that solves the problem, just replace the filter.

WHERE'S MY HEAT?
Check the filter first then the heater indicator light and make sure it is glowing. If not there is no power to the heater. You may have a bad switch or a stuck thermostat.

NOW IT'S OVERHEATING, I CAN'T WIN!
This may be caused: by a stuck thermostat or a stuck relay switch.

MY JETS HAVE LOST THEIR POWER
It is usually caused by a worn out filter cartridge.

CHAPTER 14

SWIMMING POOLS

GENERAL INFORMATION:
The majority of pool water problems are the result of the following: No free available chlorine, poor water circulation, poor maintenance, poor fresh water replacement, or poor water circulation.

MY STEPS ARE CRACKING UP
Go to your local boat store and purchase fiberglass paint and gel-repair kit. The small cracks will cause the fiberglass resin to be damaged by pool water. The gel coat does need to be fixed.

SOLAR BUBBLES????
If you have air bubbles in your pool after installing a solar heater, the pump is probably undersized. Solar systems require a larger pump than is normally on a pool.

BUGS ARE EATING MY POOL
Whoever installed the above ground pool did not use sufficient non-petroleum based pesticide and herbicide treatment on the ground before the pool was completed.

GLUB, GLUB
If your pool light fixture has water in it you need to replace the lens gasket. This was probably not done when the bulb was replaced.

THE BEST FILTER
Diatomaceous earth filters are the best. Cartridges are easier but they are not as efficient.

SOLVING POOL CLEANER PROBLEMS

SUCTION SIDE CLEANER

MOVING AS SLOW AS A SNAIL
Check the pump basket to see if there is any debris in it then be sure that the filter is clean and water is flowing properly. Also, check the throat of the cleaner for any toys or other obstructions. The hose may have a break or split, which would cause the problem.

ONLY DOING HALF THE JOB
Check the length of the hose or the cleaner may be following the flow pattern of the pool. Be sure that the fittings are positioned so that the water flows somewhat downward. If fittings can't be adjusted then there are fittings that will fit over the existing fitting.

PRESSURE SIDE CLEANERS

CHECK THE BAG REGULARLY
This type of cleaner has very few problems. The only problem that may occur is that the filter bag gets full and was not emptied. The unit will keep working but will not suck up any more debris until you empty the bag.

ROBOT CLEANERS

IT'S NOT MOVING ANYMORE?

Be sure that the indicator light is glowing on the transformer. If not, the transformer may not be turned on or the 3-volt fuse has blown. Be aware that the indicator light may still glow even if the fuse has blown. Check the electrical outlet to be sure that it is working. Make sure that the pulley belt is not broken or worn out.

If the belt is OK then the motor may have shorted out and needs to be replaced.

MOVING BUT NOT PICKING UP DEBRIS

When you lift the unit up near the surface of the water it should gush out water. If not the pump motor may be bad. Be sure that the impeller does not have any debris wrapped around it. If not make sure it is turning freely. If the unit is having trouble climbing the wall, this is another indication that the pump motor is bad.

WINTERIZE YOUR IN-GROUND POOL

The following is a step-by-step winterizing process:

1. Locate your supplies that should include the cover, water tubes, plugs for the skimmers and return jets, and the winterizing chemicals. You will also need a shop vacuum or air compressor.
2. Backwash the filter and be sure it's clean. Drain the DE filter tank and leave backwash valve open. On sand filters, unplug the filter drain plug and leave it off. Store the drain plug and other items removed in the pump basket. Be sure that the multiport valve has no water in it. If it does, blow it out. Never use acid to clean the filter before storing it for the winter.
3. Disconnect the pump and filter. Be sure that the pump has no water left in it. Remove any drain plugs from the pump and store in pump basket.
4. If you have a heater make sure that there is no standing water left inside and remove all drain plugs. Blow it out with a compressor or shop vacuum. Leave the heater tray in.
5. Loosen any quick disconnect fittings or unions at the pump or filter system. You don't want freeze cracks.
6. Remove all return jet fittings (the whole fitting). Remove all skimmer baskets.
7. Blow out all return jet pipes using an air compressor. Keep the air blowing until all the air bubbles become visible from the return jets to the pool. Place a plug into the fitting under the water when you see the bubbles blowing out at full force. Be sure that the plug is very tight.
8. Blow out the skimmer similar to #7. Place a Gizzmo-type screw plug in the skimmer when bubbles start to become visible. Be sure and place Teflon tape on the Gizzmo threads before installing. You can use black, rubber-type plugs if you prefer over the Gizzmo plug, however, there must be something in the skimmer to allow for water expansion when it freezes.

   You could use a closed empty water bottle. Don't plug the skimmer lines and forget about them since water can easily freeze in a skimmer and crack the plastic.

If you have a waterfall, you will have to drain and blow out those pipes as well. If you evacuate your lines properly you will not need to use antifreeze.

9. Blow out the main drain line and when you see bubbles coming out of the drain, plug the pipe on your end or close the gate valve. By doing this you will cause an air lock in the line and water will not enter the pipe from the poolside.

10. Be sure and place duct tape on all exposed pipes to stop anything from getting in them.

11. Be sure and remove all floats and rope from pool.

12. Place the pump, filter diving board and ladders in a shed. A sand filter can be left in place.

13. Make sure that the chemicals bring the pool chlorine level to greater than 3.0 for the winter and the products should consist of a shock-type product.

14. Make sure that there are no tears in the pool cover.

OPENING UP A POOL AFTER WINTER

The following is a step-by-step opening process:

1. Be sure and thoroughly clean the area around the pool before removing any covers to minimize the amount of debris that might get into the pool.

2. Basically, just reverse the winterizing procedures and remember to lubricate all bolts on the dive board, ladders, and rails.

YUCH! MURKY & CLOUDY WATER

The cause for cloudy and murky water are: algae, the hardness level may be too high, the filter is not working properly, too frequent backwashing, plugged filter, precipitating calcium compounds, wrong pH, the total alkalinity is wrong, or there are dissolved solids in the pool.

ALGAE

Algae spores are in the air and are always entering your pool. They are brought in by the wind, rain, and may even be in your equipment or on a bathing suit.

If the conditions are just right, the algae bloom can show up almost overnight. The conditions that algae prefer are out of balance water, warm temperatures, sunlight, the presence of nitrates, and even carbon dioxide. The usual cause is poor water circulation, lack of adequate filtration, or sanitation problems. Algae can clog the filter and reduce filtration significantly.

There are 21,000 known varieties of algae. The most common varieties found in pools are the green, yellow, black, and pink. Prevention is your best method of avoiding algae, and proper chemical balance and sanitizer residuals are the key. There are a number of specialty chemicals that you need to be aware of.

Types of Common Pool Algae

Green Algae
Common variety and may show up after a hazy condition in the water exists. If not treated immediately it will turn into a green slime. It is usually caused by poor filtration or lack of  adequate sanitation. It can be free-floating or clinging to the walls.

Yellow Algae
This may also be called mustard algae and is a wall clinger and usually on the shady, side of the pool. It forms a sheet and is very difficult to get rid of. Re-infection throughout the entire season is common. It takes a lot of chemicals to kill it.

Black Algae
This is one of the worst forms of algae and it is usually with you almost forever. It will appear as black or blue/green spots and their roots will extend into the plaster or tile grout. It can be brought into the pool in a bathing suit from someone who was at the ocean recently.

Pink Algae
It is really a form of bacteria that will appear as streaks in corners and crevices. It is a slow spreader and easily dealt with.

Algae-fighting Chemicals

Chitin
Chitin will help to bind up and remove a wide variety of impurities found in the water, allowing a sanitizer to work more efficiently to kill contaminants. It also has the ability to help the filtration system worm more efficiently. It may be sold under the name "Sea Clear."

Copper-Based

Copper has proven effective as both a mineral that will stop algae from forming, as well as killing the algae. It can be purchased in a non-foaming strength of 3-10% and is effective on all forms of algae. The only problem with its use is that it may stain white plaster surfaces.

Polymers

These are complicated chemicals that will either stop the growth of algae or kill them depending on the strength used. The percentage of strength runs from 3-60% and they do not cause foaming.

Potassium Tetraborate

If this chemical is added to the water in the proper amount it prevents the algae from converting carbon dioxide into the fuel it needs to grow. It may be sold as "Protein Supreme."

Quaternary Ammonium Compounds

This is a low-grade algaecide called "Quats." They are an effective algaestat and used as a preventive instead of a cure. If you see Quat 10 it means that there is 10% active ingredient.

Silver-Based

It works to prevent bacteria from reproducing and very effective in killing pink algae. It is non-foaming but may cause black stains on white plaster. If you are going to use it ask for a sequestering agent to add to it.

Death to Algae!

 ➤ First, balance the water and make sure that the pH is where it should be.
 ➤ Check the filter system and clean it if necessary.
 ➤ Adjust the valves for maximum circulation and allow the pool to run 24 hours a day until it is clear.
 ➤ Turn on the automatic cleaners to stir everything up.
 ➤ If you have suspended green algae you will have to shock the pool. Add as much hypochlorite as it will take to turn the pool a cloudy, bluish/gray color.
 ➤ Brush the walls and floors toward the main drain.
 ➤ Backwash the filter as needed.
 ➤ If you cannot see the bottom of the pool and it has debris and leaves in it, it would be best to drain the pool and acid wash it before re-filling.
 ➤ If the problem is ongoing, it is best to drain the pool and acid wash it.

STOP! YOU'RE EATING MY CHLORINE

Algae: actually creates a demand for chlorine and will consume chlorine that should be handling the problem.

COUGH, COUGH, I'M ALL CLOGGED UP

If your pool filter is clogged, it may just be due to poor pool maintenance, chlorine level is too low or the pool is being heated to high temperatures too often and not chlorinated enough to handle it. A clogged filter can also be caused by algae, calcification, hair, suntan lotion, improper pH, or improper total alkalinity. Clean the filter and adjust the pH and alkalinity levels.

FOAMING SOAP BUBBLES

Usually caused by too high a concentration of algaecide, or there is organic debris in the water. Adjust the pH, total alkalinity, and free chlorine residue to proper levels. You may have to super-chlorinate and discard some water.

WATER IS TURNING COLORS

Usually cause by organic debris in pool, such as leaves, etc. It can also be caused by algae. Clean pool well and super-chlorinate.

SCALING, STAINING & REDUCED CHLORINE EFFICIENCY

It is usually caused by not enough fresh water being added to pool. You may have to change the water if adjusting pH and chlorine levels do not work.

REPLACE ME, I'M GETTING OLD

Pool motors only last about 8 years before they need to be replaced or rebuilt. The motor will probably start screeching to let you know when there is a problem that needs attention.

SOLVING POOL HEATER PROBLEMS

The pilot will not light

The cause may be due to low pressure, poor air supply, or poor ventilation. Be sure that the gas is turned on and that there is gas in the tank. Make sure that there was no water runoff from the roof or the sprinkler system and that the pilot light tubing is not clogged or has a hole in it.

The heater will not reach the right temperature

Check the thermostat first to make sure that it is set at the right temperature. If the heat loss is greater than the heater output, the heater may be too small for the job or you may just not have enough of a gas supply. The heater will also respond to the outside temperature and if it is too low that may be the cause of the problem. Solar covers help to slow the heat loss and you may need one.

Every heater also has a high limit switch preventing it from overheating. If the switch is bad it could shut off the heater but if the exhaust is blocked that may be the cause for the overheating.

Heater keeps going on and off before reaching desired temperature

This may be caused by poor water flow due to a dirty filter, closed valve, external bypass needing adjustment, or you reversed the water connections or the pressure switch is out of adjustment. Occasionally, the thermostat will get out of adjustment or may need to be replaced.

Strange clicking noises and sparking coming from the heater

It is best to call a service man and shut the heater down until they come.

The heater is leaking water

Sanitizer damage may have occurred due to leaking of chemicals into the heat exchanger. The damage could also be caused by a winter freeze if the leaking started after the spring thaw. Other causes could be a faulty gasket or loose connection going to the pressure switch.

Heater is only leaking when the burner is lit

If you are heating very cold water the problem could be from condensation, a missing or damaged bypass, or excessive water that is flowing through the heater from a pump that is oversized. Also check the heat exchanger for sooting and be sure that the internal bypass is functioning properly. If all else fails, try installing an external pool heater bypass.

The exhaust is dark or the heater top has blackened

Possibly low gas pressure or a poor air supply and venting. It is best to call a serviceman.

Excessive heat has caused damage to the heater

Possibly due to low gas pressure, down drafting, poor air supply, or inadequate venting. You may have to install a high wind stack or the unit may have been installed too close to a vertical wall or in a windy area. You must have proper clearance all around a heater.

Rust going into the pool

Usually cause by an imbalance of sanitizers or chemicals. Best to re-balance chemicals or replace any damaged components. Be sure that all chemical feeders are installed properly and you may need to place a check valve in to prevent backflow.

It whistles while it works

It is probably caused by low gas pressure in the burners and it would be best to contact a serviceman. LOCATING A HISSSSSSSSSSSS

A good trick when trying to locate an air leak is to shut off the motor when it is under full pumping head pressure and look for water spray-back out of a void where the water was entering. You better be quick to locate the spray-back.

SOLVING POOL PUMP PROBLEMS

Leaking pump
The most common problem is that the threaded fitting carrying water out of the pump shrinks and allows the water to drip and eventually spray. Replace with a high temp fitting. Water can also leak from a worn out mechanical seal. The seal is located between the wet end and the dry end (motor) of the pump.

There's air in my pump basket
The pump needs to operate without any air in the basket. Check the water level in the pool first and check to see if the pump basket lid is on tight and the "O" ring is lubricated.

The pump is not being very efficient
It is possibly caused by the skimmer basket being filled with debris. Be sure that the pump basket is clean and is positioned properly. The pump basket can also have a crack in it and need replacement.

The motor is cycling on and off
When the motor runs for a short period of time, then turns off, and then on again later, it is probably overheating. If the motor is old it will have to be replaced. If the motor is relatively new then the problem may be in the electrical lines and there are connections that need to be corrected.

Motor making strange noises
If the noise sounds like screeching it is probably either the front or rear bearings and they will need to be replaced by removing the motor and bringing it to a repair shop. Another common problem: if it sounds more like a grinding noise may be that the motor is being starved for lack of water. Open more valves or find the cause of the obstruction blocking the water flow.

Motor is humming but not starting
The impeller may be clogged with debris and needs to be cleaned out. If it doesn't turn freely you will have to remove the motor from the pump and clean out the impeller.

HINTS FOR CARING FOR YOUR SOLAR BLANKET

- ➢ The best way to store a solar blanket is on a roller.
- ➢ If you need to clean the solar blanket use "solar cover cleaner."
- ➢ Never leave the solar blanket outside in the winter.
- ➢ Make sure that the pool is always chemically balanced.
- ➢ When it starts to flake, buy a new one.

CHAPTER 15

GENERAL PROBLEM AREAS

AIR CONDITIONERS

CENTRAL AIR CONDITIONING

GET OUT THE BUCKETS
If the roof unit is leaking water into the house, the drain line is probably plugged up causing a backup and should be cleaned out as soon as possible.

Attic fans are a must!

INSULATE THOSE DUCT
The ducts in the attic should be insulated.

IT'S COOL UP HERE
If the upstairs is too cool, place a gable fan in the attic and be sure the attic is well insulated. You can also try closing the bedroom doors.

WHERE'S THE AIR?
If the airflow stops after the unit turns on and will not start up again unless the unit is turned off for hours, the refrigerant level is probably low. I would try adding refrigerant before going further to see if that solves the problem.

WHY CAN'T I RUN?
This problem may be that the thermostat is set incorrectly or there is no power to the unit. You need to be sure that the room temperature is above the thermostat setting. Be sure and check the fuses and breakers.

NOT COOL ENOUGH!

If there is not enough cold air coming out to reduce the temperature to the set point, the blower motor may be going bad or the unit is low on refrigerant. If the refrigerant is too low, you will have to call a professional to fill it. You also need to check for a clogged filter.

NEW COMPRESSOR, BUT AIR NOT COOL ENOUGH

Since the problem is not the compressor, it is probably the blower motor or the refrigerant level is low. They may have installed the compressor wrong as well.

KICK IT!

The fan on the outside unit only turns when I hit the top of the unit. The fan probably needs oil. Do not use WD-40. If that does not fix the problem, it may be the run capacitor, which is only about $10.00.

ON & OFF, ON & OFF

If the system is cycling too often it may indicate that you have an airflow problem or a defective thermostat. Best to check the condensing unit's airflow then check the blower and the filter as well as the thermostat.

WINDOW AIR CONDITIONERS

GENERAL INFORMATION:

Window air conditioners work similar to your refrigerator. They have a system that cools the air as it enters the unit allowing the air to condense on the cold coils and allows water to drip into the tray at the bottom. The warm air that is in the room is then drawn over the evaporation coil, which then collects the heat. The heat is then conducted into a refrigerant gas, which is then circulated to the condensation coils on the back of the unit and dissipates back to the outside.

WHERE'S THE AIR?

If you are not getting adequate airflow, the filter is probably dirty. The filter should be cleaned at least twice a month for maximum efficiency. Wash the filter in lukewarm water then gently shake off the excess water.

CAN'T HEAR A THING?

If the air conditioner will not operate it is normally that the plug has gone bad, the outlet has a short or the fuse or circuit breaker has blown.

OILY WATER IN DRIP PAN

If your air conditioner is not cooling properly and you see oily water in the drip pan, this indicates that you have a Freon leak. It is best to call a serviceman.

TOO WARM IN HERE

If you do not feel cold enough air coming out it may be that the temperature setting is incorrect, the air filter may be clogged with dust or the air flow from the outside is obstructed. If you cannot find the problem, turn off the air conditioner and bring it to a repair center.

HUMMMMMMS: BUT NO AIR?

The fan motor has seized up and you will have to replace it.

WATER FROM THE FRONT

If there is water coming out the front, the drain system is plugged and the unit needs to go in for a complete servicing.

OILING, BUT WHERE?

Some fan motors have oil plugs, which should be removed and a few drops of oil placed into the hole.

A BIT CHILLY

If you run your air conditioner for 4-6 minutes during the winter it will keep the seals in good shape for the summer.

FINDING THE RIGHT SIZE UNIT

ROOM SIZE/SQ.FT	CAPACITY UNIT/BTU PER HOUR
150 to 250	6,000
250 to 325	7,000
325 to 375	8,000
375 to 425	9,000
425 to 475	10,000
475 to 575	12,000
575 to 725	14,000

If the room gets direct sunlight increase the capacity by 10%. If the room is well shaded decrease the capacity by 10%. Kitchens will need a higher capacity unit depending on the size of the kitchen.

CEILING FANS

GENERAL INFORMATION:
Ceiling fans are an excellent addition to any home in all parts of the country. They will make a room warmer in winter with better air circulation and assist an air conditioner to keep the home cooler with less energy expenditure in the summer.

REVERSE IT
In the winter, reverse the fan and place it on low to draw warm air up to the ceiling and force it back down to the floor.

CERAMIC TILE

SECRETS FOR SELECTING THE RIGHT TILE
When selecting tile you should know the right tile for the job to get the best results. Water can cause cracks in tile since they can absorb water and can cause damage beneath the surface. Buying ceramic tiles that have been kiln-dried for longer periods at high temperatures will absorb less moisture. However they are more expensive, which is why it is best to choose the right tiles for the specific job.

Non-vitreous
Best used for decorative purposes indoors and in dry locations. It may be used around a fireplace or in a dining room but not in the kitchen.

Semi-vitreous
It is best used indoors in dry, and occasionally moist, locations. This will include a kitchen wall or in a serving area.

Vitreous
Good multi-purpose tile that can be used indoors or outdoors either in a wet or dry location. It can even be used on a bathroom floor, walls or patio floor.

Impervious
This is a more expensive tile that is normally used in hospitals and restaurants or other commercial buildings. The tile can be thoroughly cleaned and will not absorb moisture.

IT'S GETTING GLAZZZZY

The glaze on tile is placed on as a protective coating that is colored and fired into the surface of the tile. The glazes may be glossy, matte, or have a textured surface. Glazing will keep moisture from entering the surface, but the bottom, which has not been glazed, will still absorb moisture.

TIPS ON CHOOSING THIN-SET MORTARS

Water-mixed mortar
This is also referred to as dry-set mortar and is a blend of Portland cement, sand, and some additives. It needs to be mixed with water.

Latex/Acrylic-mixed mortar
Similar to water-mixed mortar, but it has either latex or acrylic added to it. These additives will improve adhesion and also reduce moisture absorption. They can be premixed with the mortar in dry form, or added as liquid by the mixer. Best for wet or dry installations!

Epoxy mortar
This is a mixture of cement, sand, liquid resins and a hardener. It is expensive, but it is excellent when used with any setting materials. Especially good: when used on a substrate that is not compatible with other adhesives.

Medium-bed mortar
This adhesive will stay stronger than standard thin-set mortar when applied in layers of more than ¼-inch. Best used with tiling that doesn't have uniform backs, which would include handmade tiles.

KNOWS YOUR GROUT

All grout is a mortar that is used to fill the joints between the tiles. It helps to prevent moisture from seeping into the joints and stiffens the installation.

In most cases just add liquid and mix to a pasty consistency. However stores are now selling grout-calking guns, which work very well.

Plain grout

May be referred to as un-sanded grout and is a mixture of Portland cement and special additives. Normally, used for grout joints of $1/16^{th}$ of an inch or less. Commonly used for absorptive tile and marble.

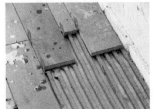

Sanded grout

Similar to plain grout but with sand added to it. It is usually used for grout joints more than $1/16^{th}$ of an inch.

Epoxy grout

Contains epoxy resin and hardeners and is normally used when chemical and stain resistance is necessary or when high temperatures are expected.

Colored grout

It is sold in pre-mixed packaging and in a large assortment of colors, which makes it easy to match any color tile. It is capable of filling any type of grout joint. If you prefer the look of cement, natural colored grout can be used.

Mortar

Similar grout to the sanded grout is normally used for joints between brick pavers, slate, or other types of masonry material.

Pre-mixed grout

These are container-mixed grouts and are ready to use from the container. Not a big variety of colors, and are somewhat costly. Best for small jobs!

CLEANING

CLEANING SOLUTIONS

Carpet Matted down

Place an ice cube on the area that is matted down from the furniture leg and allow it to remain overnight.

Decals

Transparent decals may be easily removed using a solution of lukewarm water and ¼ cup of white vinegar. Place the solution on a sponge and dampen the area thoroughly for a few minutes. If this doesn't work saturate the decal and allow it to stand for 15 minutes then try again with very hot water.

Flower Vase

To clean the insides of a flower vase or wine bottle just use a solution of 2 tablespoons of salt, some raw rice, and 1 cup of white vinegar. Shake vigorously for a minute or so.

Ink Stains
Place rubbing alcohol on the stain and it should make it disappear. If you get ink on the walls just use bleach on it.

Kitty Litter
To keep the cat litter fresh smelling just mix some baby powder in the litter.

Permanent Marker
Dab a sponge in rubbing alcohol and dab lightly on the stained area (do not rub). Don't overdo any one area.

Shower Doors
One of the best cleaners is Resolve® to get rid of the soap scum residue.

PORCELAIN SINK STAIN REMOVER
The following ingredients will be needed:

1	**Teaspoon of liquid detergent**
½	**Cup of liquid chlorine bleach**
½	**Cup of white vinegar**

Place a closure over the drain and then place 2-3 inches of warm water in the sink. Place all the ingredients into the sink, mix well, and allow the mixture to remain for about 8-10 hours. Rinse with hot water.

DEHUMIDIFIER

GENERAL INFORMATION:
Dehumidifiers remove moisture from the air and protect the home from excess damage from the moisture. They will help prevent mildew, rusting of items, swelling of floors, drawers, and doors. It does this by passing moist air over a cold coil. The moisture condenses out of the air onto the coil and drains the moisture into a bucket that must be emptied.

DEHUMDIFIER DOESN'T LIKE COLD ROOMS
The room temperature has dropped to 65°F or below making the room too cold for the dehumidifier to work efficiently.

DEHUMIDIFIER IS ICING UP
If the unit is icing up you will need to move it to a warmer location or increase the temperature of the room. The room is getting too cool and forming ice on the coils.

Other reasons may be that the condenser fins have clogged up with dust or the unit is too close to a wall or draperies.

IT'S STOPPED WORKING
If the dehumidifier does not work it is usually due to an electrical problem such as a fuse blown or bad cord or the water bucket is full and needs to be emptied.

I STILL HAVE A LOT OF MOISTURE?
Not removing moisture: can be caused by a slow fan or a fan motor that is not working. If the coils are too dirty this can also cause the problem.

IS THERE A MOUSE IN DA HOUSE? IT'S A BIT NOISY IN THERE
Squealing noises are usually caused by a bad fan motor that will need to be replaced. However, that sound can also be caused by screws, trim, or exterior panels rattling or vibrating. The other common problem is that the rubber in the mounts have hardened over time.

CLICK, CLICK, NO WATER
The clicking noise is caused by the compressor trying to start but cannot. The problem is either a bad start relay or a bad compressor.

GETTING EXPENSIVE
Your electric bill will be higher when running a dehumidifier. It is almost equal to running a window air conditioner.

IT'S RUNNING AWAY
The unit should not run all the time unless you are finding the water reservoir filled frequently. This just means that there is a lot of humidity. If it is running all the time and the reservoir is not filling there is a mechanical problem that needs to be repaired.

RUN, RUN, RUN, I'M GETTING TIRED
Dehumidifiers usually do not need to run all year long. In northern climates they only need to run during the hot months. In southern climates if you run an air conditioner you probably don't need to run the dehumidifier at all. If you have a damp cellar or basement, you may have to run one all year round in that location.

DOORS

COLD AIR COMING UNDER THE DOOR
Because of carpeting, it is necessary to have room under the door so that they will close and not hit the carpet. You will need to install a door sweep, which works by lifting up whenever the door is closed by keeping the warm air in and the cold air out.

MY INTERIOR DOOR IS STICKING

❖ This is normal due to humidity causing door, jamb expansion. It can also be caused by settlement or swelling from moisture. You will need to adjust striker, hinges, or jambs.

❖ Check the hinge screws on the door and the hinge screws on the jamb. They may be loose and just need to be tightened. If they are loose the door will sag and rub against the frame. Open the door as far as it will go and tighten the screws.

❖ If the holes have become enlarged just pack the holes with wooden toothpicks that have been dipped in glue. Make sure that the glue has set completely before attempting to place the screw back in.

❖ If one of the hinges needs to be adjusted, just cut a piece of sturdy cardboard the same size as the hinge and place it behind the hinge before you replace the screws. It may be either the top hinge or the bottom hinge. If one thickness does not work, use two thicknesses.

DOOR WON'T STAY CLOSED
The striker plate is out of adjustment.

REMOVING A STUBBORN HINGE PIN
If you have a problem removing a stubborn hinge pin, just insert a nail into the hole from the bottom of the barrel. Tap the nail with a hammer, forcing the pin out of the hinge.

SQEAKY HINGES
Use a silicone spray, you have metal rubbing.

REMOVING A HINGED DOOR EASILY
Try removing every screw except the top one in the top hinge. You can then control the door as you remove the last screw.

BAD LATCHING ON ENTRY DOOR
Weather stripping needs to be replaced or adjusted.

OFF WITH THE DOOR HANDLE
To remove a door handle on an interior door, just look closely at the shank of the interior door handle and you will see a tiny slot or hole. Push a small screwdriver head or nail set tip into the hole and when you tug on the knob it will come right off.

HELP! MY PANEL HAS CRACKED
It is caused by expansion or excess humidity. Putty the crack and seal the panel by either re-painting or applying a clear coat of varnish.

EXTERIOR DOOR IS LETTING AIR & WATER IN
The threshold is out of adjustment or the sweep needs to be adjusted or replaced.

WOOD DOOR TRICKS
Wood entry doors are not as popular as they used to be. They are subject to shrinkage and swelling with changes in weather. Because of this wood doors only carry a 10-year warranty. However if they have cracks in them, just purchase some plastic wood and coloring stain to match the door, patch and sand lightly.

DID SOMEONE STEEL MY ENTRY DOOR?
They are sturdy and resistant to shrinking, swelling, warping, or splitting. They have a core of foam insulation making them very energy efficient. They also carry a 25-year warranty.

IS A FIBERGLASS DOOR PRACTICAL?
These are now manufactured with a "porous fiberglass" and can be stained with wood gel stain. They look like a wood door and are more expensive than steel doors but will last the lifetime of the home.

DOOR, STOP!
A solid brass stop or a flexible spring base stop can be mounted onto the door or on the wall and is just screwed in. A doorstop can be placed into position by removing your hinge pin and inserting the stop.

REMOVING THE OLD DOORKNOB
Remove the trim carefully by either unscrewing the plate or placing a screwdriver gently under the plate and lifting it up. There are two long screws holding the doorknob. Remove the screws one at a time. The two parts of the knob can now be pulled out.

You will then notice two screws. Remove them and the bolt. The strike plate can be replaced if you wish.

DOORKNOB TIPS

- ✓ New bolts and strike plates that feel loose sometimes and can be fixed by using screws that are little longer than the original ones.
- ✓ When removing the parts, place them in order on the floor so that you will remember how they go back.

SOLVING BI-FOLD DOOR PROBLEMS

- ✓ If you don't know how to remove the door just lift it up out of the bottom pivot and swing it away from the bottom bracket. Then pull the top pivot out of the bracket.
- ✓ When the door has been removed you can easily loosen the adjusting screw and then slide the bracket into the desired position. If the doors do not meet then move the top and bottom brackets toward the center. If the doors are pressing together too hard and won't close at all, just move the brackets away from the center. If the door is uneven and looks like it is sagging toward the center, only move the top bracket just slightly away from the center position.
- ✓ All bi-fold doors have a liner down the inside that helps hold them closed and normal wear and tear may bend them. If this happens, gently bend the liner back into shape with a pair of pliers.

PEEK-A-BOO, I CAN'T SEE YOU!

If you have a solid door and need to install a viewer, this is the best method to follow:
- ✓ First, determine how high you want the door viewer to be and mark off the height in the center of the door on both sides.
- ✓ Next you will need to drill a hole, straight through the door. Make sure you use the right size drill bit or you will have a BIG problem.
- ✓ Roll up a piece of sandpaper that is small enough to fit through the hole and pull it back and forth several times to smooth it out.
- ✓ Insert the door viewer then screw both sides into each other.

STOP THAT WARP, STOP THAT WARP

Warping can be a serious problem! To prevent warping, which happens as wood expands and contracts just use the same type of sealant (polyurethane or lacquer) on all six sides of the door. Be sure and seal the inside and outside faces as well as the top and bottom, left and right edges. If this is not done the door will swell and eventually warp.

DOOR LOCKS

SUPER GLUE TO THE RESCUE

If you broke off your key in the lock just place some super glue on the broken part, wait a few minutes, and pull it out.

REPLACING A DOOR LOCK

The following are the steps necessary when replacing a door lock:

Latch-plate

It may be necessary to deepen the latch-plate mortise to enable the faceplate to sit flush with the door. Use a wood chisel and deepen the mortise area just a little.

Template

The new template should enable you to determine whether the hole on the face of the door is the right size (diameter) to accept the replacement lock. If you need to enlarge the hole, use a wood rasp.

Strike-plate

The existing strike-plate can be allowed to remain in place but you will want to replace the screws with ones that are 3-inches long. Check the hole and be sure it is deep enough to accept the new latch-bolt. It has to be in the proper position to depress the plunger on the deadlocking latch. If you do change the strike-plate assembly, you will find additional hardware available that is stronger and more resistant for this purpose.

If needed, you can reduce the gap between the door and the frame by just placing a cardboard shim behind the strike-plate. Be sure and use 3-inch screws.

CROOKS LOVE KEYPAD ENTRY SYSTEMS

The keypad entry system has gained in popularity over the last few years and crooks are having fun checking them out and finding them easy to open. The keypad tends to give many clues to the crook to figure out the code. It is best to clean the keypad regularly to remove the fingerprints and smudges making it easy to decipher the code.

HELP! MY KEY HAS STOPPED TURNING AROUND

The following are solutions to the problem of a key not turning in the lock, even though it is the right key:

- ❖ Try using penetrating oil in the lock, but if you don't have any use spray vegetable oil both in the lock and on the key. Turn it back and forth several times to lubricate all the moving parts as best as you can.
- ❖ Pencils are made of graphite and they can be used to rub on the end of the key. After it builds up a little insert it and try moving it around. If it does work, move it around several times to lubricate all the insides. Be sure and use a "soft" pencil.
- ❖ If you don't have a pencil, try using talcum powder, which has a similar effect as the graphite. You can also get a small plastic bottle and spray the talcum powder into the lock.
- ❖ If you live in a cold climate and your lock is frozen just heat the end of the key with a match or the cigarette lighter and try it again. The heat from the key should melt the ice and loosen it. A hair dryer will also do the job.

DRINKING WATER

GENERAL INFORMATION:

Most drinking water in the United States is safe to drink and is tested regularly. However, more and more pollutants are being released into our water supplies and the safety may be more difficult to obtain in some areas. If you trust the drinking water in your area than drink it! If not best to have a filter system on your home or drink bottles water to be on the safe side.

If you have a well on your property and that is the source of your water it should be checked regularly, especially if you have children since they are more susceptible to waterborne diseases than adults. Remember children's immune systems are not as strong as adults therefore the quality of the water is even more important.

MY PIPES ARE KILLING ME

If the pipes that carry water in your home are too old they may be releasing harmful contaminants since some older homes still have lead pipes. When cooking use only cold water since hot water tends to have more contaminants from the pipes.

WATER PURIFICATION METHODS

There are numerous methods of home water purification systems. If you decide to purchase a system, be sure to investigate the different types and the availability of service for that particular system. A number of units only produce a minimal quantity of pure water, which would not be sufficient for many families while other units do not provide the level of desired filtration.

Activated Charcoal Filtration Units

A number of the more popular units filter the water through activated charcoal filters. This method is very efficient in filtering out insecticides, pesticides, chlorine, and organic matter. However this type of filter is not very effective in filtering out bacteria and un-dissolved metals such as lead, copper, iron, and manganese.

Filters need to be checked regularly and changed or the system will be useless. If you do choose this type of unit, be sure it does not contain silver to neutralize bacteria. Silver is not that effective and a percentage may end up in your drinking water.

Chlorination

Systems that utilize chlorine to kill bacteria usually produce water with a somewhat off-taste and odor to the water. The system must be functioning properly at all times or there is the possibility of the chlorine forming a dangerous element.

Multi-Stage Filtration

These units are one of the most effective and usually recommended above most other units. They utilize a number of filtration methods such as a pre-filter, which will remove iron, rust, dirt particles, and sediments as small as 5 microns.

They also have a lead-activated carbon filter, which removes lead and chlorine as well as a carbon block filter to remove chlorine, improve taste, remove odors, and most organic impurities.

Micro-strainers

A good method of filtration, but it is not able to remove most nitrates and nitrites. It will remove almost all chemicals and bacteria.

Reverse Osmosis

This is one of the most popular units sold in the United States and utilizes a duel sediment filter system. The system is effective in removing up to 90% of the minerals and inorganic matter. The system works by forcing water through a thin membrane which removes the inorganic metals. Most units only store 5 gallons of water or less. This system only produces 20% drinking water and discards 80% as waste. Commercial systems are used to remove salt from seawater producing drinking water.

Distillation

Distillation is one of the most effective methods of filtration. Water is boiled producing steam, which is then cooled to produce water vapor, which is then trapped. But certain gasses are not removed through this method. The more efficient distillers utilize activated charcoal filters as an additional organic material remover. Be sure and de-scale your distiller regularly or the efficiency will be greatly reduced.

Aeration

Radon gas is a continuing water contamination problem, especially in the Midwest United States. An aeration filter is the most effective type of filter to resolve this problem. A survey conducted by the Environmental Protection Agency estimated that over 8 million people are at risk from radon contamination.

Ultraviolet Radiation Purifiers

These types of filters are very effective in filtering out bacteria and are normally installed on wells in conjunction with other types of filtration units. This system does require a constant electrical line voltage. It does not remove cyst contamination.

Ozonators

These filters are being used more extensively than ever before and are frequently found on swimming pools built after 1992. They utilize activated oxygen that is capable of purifying and removing bacteria without chlorination. Recommended more for swimming pools rather than drinking water since the system may produce bromate, which may be related to tumors of the kidney.

Carbon Filters

These filters utilize carbon to attract the contaminants, which then adhere to the carbon. They are useful in removing odors, improving the taste of water, and eliminating organic chemical compounds. Their drawback is that they do not remove harmful heavy metals.

Magnetic Water Conditioners

 Since all home appliances or equipment that use water build up scale over a period of time, these conditioners are a must for the homeowner who wishes to protect their investment with a minimum of repairs from water scale damage. These systems do not affect water purity but they condition the water, magnetically altering the physical characteristics of water-borne minerals. The mineral will no longer be able to cling to the insides of the water pipes and no scale can be formed.

CHECKING YOUR OWN TAP WATER

Hints that will help you evaluate you own tap water for possible contamination or problems:

- If your sink has a dark reddish-colored stain it may be the result of rust in your pipes.
- If your sink has greenish stains it is probably from copper leaching from the pipes.
- If you notice a rotten egg smell, it's probably hydrogen sulfide produced from bacteria.
- If the water is cloudy it can be from dirt particles, iron, or bacterial contamination. Cloudy water can also result from small air bubbles forming when the water is under pressure as it leaves the tap and soon dissipates. This is harmless and no need for concern.

COMMON CONTAMINANTS IN TAP WATER

Copper

This is usually more of a problem in older homes stemming from the metal leaching out of the pipes.

Fluoride

Water companies add fluoride to reduce the incidence of tooth decay. While fluoride does reduce the incidence of cavities, it is also a very toxic chemical and must be carefully controlled.

Chlorine
It is sometimes added as a disinfectant. People who frequently swim in pools that are chlorinated have reported arthritis and immune system disorders.

Lead
It is leached out into tap water from older pipes.

Chlorocarbons
If chlorine is present it may react with organic compounds producing a harmful contaminant.

Organic Molecules
It includes hydrocarbons, gasoline, and cleaning solvents.

PVC's
Plastic materials: from water pipes.

Radon
Naturally occurring contaminant!

Minerals
Sodium content of some water may be too high.

Pesticides/Fertilizers
Filter through the ground and end up in our water supplies.

Microorganisms
Include fungi, bacteria, and parasites.

Nitrates
Residues from fertilizers!

Drugs
Reside from prescription pharmaceuticals.

WATER TIPS

RISK OF DYING FROM PESTICIDES IN WATER SUPPLIES
The risk of getting cancer from drinking pesticide contaminated water is about 1 in one million if you drink 8-10 glasses per day. The chances of getting cancer from smoking cigarettes (1 pack per day) are about 80,000 in 1 million.

YOUR TAP WATER MAY BE DRUGGED
Reports are surfacing that show drug residues in tap water, surface water and groundwater. These residues are from antibiotics, chemotherapy agents, numerous pharmaceuticals, tranquilizers, hormones, etc. They are excreted by humans and domestic animals and may be spread by flushing toilets, manure fertilizers and most types of sewage. German scientists have identified 30-60 drugs in typical water samples.

GIVE IT TO THE PLANTS

Tap water should always be allowed to run for 2-3 minutes first thing in the morning in case contaminants have seeped in during the night.

YOU NEED TO GET THE LEAD OUT

Over 5 million private wells in the United States may be exposing millions of people to high levels of lead. A warning has been issued by the Environmental Protection Agency that certain types of submersible pumps may leach lead into the water. The problem pumps have fitting made from brass that contains copper and zinc and 2-7% lead. It is possible to drink water with 51 times the allowable limits of lead in water prescribed by the EPA. Pumps should be made from stainless steel or plastic to eliminate the risk. For more information call the EPA's

---

Safe Drinking Water Hotline (800) 426-4791

ELECTRICAL

When it comes to any electrical problem, we recommend that a qualified electrician be called in all instances. The following information is only to assist you in identifying the problem not fixing it on your own.

BAD OUTLET

If one or more outlets on the same circuit breaker are not working, you have an open line somewhere which can be dangerous and possibly start a fire. If you have recently done any work on the line, check your work.

BAD SMALL APPLIANCE

If one outlet is not working after plugging in a small appliance, but the rest do on the same circuit, this is probably a GFI (ground frequency interrupter) that has tripped and should be checked first. Know the location of all GFI's in the home. If the problem is not a tripped GFI or a circuit breaker then it is probably a loose wire in one of the outlets or wall switches. If you push the red button it may fix the problem.

THAT WAS SURE BRIGHT
If the lights get bright for a few seconds after turning on a small appliance you may have a neutral wire in your panel box that is loose. This is dangerous and needs to be fixed immediately. When you call a serviceman, mention that you have a "loose neutral" and he will be there very quickly.

SMALL APPLIANCES ARE TRIPPING GFI
If this only happens at night it means it is a low voltage problem and one of the wires coming into the house has a partial connection that has become loose.

HELP! EVERYTHING HAS GONE OFF
Reset the main breaker. Call the power company.

RECESSED LIGHTS KEEP TURNING ON & OFF
The light fixture is overheating. You may be using too high a wattage   bulb.

WIRE COLOR & FUNCTION

Bare Copper
Used as a grounding wire.

Black
Be careful, this is a hot wire carrying current at full voltage.

Green
Used as a grounding wire.

Red
Be careful, this is a hot wire carrying current at full voltage.

White
This normally is a neutral wire that carries current at zero voltage.

White & Black
Be careful, this is a hot wire carrying current at full voltage.

Know your wire colors!

ELECTRICAL SAFETY TIPS
- ✓ Make a plan of attack for every project. Know what you are going to do before you do it.
- ✓ Did you turn off the power?
- ✓ Be sure you look at the unit and how it was originally installed. Make a sketch if you have to. It is best to use an instant camera to take a picture before starting and always keeps the original instruction books.

- ✓ Be sure and have a few small holders to place the tiny parts in.
- ✓ Save all the screws and small parts that you replaced for possibly future use.
- ✓ Make sure that you use the exact replacement parts unless you are upgrading the unit.
- ✓ Be sure that all electrical parts have the Underwriters Laboratory (UL) stamp of approval.

NOT A SHOCKING EXPERIENCE

To remove a broken light bulb first turn off the electricity then try placing ½ a raw potato or ½ a small apple into the broken base and screwing it out - or just use needle-nosed pliers.

BE CAREFUL EXTENDING

Extension cords have caused thousands of fires and are a hazard when not used properly. If you have to use one be sure that it is rated and is thick enough to carry the load. If the cord is rated for 15-amps you can't use it on a 30-amp appliance. If it gets hot it may start to burns and hopefully the circuit breaker or fuse will blow first.

FIREPLACE/CHIMNEY

GENERAL INFORMATION

The chimney needs to be checked before the winter season starts to be sure that the damper is working properly. Check and see if all the bricks are in place and that no mortar has fallen out. Be sure and close the flue after you have used the fireplace to reduce heat loss in the house.

FORGET THE ALUMINUM FLASHING

Aluminum is commonly used as flashing and extended around the chimney. However, it would be best to remove the aluminum if there is any brick near the chimney and use either copper or galvanized steel flashing. Lime from mortar will cause the aluminum to corrode.

CALL THE CHIMNEY INSPECTOR

If you have the chimney cleaned at least once a year, the chimney sweep should do the inspection free.

PUT A LID ON IT

It is a good idea to place a chimney cap on top of your chimney to keep the squirrels, bats, and birds out of the house. It will also shed rainwater, but make sure it is not one that will impede the airflow.

CONTROL THAT BURN

Controlled burns to clean out chimneys are done but they are not recommended since they do pose a risk.

FIRE WILL NOT STAY LIT

The wood is probably wet or unseasoned. The firewood used to start the fire may be too large.

FIREPLACE LOG STARTER

The following ingredients will be needed:

5	**Pounds of sawdust (clean)**
1	**Quart old auto oil**

Place the ingredients in a safe container and mix well, then allow at least an hour for complete absorption. Sprinkle a small amount around the smaller logs or twigs and then light.

TOO MUCH SOOT ON INSIDE OF FLUE

It is caused by burning poor quality wood or items that are not wood.

FINISH GETTING DULL ON FIREPLACE

It needs to be re-painted with a heat-resistant paint.

HOW TO MAINTAIN STONE HEARTH & WALL

Hopefully a layer of penetrating-sealer was applied with tung oil. This is moisture-resistant and will form a coating tough enough to clean. To remove the soot dissolve 4 ounces of yellow laundry soap in boiling water then allow it to cool.

Add ½ pound of powdered pumice and ½ cup of household ammonia to the mixture and mix well. Use a stiff brush and remove as much soot as possible, then apply the mixture with a paintbrush and allow it to remain for ½ hour. Finish by washing it off with a stiff brush and warm water.

COLORED FLAME FROM LOGS

The following ingredients will be needed:

½	**Pint of methanol (denatured alcohol)**
¼	**Teaspoon strontium nitrate (red flame)**
¼	**Teaspoon barium nitrate (green flame)**
¼	**Teaspoon table salt (yellow flame)**
¼	**Teaspoon copper sulfate (blue flame)**
¼	**Teaspoon copper sulfide (purple flame)**

Place the methanol into a spray bottle and add one of the above chemicals to the solution and mix. Spray the logs to be used and allow them to dry before lighting the fire.

CAUTION: Never spray the logs while the fire is lit. Methanol is also poisonous.

ASHES TO ASHES
Remember to save the old ashes from a fireplace, dry them, and use them as a fertilizer in the spring to increase the pH (alkalinity) of the soil.

CHIMNEY CLEANING TIP
One method of keeping your chimney clean is to place ½ cup of salt on burning logs. The salt will place a lot of the soot in the chimney into the air leaving the chimney.

FIREWOOD

Beech
Very tough to split and slow to dry out, however, it will burn good and provide plenty of heat.
Elm
This wood is best if cut in the dead of winter and dried for at least 2 years. Very hard to split and is not one of the better woods to burn.
Hornbeam
This may be called ironwood and burns hot and will last longer than any other wood. Very hard to find and only harvest dead trees.
Oak
It is one of the best for firewood but needs to be seasoned. Tends to spit and sizzle if kept too long under cover.

Red Maple
Easy to cut, dry, and split, but it doesn't burn as hot as other wood.

Sugar Maple
Dries slowly and splits hard, but it burns hot and lasts a long time.
White Birch
This wood burns fast and not very hot. It is good for a quick fire and to keep slow burning wood going. It is best to use as a fire starter if you strip off the bark.

HOW CAN I BE OLD AT 10?
If you have a masonry chimney over 10 years old it is probably due for inspection by a professional.

Many of the old chimneys are not lined and the mortar between the bricks can break down over the years from heat gasses and wood emissions. Even if you have a clay liner, it can deteriorate and crack over time. These possible problems can cause a chimney fire.

HEATING

GENERAL INFORMATION:
Heating leaks are notorious for causing your winter heating bills to rise. Before the winter hits you need to check any area that may allow outside cold air to enter.

AIR AROUND THE ELECTRICAL OUTLETS
Hardware stores sell inexpensive foam gaskets that can be placed around the outlets to seal them up. They also have special plastic outlet covers.

STOPPING THE COLD AIR AROUND THE WINDOW UNIT
Window air conditioners should have a cover for the winter that goes inside as well as outside.

COLD AIR COMING IN MY DRYER VENT
The dryer vent needs to be caulked all around the exterior opening.

CLOSE THOSE REGISTERS
Since hot air rises, it would be best to close some of the registers upstairs.

ARE FILTERS IMPORTANT IN WINTER?
Filters should be changed twice a year or purchase special filters that can be reused and vacuumed.

DIFFERENT TEMPERATURES IN DIFFERENT ROOMS
There may be an obstacle in the register or you may have to close off some vents.

RATTLING REGISTERS
It is caused by loose louvers. If not, call professional service.

LOW AIR FLOW FROM REGISTERS
This is usually a   dirty filter problem. Replace or vacuum.

Good way to save money!

STOPPING WINDOW LEAKS
Window leaks can now be stopped using an expandable foam spray that will seal the area around the windows. This will only cost about $15.00 to do the entire house and will probably save you $60.00 every year.

HUMIDIFIER

GENERAL INFORMATION:
Humidifiers usually work when there is a furnace running and the home needs some moisture placed into the air. The humidifier works by allowing water to flow either into a reservoir that has a pad mounted to a cylinder that turns or the water goes through a screen or wick then into a drain.

A fan then blows air across the damp area, and the water evaporates into the air. The warmer the air, the more evaporation takes place. Most humidifiers are placed near a furnace. The colder the weather, the more humidity you will probably need since colder air is usually drier air.

The humidifier has the following components:

Water
This comes from a small valve that is attached to the household's water supply.

Pad or screen
If there is a pad, it will be mounted to a cylinder and there will be a small motor rotating through a small reservoir of water. If there is a mesh or screen, the water will flow through a trough located at the top of the screen in order to distribute the water evenly across it.

Fan
It is usually the furnace blower fan that will blow air across a damp medium and cause the evaporation of the water.

Valve
This may also be a float, which allows the water to flow either into a reservoir or across the pad or screen then into a drain.

Humidistat
This will determine the amount of moisture the air needs and will turn on the humidifier when needed with the furnace blower.

CAN HUMIDIFIER BE LEFT ON ALL YEAR?
The humidifier should be turned off after the cold season is over.

BEST TYPE TO PURCHASE
The most efficient are the type that is attached to your furnace and works when the furnace blower is on.

INDOOR AIR QUALITY

GENERAL INFORMATION:
Indoor air can be unhealthier than the air you breathe outside! It can actually be harmful to your family's health.

The basement especially can contain the most polluted air in the home since it is next to the ground. It is susceptible to a radioactive gas called "radon," which is a known carcinogen, a major risk factor for cancer.

Moisture tends to be more of a problem in basements, leading to mold and mildew problems, and can cause an allergic reaction in many individuals. Condensation may form on walls and the basement is a source of sewage leaks. Carbon monoxide may also be a problem from heaters, furnaces, or poorly vented dryers.

SIDE STREAM CIGARETTE SMOKE
Try not to smoke in the home since this is a source of many pollutants that can get into the furniture and carpets.

FOOD SPILLS = INSECTS
Remove food spills immediately.

HOUSEHOLD & PEST CONTROL CHEMICALS
Keep windows open whenever possible or run fans to circulate the air.

DRY CLEANING & CARPET CHEMICALS
If installing new carpeting, have the store unroll the carpet and allow it to air out for at least one day before laying it in the house.

PETS BRING IN ALLERGENS
Be sure the pets are clean.

BASEMENT MOLD, HARMFUL GASSES, MOISTURE
Have your basement tested for radon gasses. Make sure to ventilate the basement. Clean all areas with a quality bactericide product. Make sure that all furnaces are tested for leaks and sealed. Check that all vents from the furnace and gas-dryers are free of debris and cleaned of any mold at least twice each year. Purchase a carbon monoxide detector for the basement.

BASEMENT ROOMS A PROBLEM
Seal up any possible areas that could allow moisture to enter reducing the possibility of mold growth and other allergens to survive. If the humidity is high in the home don't have a lot of houseplants around the home. Be sure and wipe down walls in showers with a squeegee. Clean-up mold: using 10 cups water to 1-cup bleach. Improve air circulation with air-conditioners or other ventilation. Never use a charcoal grill inside the home.

CARBON MONOXIDE POISONING SYMPTOMS

Headache..........Nausea..........Vomiting..........Dizziness..........Confusion...........
.......Tiredness..........Breathing Problems..........Sleepiness.........Chest Tightness....

PLUMBING

BOY! DO I SWEAT
Sweating pipes can be fixed by placing foam pipe insulation around the pipes. This will keep the humid air from condensing on the pipes.

MY COPPER PIPE HAS A LITTLE LEAK
You will need a piece of firm, but flexible, rubber and a hose clamp. Place the rubber around the area that is leaking and put the clamp on it and screw it tightly shut.

TOILET BLOCKS & DRAINS HAVE A BAD ODOR

This problem may be caused by the vent stack through the roof being blocked, causing the traps to be suctioned of water every time you flush the toilet. Chances are that if you hear a gurgling noise that is definitely the problem. Just run a snake through it and unplug it.

DRAINS ARE NOT FREE-FLOWING & STINK

To keep drains free flowing and to have a better odor, just place ¼ cup of baking soda in the drain and slowly add ½ cup of white vinegar. This works well for smaller drains. For larger drains double the amount.

NOW I CAN FISH IN THE TOILET

The worms are coming in through a break in a pipe and the break needs to be found and repaired as soon as possible or this will cause more serious problems.

SCREENS

GENERAL INFORMATION

In the early days, screening material was made from horsehair and it wasn't until the 1920's when galvanized screening material was introduced to the public. Steel wire has the tendency to rust and eventually aluminum was used. Screening today is produced from either aluminum or vinyl-coated fiberglass (the more popular).

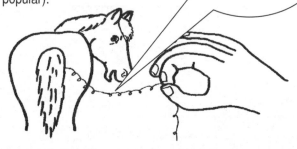

OUCH! There must be a better way to make a screen!

The vinyl-coated fiberglass is the most popular screening material and won't corrode, rust, or stain. But it will stretch and tear more easily than aluminum. If you get a tear or hole in a screen door or window the bugs will invade your home. There are a few easy methods of repairing these holes.

SCREEN WEAVER

Get a long needle and try weaving the screen back together.

Once you have everything back in its place, be sure and paint both sides with a clear coat of nail polish then allow it to dry. If you don't have nail polish, try using rubber cement or even airplane glue.

BIGGGG HOLE

If the hole is too large to weave back together, you will have to patch it or buy a new screen. To patch it just cut another piece of screen about ½-inch longer than the hole. Be sure and unravel a few strands on each side then bend the wires and insert the patch over the hole. Use the long needle to weave the wires back into place.

THERE'S A LITTLE HOLE IN THE SCREEN

The small hole can be fixed either by using a number of layers of clear nail polish or use waterproof glue. If the screens are plastic, you will need to use acetone-type glue.

SEPTIC TANKS

GENERAL INFORMATION:

The septic tank is a large metal tank that sits underground on your property and accumulates your household wastes. Most people do not know how to maintain the tank and problems will occur. There are also natural failures that can occur if the ground fails where the tank is located. Septic systems can cost up to $20,000 to replace if not cared for. Every year approximately 1200 people die from contaminated water and failed septic systems.

ENOUGH ALREADY

Be sure and have a very efficient water softener that will not put too much water into the system every day.

THE EFFLUENT IS BEING KILLED BY HOUSEHOLD CLEANERS

Replace the bacteria in the tank regularly since the household cleaners may be killing them off. Products are available in most supermarkets.

I'M GETTING SICK, PUMP ME OUT

Have the tank pumped every 2-3 years.

SPECIAL FILTER
Effluent filters should be installed (by a professional) in the exit baffle to stop larger solids from clogging the drain field lines.

CHLORINE IS KILLING ME
Using oxygen bleach will help your system stay healthy. The oxygen bleach works better than other types of bleach.

NOTE:
Divert other runoff from roofs, patios and driveways away from your drain field.

STONE TILE

Marble
This is a natural stone composed of crystals that can be found in different colors and patterns. Used in many famous buildings worldwide and known for its durability and beauty. It must be sealed and can easily be scratched and stained by most liquids.

Granite
Has a tough, glossy appearance with colors ranging from light to dark and patterns will vary with graining. It is harder than marble and will resist scratching better, even resists acids. Can withstand freeze/thaw cycles. Be sure and get the hardest quality granite since some are softer than others.

Silestone™
Produced from quartz and is superior to granite for use on kitchen countertops. Will not scratch or stain and does not have to be sealed like marble or granite.

Slate
It is rough-textured tile that is produced from quarried stone and can be purchased in slabs or tiles, which are about 12-inches square. It also comes in two types: gauged slate, which is ground smooth on the bottom or un-gauged which is rough on both sides. Very reasonably priced but somewhat brittle and does not have much of a range of colors. The darker slate has a tendency to fade in direct sunlight and may be somewhat difficult to work with.

STORAGE PROBLEMS

GENERAL INFORMATION:
There are many places in a home that could increase storage capacity without any major construction. Most homes have enough storage space, but people are not aware of how easy it is to better utilize the space.

STORAGE SOLUTIONS

Most people feel that increasing storage space is too expensive and their home may need structural changes. Finding the locations for more storage space is easy.

> ➢ Extend upper cabinets to the ceiling. This usable space that is left unused or filled with soffits. These areas can easily be accessed with the use of a step stool and you can store items that are rarely used.
> ➢ Closets that are not in full use can be converted to provide shelves or a bookcase by adding the space to a room behind the closet.
> ➢ Access lost cabinet space that is at the back of the shelves by installing pullout shelves or lazy Susan's.
> ➢ Low closet doors make access to storage areas on top of closets. Install ceiling height doors.

VINYL FLOORS

TIPS ON LAYING A SELF-ADHESIVE VINYL FLOOR

Follow the directions!

Step One:
Be sure and remove all the rooms' shoe molding, if any exists, including the toilet if you are working in the bathroom.

Step Two:
Snap a chalk line from the center point to the center point of opposite walls. At the point where the lines intersect will be the center of the room. Using a carpenter's square be sure that the two chalk lines are at a 90^0 angle where they meet. If not, adjust!

Step Three:

Place the tiles without removing the backing in a dry run along the chalk line. Make sure that you have at least ½ of a tile going around the perimeter of the room. If this is not the case, you may have to change where the chalk lines intersect.

Step Four:
Start installing the tiles at the point where the chalk lines intersect. Peel off the backing from the first tile and set it, making sure that it aligns with the chalk line. Press it down firmly!

225

Step Five:
The tile should be laid in one quadrant at a time, follow the chalk line and keep butting the tiles edge to edge.

Step Six:
When you come to the perimeter of the room be sure and cut those last tiles to make them fit. Measure the tile that you have to cut by placing two full tiles on top of the last full tile. Then you will need to slide the top tile over so that it is about ¼ inches away from the wall. Use the top tile as a straight edge and draw a pencil line on the tile sandwiched in between.

Step Seven:
Now use a utility knife and straightedge to score the tile along the pencil mark, and then just snap the tile in two. Peel the adhesive back and fit the trimmed tile into place. Be sure that the factory finished edge goes next to the adjoining tile leaving the trimmed side next to the wall.

Step Eight:
After all the tiles are in place roll the floor with a rented tile roller or use a rolling pin.

Step Nine:
Re-install the shoe molding or if it in a bathroom, it would be best to re-caulk the areas around the toilet and tub.

REPAIRING A GOUGE

Gouges and dents in a vinyl floor can easily be repaired. Just shred a scrap of the vinyl with a food grater and watch your fingers then add a small amount of clear acrylic glue to the shreds and make a paste. Work the paste into the gouge or dent until it's flush with the surface.

WALLS

WALLBOARD REPAIR

A large hole can be repaired by using a scrap piece of wallboard and placing a backup plate behind it. The following is a step-by-step method of completing the repair:

> First, using a sharp utility knife or small saw make the hole into an even square.

> Use a piece of wallboard that is cut to about two inches larger than the hole, but barely narrow enough to fit through the hole. Drill a hole in the center of the back plate just large enough to place your finger in.

- Place glue around the overlapping area and carefully place the back plate through the hole and force it gently next to the hole until the glue catches. Remove your finger and allow the glue to dry fully before going any further.
- Cut a piece of wallboard about 1/8th of an inch smaller than the hole and glue it to the back plate even with the rest of the wall.
- Next fill the area around the patch with joint compound, allow it to dry then sand and match the texture of the balance of the wall.

HOW FIRM I AM............

If you dip screws into water before you drive them into a plaster wall, the damp plaster will set up around them and hold them firmly in place.

MY STUCCO HAS A CRACK

This is caused by expansion or contraction. Repair by caulking or re-painting.

REDUCE SANDING TIME & TROUBLE

When you are going to fill a hole or repair a dent in drywall, just reduce the sanding time by rubbing the dried joint with a damp sponge. The texture you create will help blend the patched area into the rest of the wall.

WATER PIPES

KNOCK, KNOCK: WHO'S THERE?

If the problem is banging, you will need to locate the pipe that is not fastened down and fasten it securely.

The hammering can be fixed by draining the water out of the pipes and adding some air. An air cushion chamber can be installed in the line to solve the problem.

INSULATE ME

Be sure and clean the pipes well. If you choose foil or fiberglass, be sure and wrap it around the pipes with a ½" overlap before taping it closed. If you use fiberglass, wear the proper protection and wrap them in plastic after the fiberglass is installed to keep them from dripping condensation.

WINDOWS

GENERAL INFORMATION:

Quality windows can increase the value of a home and save money on energy costs, especially if the home has older windows. There are many indications that will influence the purchase of new windows such as the condition of the present window frames, poor insulation, and single pane without storm stutters. There are also different window finishes for different locations throughout the house.

KNOWLEDGE IS PRICELESS

When replacing windows, lack of knowledge is common regarding the different window types, poor evaluation of your present window frames, or purchasing inexpensive windows that will not really do the job. That being said, you can work within a budget and get good quality windows.

Choose a well-known company to evaluate and install new windows and remove the old ones. Learn about the four major types of frames: vinyl, aluminum, wood and fiberglass composite (new one). Choose energy efficient windows:

Low "E"

This window eliminates the majority of UV light that can damage furniture, paint, and other objects. You still get the light but not the harmful rays.

Double-Pane

These windows have a gas between the panes that is pressure sealed. The gas acts as an insulator between the outside temperature and the inside temperature.

WINDOWS ARE FOGGING UP

These are probably double-paned windows and the seal is shot. There is no way to fix it and the windows need to be replaced.

ALUMINUM WINDOWS BIND

This may be caused by a broken window balancer, which needs to be replaced. Or the tension adjusted.

KEEPS SHUTTING, WON'T STAY OPEN

The balancer is probably weak and needs to be replaced. If the balancer seems OK then try and adjust the tension.

TENSION ROD IS JAMMED
The tension rod is jammed. Call a repair company.

HELP! MY WINDOW IS STUCK
To release a stuck window: take a sharp blade (large X-Acto™ knife or spackling blade) and go around the edge of the frame. You could also take a two-by-four and lay it flat against the frame and tap lightly with a hammer.

GETTING ON THE RIGHT TRACK
Windows will slide more easily if you rub a bar of soap across the track occasionally.

THE CASE OF THE RATTLING WINDOW
Almost all old windows tend to rattle and the answer is easy, just glue ordinary "corn pads" to the frames and they will quiet down immediately.

MY WINDOW HAS MOISTURE ON IT
Usually the humidistat is set too high. Moisture accumulates on windows when they are cold and you have taken a long hot shower or are boiling water. Turning on a ventilation fan should help the problem.

FIXING A HOLEY WINDOW
If you have a few very tiny holes in a windowpane, you don't have to replace the window. Just place a small amount of clear finger nail polish in the hole.

METHOD OF REPLACING A BROKEN WINDOW

1. Make sure you are working on a horizontal surface and remove all the broken glass pieces from the frame. Best to wear safety glasses and leather gloves. Place a piece of newspaper over the window and tap it with a rubber mallet to loosen all pieces of glass.
2. You will need to remove all the old putty using a heat gun on medium or possibly a hair dryer on the high setting. Use a putty knife or small chisel to scrape away all traces of the old putty.

3. Remove all the old metal glazing points. There are usually 2 or more on each side of the frame. Be sure to find all of them.
4. Dip the end of a sponge in boiled linseed oil and then wipe around all four sides of the frame. The oil will prevent the glazing putty from drying out too fast.
5. Place a small rope of putty on the back-bed to keep the glass from rattling.
6. Position the new piece of glass in the frame and gently push it into the back-bed putty. Reposition the glazing points using the putty knife then place a small amount of putty around all sides of the glass. Smooth it out with the putty knife and scrape away any excess.

WINTERIZING A HOME

KEEP MY PIPES WARM
Be sure and insulate your pipes if you live in a cold climate. Insulation will go a long way to prevent freeze-ups. You will need to cover every square inch of pipe including the connections. You can purchase pipe jacketing in standard lengths that can easily be cut with a knife. Secure it with electrical tape. If you prefer you can use standard insulation and just cut it to the length you need and tape it securely.

FILL THOSE CAVITIES
At the end of many pipe runs there is an area that may be a small cavity. Be sure and stuff insulation in all open cavities regardless how small the opening may appear to be. Be sure and don't compress the insulation too much or it will not be as effective.

SOMETHING NEW ON THE HORIZON
When trying to keep pipes warm, try using heat tape. This is electrically charged tape that draws only a fraction of power and is safe and inexpensive. Just wrap the tape around the pipe and then plug the tape into an outlet. The tape contains a thermostat, which turns the tape on and off as needed. The only drawback is that the tape will not work during a power outage.

PROTECT YOUR HOSE BIB
Before winter arrives, be sure and remove all hoses and drain them of all water. Allow all water to drain out of the hose bib (sill cock) and leave it open. If you do not have an indoor shutoff, it would be best to install one or install a freeze-proof sill cock. Newer homes may have these already installed since many local codes require them.

TRICKLE, TRICKLE

To prevent a problem on very cold days and especially nights, turn on any faucet that you are concerned about and let the water just trickle out continuously. If there is a cabinet underneath, open the doors and allow warm air to enter.

WINTERIZING FOR EXTENDED PERIOD

When closing a home or cabin down for the winter, it is not necessary to leave the heat on to avoid a problem. Utilities can safely be turned off if the house is properly prepared with no damage taking place. You will need to have the water shut off and drain the entire system making the plumbing system dormant.

CALL THE WATER DEPARTMENT

The first thing to do is to call the local water department and ask them to turn off your water to the property. They may just tell you to go to the valve on the street and do it yourself.

OPEN SESAME

The next step is to open all faucets in the home, starting at the top of the system. Shut down and then drain the water heater. Detach all drain hoses on the washing machine and dishwasher.

If you have a drainable valve or two (usually near the water meter) open the drain cock on each and drain the supply lines completely. If you locate a low-lying pipe that doesn't have a faucet or drain cock, just open a union where two pipes join and allow any water to leave.

ANTIFREEZE YOUR TOILET

You will need to replace the water in your toilets with antifreeze solution (use non-toxic antifreeze mixed with water according to directions on container). Place the liquid into the bowl and it should start a mild flushing action with some of the antifreeze remaining in the bowl and toilet trap.

TRAP THAT ANTIFREEZE

Next you will need to pour the antifreeze solution into all fixtures that have a trap, which includes all sinks, showers, bathtubs and even the washing machine standpipe. If the house has a main house trap, you will need to fill the elbow portion with full strength antifreeze for maximum protection.

GOODBYE WINTER, HELLO SPRING

After winter is over it's time to get the house back in working condition and reverse everything you did.

- ❖ First turn all faucets off, including all sill cocks. Best to remove all aerators on faucets and clean them out.
- ❖ You will have to reconnect all the pipes you disconnected and close down all drainable valves.
- ❖ Replace any hoses you removed.
- ❖ Have the water company turn on the water supply.
- ❖ Be sure and turn on all the faucets slowly and begin at the sill cock. The water will spit out for a while getting any air out of the system before a normal flow starts.
- ❖ Be sure and replace the aerators.

WOOD FLOORS

A turpentine product is recommended. In fact most wood floors will be damaged if water is used since the water tends to raise the grain and permanently dull the wood. The only exception to the rule is if the floor has been water-sealed. If the wood has been oiled, it would be best to just clean the floor with a mild solution of dish soap and just damp mop it to remove the suds and any scum leftover.

GENERAL CLEANER FOR WOOD FLOORS

The following ingredients will be needed:

2 ¼	**Cups of mineral oil**
¾	**Cups of oleic acid (from drug store)**
2	**Tablespoons of household ammonia (toxic)**
5	**Tablespoons of turpentine (toxic)**
2	**Quarts of cool tap water**

Place the mineral oil and oleic acid in a container and mix well, then add the ammonia, turpentine, and mix well. Place 1 cup of the mixture into the 2 quarts of water and then apply to floor with a sponge mop. Rinsing will not be necessary. **Keep out of reach of children.**

INSTALLING CARPETING OVER SQUEAKY FLOOR

Be sure and nail down all squeaky floor areas with deck screws through the subfloor and into the joists.

THE SECRET TO SCREWING SCREWS

If you want to make screws go in easier, just push the screws into a bar of soap before trying to screw them in. They will also never come loose if you place a drop or two of clear nail polish in the hole before you finish tightening it up.

STOP SCRATCHING ME

The easiest method of stopping furniture from scratching wood floors is to place a few layers of masking tape on the bottoms of the legs or the bottom of rocking chair rockers. Place at least 2-3 layers so that the tape cannot be seen.

PINE BOARDS DON'T LOOK LIKE THE OLD ONES

If the new area gets sunlight it will gradually darken and look like the old flooring.

NEVER ON JOISTS

It is best to never lay a finish floor on joists. When you do this, you lose strength and the looks of the floor. Use a subfloor, which can be either planking or plywood.

POSITION IS EVERYTHING

Knots reduce the strength and do not look too good. If you have to use them, try placing the area with the knot positioned at the top of the joist.

WHAT DIRECTION FOR SUBFLOORING?

Board flooring works best when installed diagonally. This will make your home more rigid and you can nail a finish floor on top of it in either direction.

THERE MUST BE A MOUSE UNDER THE FLOOR

If you have squeaky floorboards, purchase some powdered graphite in a squeeze tube and force the powder between the two floorboards. You can use a putty knife if necessary. The squeaks can be temporarily quieted using liquid soap. Just pour some between the floorboards and the squeaks will be gone. You can also temporarily stop the squeak by sprinkling talcum power in the area and then walking over the area, forcing the powder in the cracks. The oil from the powder will lubricate the boards and quiet them. It works great on stairs as well.

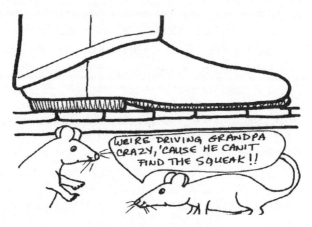

WOOD STOVES

GENERAL INFORMATION:
When using a wood stove, be sure and only burn seasoned wood that has been split and covered for at least 7-8 months. If the wood is too green, it will burn cooler and cause a buildup of creosote.

CAN I USE THE ASHES ON MY PLANTS?
Wood ashes can be used as fertilizer to help neutralize the acidity in the soil. However never use coal ashes or you will kill your plants.

CAN TREATED WOOD BE BURNED IN A WOOD STOVE?
Treated wood should not be burned in a wood stove or you risk dangerous gasses and ashes.

VACUUM CLEANER

SMELLS DUSTY IN HERE
Try placing a small piece of cotton inside the bag with a few drops of vanilla on it and remember never over fill the bag or you may hurt the motor. Change the filter regularly unless you have a machine with a filtered bag.

SNEAK-A-PEEK
Always check the floor for objects that may get into the vacuum cleaner fan and cause a problem. If you do hear a strange sound, turn the machine off immediately, and clean out the foreign object.

VACUUM CLEANER PROBLEM SOLVERS

MOTOR WILL NOT TURN ON
1. Power is off at outlet – first check wall outlet to be sure you have power there. Look for a frayed or damaged cord.
2. Motor hums and will not run – you will have to take the cleaner apart and see if the fans are jammed – remove any foreign object.
3. Switch to motor cord broken – upright vacuums all have a handle cord that is connected to the on/off switch that may be bad.

MOTOR RUNS BUT NO SUCTION
1. There is most likely an obstruction in the air passage – clean out the hose or check and see if the bag is full. There may also be a leak in the hose or housing.
2. Fan loose or obstructed – disassemble vacuum and clean out the fan, or the shaft controlling the fans, may not be rotating.
3. Motor binding – poor lubrication, worn brushes, a binding rotor, or a dirt commutator. It may also be a shorted wire in the field.

VACUUM CLEANER IS BLOWING FUSES
1. Circuit overload – check and see if there are too many appliances on the same circuit.
2. Short circuit in power cord or plug – replace cord or plug.
3. Short circuits in switch to motor cord – fix, repair, or replace cord.

VACUUM CLEANER IS TOO NOISY
1. Power brush noisy – brush may be hitting the bottom plate and needs to be adjusted.
2. Fans blades loose or broken – tighten or replace fan blades.

VACUUM CLEANER IS SHOCKING YOU
1. Power cord frayed – best to replace it.
2. Leakage current problem – if you are getting a shock from a metal part take the machine to an authorized dealer.

GLUB, GLUB, BETTER BUY A NEW ONE
Unless the vacuum is made for water pickup, never pick up any liquid or moisture with a standard vacuum cleaner or it will rust the insides and ruin the machine.

COMB OUT THE BRUSHES

Use a common comb to comb out the debris and hair from the brushes regularly to increase the efficiency of the vacuum cleaner. The machine will not pick up efficiently if the brushes are dirty. Hair will also work its way to the ends of the roller and get around the end bearings causing the brush to slow down and place a load on the motor.

MISCELLANEOUS

BRONZE WOOL INSTEAD OF STEEL WOOL

If rusting is a concern when working on a project, try using bronze wool, which is available at most hardware or marine supply houses. Bronze wool will not rust so the small slivers that end up sticking to your project will not have a rust problem.

COLA WORKS GREAT TOO

If you're having a problem with a rusty nut or bolt try placing a few drops of ammonia or hydrogen peroxide on it for 30 minutes.

HOW DO ELECTRIC AIR CLEANERS WORK?

The newer electric air cleaners draw the air over a series of electrically charged metal plates that attract dust and pollutants. The plates must be removed periodically and cleaned. Another type is the porous silicon plate, which traps the particles like a magnet. This type of unit utilizes a blower motor to pass the air over the filters, which need to be washed.

SNOW SLIDE

If you want the snow to slide off your snow shovel with ease all you have to do is save your empty butter wrappers and wipe the shovel off before using it.

HOW TO GET A RUN IN YOUR PANTYHOSE

Whenever you are using sandpaper to finish a wood surface, try placing an old nylon stocking over your hand and running it over the surface, the slightest rough spot will be found.

FINDING A REAL STUD

If you don't have a stud finder, try using a compass, holding it level with the floor and at a right angle to the wall. Then slowly move the compass along the surface of the wall. When the needle moves that's where you will find a stud. Another method is to locate studs using an electric shaver. Just run it along the wall and when the tone of the razor changes, you found the stud.

OUCH
Use a split piece of old garden hose to cover the blades of a saw when storing it to be safe.

DO WINDSHIELD DEICERS REALLY WORK?
Most windshield deicers are made from alcohol and are overpriced products. They do work fairly well depending on the thickness of the ice. If the ice is very thick it will take quite a while for the ice to melt. Never place hot water on your windshield it may cause the glass to expand from the heat and then contract when it cools, cracking the windshield. Most deicers are similar to antifreeze. You can place a solution of homemade deicer in your window washer unit. Just mix 1 part of any commercial antifreeze with 9 parts of 50/50 mixture of alcohol and water.

DRIP, DRIP, DRIP
If you're worried about your water lines freezing just leave one of the taps running very slightly to avoid the problem. If you have a two-story house, open one on the first floor.

HANDY RULER
Remember a dollar bill is 6 inches long and almost 3-inches wide.

AND A LONNNNG EXTENSION CORD
If your pipes freeze and do not burst: try using a hair dryer to defrost them.

TRY TO KEEP IT TOGETHER
Lightweight materials that need to be glued together are easily held in place with spring clothespins.

'TILL YOUR OLD AND GRAY
If you "weather" wood before applying stain, the stain will last years longer.

DON'T CRACK-UP & SAVE YOUR FINGERS
To prevent plaster walls from cracking when driving a nail in for a picture hanger, try placing a small piece of tape over the spot before hammering in the nail. If you are using small nails, like brads, try holding the nail with a small plastic comb to save the fingers.

BUBBLE, BUBBLE, TOIL AND TROUBLE
Varnish never needs stirring. Stirring only creates air bubbles, which may ruin a smooth finish.

ODE DE CEDAR CHEST

If you would like the original cedar odor from an old cedar chest, try rubbing the inner surface lightly with fine sandpaper.

Kerosene is a fire hazard!

KEROSENE KILLS RUST

If you brush a small amount of kerosene on a rusted screw then wait 10 minutes before removing it, it will come out easily. You can also dampen a rag with white vinegar, wrap the rag around the rusted screw, and wait at least an hour before trying to remove it.

STOP SPLITTING WOOD

If you want to avoid splitting wood when driving a finish nail in near the end of the plank, just flatten the chisel end of the nail with a few hammer blows before hammering it in. The nail will tear through the wood instead of splitting it.

I WONDER WHERE THE IVORY YELLOW WENT!

If your piano keys are getting yellow, just dip ½ of a lemon in salt and rub on the keys to whiten them up.

GET THE STINK OUT OF GASOLINE

To deodorize gasoline just add 20 drops of sassafras oil to every gallon or solvent. Heat is then transferred to the substrate.

POOR DRYER DIED

When a dryer will not run it is usually an electrical problem, a clogged vent tube, or a broken belt. These three things can easily be checked and repaired.

I'M GROWING A BEARD

If the dryer takes too long to dry clothes, the problem is usually that the vent is restricted or clogged. Move the dryer away from the wall and check the vent. Another reason is that the blower has excessive lint buildup.

DRYER ON, CIRCUIT BREAKER OFF

The circuit breaker is probably bad, not the dryer. Replace the circuit breaker first and if that does not work, it is probably in the dryer.

OUCH, OUCH

If the white vinyl tubing is getting hot and dust or lint collect easily, you have an older dryer. Most building codes in the United Stated now require metal aluminum tubing for clothes dryers. Lint will not collect as easily in a metal vent.

VENTS ARE PROBLEMS

Many birds tend to nest in vents, especially dryer vents. It is best to cover these vents with a netting to prevent the problem. Special plastic bird netting is available through a garden supply house or from InterNet, Inc. at (800) 328-8456.

MY DRYER IS NOT ON THE LEVEL

If your dryer is not leveled properly, you will wear out a number of the parts prematurely.

DRYER SHUTS OFF WHEN IT FEELS LIKE IT

If the dryer all of a sudden shuts down it is probably the split coils that are on top of the burner. If you tap the coils and it starts that will answer your question.

IT'S NOT MY CAR TIRES

If you hear a knocking and smell rubber burning, it is probably the drum rollers supporting the drum. These will wear out and may need to be replaced or lubricated.

SOUNDS LIKE A PIG'S IN THERE

If you hear squealing, it is probably bad drum gliders or rollers. WD-40 will sometimes help but if the bearings show through, it would be best to just replace them.

BELT ALERT

It is not too hard to replace the belt. Just lift the lid and unscrew the front to get to the drum. Remove the drum with the belt on it and replace.

DRYER TIPS

> ➢ Always clean the filter between loads.
> ➢ Replace damaged filters immediately.
> ➢ Metal vent tubing is much better than plastic.
> ➢ Be sure and clean out any lint in the motor compartment.
> ➢ Check the belt every 8 months.

DRYER SHEET TIPS

FLYING INSECTS

If you place an anti-static dryer sheet in your pocket and allow it to stick out a little it will keep the bees, yellow jackets, and mosquitoes away from you.

BED BUGS

Place 4 sheets between the mattress pad and the mattress to get rid of bed bugs then place duct tape (sticky-side out) around the legs and bed rails.

ANTS & UNCLES

Ants will not come near any area that has an anti-static dryer sheet.

MOUSE REPELLANT

Place a dryer sheet anywhere you have a mouse problem and they will run the other way.

ELIMINATE BOOK ODORS

Place a dryer sheet in any books that you do not use very often to eliminate the musty odor.

A LITTLE PIECE WILL DO YA

To save on money, try tearing a dryer sheet in half. Half a sheet will work just as well as the whole sheet.

NO STATIC SCREENS

Wipe your TV or computer screen with an anti-static sheet to eliminate static electricity.

NO SOAP SCUM

Clean the shower doors with a dryer sheet to remove the soap scum.

FRESH CLOSET

Hang a dryer sheet in the closet to keep the air fresh and clean. You can also place a sheet in the dresser drawers.

VACUUM CLEANER AIR

To keep the air smelling good while you vacuum just place an anti-static sheet in the bag.

NO TANGLES

To prevent thread from tangling, just run a threaded needle through an anti-static sheet.

SUITCASE SMELLS

Place a dryer sheet in all your suitcases to get rid of any musty odors.

IMPORTANT NEWS YOU CAN USE

Dryer sheets have caused many dryers to either burn out the heating unit or cause a fire by blocking the filter. Even though you clean out the lint filter every time you use the dryer, there is a buildup of residue from the dryer sheet that sticks to the mesh and cannot be seen. The coating is invisible to the naked eye.

Try running water through the mesh filter and if the water will not go through easily it may be partially or completely blocked and you will see

the problem for yourself. Use an old toothbrush every 3 months to clean the screen and you will see the difference. This will lower your electric bill, make the dryer more efficient and protect your property.

UNDER THE SEAT
To keep the car smelling fresh, just place an anti-static dryer sheet under one of the seats.

BAKED-ON FOODS
To clean baked-on foods after using a pan, just place a dryer sheet in the pan and add water. Allow the sheet to remain overnight and you should be able to just sponge it clean the next day. The soapy agent in the sheet will loosen the dried on foods.

BASKET BOTTOMS
Place a dryer sheet in the bottom of all the waste cans and garbage cans to eliminate the odors.

HAIR REMOVER
If you rub a dryer sheet over the furniture, it will remove cat and dog hair.

A BLIND TRICK
Wipe the Venetian blinds with an anti-static dryer sheet and the dust will not adhere to it.

VERY TACKY
Sawdust can be removed using a dryer sheet. The sawdust will adhere to the sheet like a magnet and do the same job as tack cloth.

SMELLY UNDERWEAR TRICK
Place a dryer sheet on the bottom of the hamper and you will not have a smelly experience when you open it.

FEET SMELL?
Try placing a dryer sheet in shoes or sneakers overnight to eliminate the odor.

SUPER SOFT FABRIC SOFTENER
The following ingredients will be needed:

1   **Tablespoon of unflavored gelatin**
1 ½   **Cup of boiling water**

Place the gelatin in the boiling water until it is fully dissolved. Add the softener to the final rinse after the washing cycle is completed.

MAKING YOUR OWN DRYER FABRIC SOFTENER

The following ingredients will be needed:

½   **Cup of baking soda (fresh)**
1   **Tablespoon of cornstarch**
1   **Tablespoon of arrowroot powder**
2   **Drops of essential rose oil (optional)**

Place all the ingredients into a small bowl and mix well. Place a small amount in a small cloth bag that can be well secured with a drawstring, or tied, and place it into the dryer with the load. Be sure the bag is well sealed or it becomes a bit messy.

IRONING

BEATS IRONING

If you want your sheer curtains to come out of the washing machine "wrinkle-free," just dissolve a package of unflavored gelatin in a cup of boiling water and add it to the final rinse. The protein has a relaxing or softening effect on the fabric.

WASHING MACHINE

GENERAL INFORMATION:

The standard washing machine consists of a tub with holes for water to enter and an inner tub to hold the water with an agitator at the center that rotates both clockwise and counter-clockwise. This forces the clothes from the top to the bottom and back again. This motion will allow the detergent and water to reach all areas of the clothing.

The motors are on most models reversing so that they can run clockwise and counter-clockwise. The motor operates through a clutch, or a type of transmission to spin the tub at speeds that vary from 400-800 rpm's. The pump removes the water by centrifugal force.

BOUND-UP WATER FAUCETS

Faucets that supply water to the washing machine should be closed and opened once a month to avoid bind-up.

I'M GETTING DIZZY

If the washer is wobbling, the washer is no longer level and needs leveling.

WHAT DETERGENT IS BEST?
If you have a front-load washer you should be using a low suds detergent. Top loaders are a little more forgiving when you add too much detergent.

LIQUID LAUNDRY DETERGENT
The following ingredients will be needed:

1	**Cup of soap flakes (grated)**
½	**Cup of washing soda**
½	**Cup of borax**
4	**Tablespoons of glycerin**
4	**Cups of very warm tap water**

Place all the ingredients in a large bottle and mix well. Be careful not to mix too rapidly or it will result in too many suds. Add ½-3/4 of a cup to your tub in warm water and then use a cold water rinse. This makes about 24 ounces and can be reduced or increased as desired.

TOP LOADER OR FRONT LOADER
Front loaders are more efficient than top loaders, even though they are a little more expensive to purchase. You will save money through using less detergent and water.

MACHINE ATE MY CLOTHING
When a piece of clothing comes out torn, it means that you have overloaded the washing machine. If you have a top loader only place clothes to the top of the agitator and place them loosely. Front loaders can be filled up but loosely.

MY MACHINE IS RUNNING AWAY
Can I let an unbalanced load finish running? No! Be sure and balance a load or you will damage some of the delicate components.

WHY AM I INSIDE OUT?
Some clothes need to be turned inside out or they will receive abrasive damage. This protects the more delicate clothes.

I NEED A NEW RUBBER HOSE
All rubber hoses should be replaced every 4-5 years.

IT REALLY HITS THE SPOT
If you are going to wash a load of greasy clothes, try adding a bottle of cola to the load. It will really improve the cleaning action of most detergents. Colas contain a weak acid that will help to dissolve the grease. Cola can also be used to clean the rings off toilets.

DO DRY BLEACHES WORK BETTER THAN LIQUID BLEACHES?

There is a misconception that bleaches remove stains. Bleaches do not remove stains they only mask the stain so that you will not see it. This process is known as oxidation and utilizes one of two types of bleach.

The dry bleach is composed of sodium perborate, which is converted to hydrogen peroxide, which continues to break down liberating oxygen gas, which then oxidizes the clothing. Liquid bleach contains the chemical sodium hypochlorite, which causes the release of chlorine gas that oxidizes the clothing, thus bleaching the stain out. The more powerful of the two bleaching agents is the liquid bleach.

MAKING YOUR OWN WASHING MACHINE FABRIC SOFTENER

The following ingredients will be needed:

1	Cup of white vinegar
2	Cups of baking soda (fresh)
3	Cups of cold tap water

Place all the ingredients in a small bucket and mix well. Store in small plastic or glass sealed jars. Before using be sure and shake well. Add ¼ cup of the softener to the final rinse for the best results. Keep out of reach of children.

A LITTLE PREVENTION

Water faucets

They feed your washer and should be turned on and off at least once a month, especially if the water you are using is hard water. If you don't do this, they may bind-up when you do want to close them off and they may also leak. Replace the washers in the hose ends every 2 years. The best hoses are the braided high-pressure hoses for trouble-free operation. Also, be sure and clean the screens every 6 months.

Belts

Should be checked regularly and replaced before they break. Be sure and change the settings on push button machines at least every 10 loads. Just press all the buttons in and out once.

The Tub

It should be cleaned once a year if you use the washer heavily. Fill the tub with hot water then prepare a solution of ½ cup of TSP, ½ cup of household bleach and 2 quarts of water. Pour the solution into the washer and run the washer through the rinse and wash cycles.

SOFT WATER VS HARD WATER

Soft Water
- Will save up to 50% of the cost of soap and detergents.
- Saves on energy.
- Reduces deposits on appliances and showerheads.
- Reduces cleaning times.
- Eliminates rings around the bath tub and toilet.
- Clothing will last longer.
- Saves money on the purchase of abrasives and cleaning supplies.
Hard Water
- Leaves mineral deposits everywhere that can only be cleaned off with an acid such as vinegar or phosphoric acid (4%) or most colas.

USE YOUR TOOTHBRUSH
If you really want a clean filter in your washing machine use an old toothbrush to remove any lint buildup. Then soak the filter in white vinegar for 12 hours before rinsing with warm water.

NATURAL SOFTENER
If you run out of softener sheets just use 1 cup of white vinegar during the rinse cycle.

BOIL THE SOCKS
If you're white socks are grimy and you can't get them clean, try boiling them in water with a slice of lemon.

SOLVING WASHING MACHINE PROBLEMS

TUB NOT FILLING WITH WATER
1. No power at wall outlet – replace fuse or check circuit breaker.
2. Water inlet hose kinked – reposition the hose or replace it.
3. Inlet valve screens clogged – clean valve or replace it.
4. Power cord is defective – test cord and replace.
5. Timer or selective switch faulty – replace if defective.

WATER WILL NOT SHUT OFF
1. The air hose on water level switch has fallen off – re-attach.
2. Inlet valve defective – replace any defective part.

WATER IS AT THE WRONG TEMPERATURE
1. Faucets are probably connected wrong – check hoses.
2. Inlet valve screen clogged or defective solenoid – clean screen or replace solenoid.

TUB FILLS NORMALLY BUT MOTOR WILL NOT START

1. Lid safety, switch out of adjustment or defective – adjust or replace.
2. Overload tripped or defective – reduce wash load in tub and wait 15 minutes for it to reset. If it doesn't reset it needs to be replaced.
3. If the motor hums, the motor is faulty – replace the motor or possibly the drain plug is jammed and needs to be un-jammed.

WASHING MACHINE IS AGITATING BUT WILL NOT SPIN
1. Machine is not balanced or is overloaded – re-distribute wash load, if this does not work reduce water in tub.
2. Lid safety, switch out of adjustment – adjust or replace.
3. Drive belt slipping or loose or broken – tighten or replace.
4. Timer may be defective and needs replacement.

MY MACHINE IS EATING MY CLOTHES
Possibly too much bleach is being used or the agitator van is broken. The basket surface may also be too rough.

I'M NOT GETTING AGITATED

If the motor is running and the agitator will not turn, the belt is probably broken and you will need to replace it. If you are able to do this yourself, the belt should be replaced every 2-3 years if the machine is used 2-3 times a week.

MY CLOTHES ARE SWIMMING
Usually if the water will not leave the washer, there is probably a small piece of clothing or a sock stuck in the pump or the hoses that are connected to the pump.

CHAPTER 17

SEWING ROOM

GENERAL INFORMATION:

The following is information regarding the needs to set up a sewing room in your home:

1. **The Hanging Area** – This will require about 70 inches off the floor to hang full-length garments.
2. **Mirrors** – You will need a full-length mirror to see a person's head as well as their feet. Preferably one mirror and two side mirrors at 45^0 angles.
3. **Fitting Room** – This may just be a fitting area that is elevated in front of the mirrors.
4. **Work Area** – There are three basic areas for cutting fabric, sewing, and pressing. You should be able to move freely between areas for the most efficiency.
5. **Electricity** – Try and use electrical outlets instead of extension cords. Power strips and surge protectors are recommended.
6. **Cutting Surface Size** – The table should be 30 inches wide and 60 inches long and should be easy to reach from all sides.
7. **Ventilation** – Remember dry cleaned fabrics and even new fabric may contain chemical residues, which release fumes when heated. Also dust and lint can become a problem. Be sure that you have a good ventilation system.
8. **Stools** – Be sure and purchase a stool that is adjustable.
9. **Machine Height** – The height of the machine should be 25-29 inches high. The depth of the sewing table should be about 20 inches high.
10. **Pressing Surface** – Use an adjustable ironing board. If the height is fixed that you will be ironing on make sure that it is a comfortable height that will not hurt your back.

SEWING MACHINE

MACHINE STOPPED WHILE SEWING
The machine may have been run at a low speed for a prolonged period of time. The machine has shut off to prevent the motor from overheating. Turn off the power and wait about 20 minutes and the machine should work fine.

NEEDLE NOT MOVING

The upper thread may have run out, the presser foot is in the up position, the bobbin winder shaft was left in the winding position or the buttonhole lever was not lowered when the machine was placed in the buttonhole mode.

MACHINE WILL NOT RUN
The presser foot may not be the right one and the needle is hitting the foot or the needle has come loose and is in the hook of machine.

UPPER THREAD KEEPS BREAKING
Any one of the following may be the problem:
- ❖ It may be threaded wrong
- ❖ The needle has been inserted incorrectly
- ❖ The thread has a bad knot in it
- ❖ The thread tension is too tight
- ❖ The needle may be bent or blunt
- ❖ The needle and thread may not match
- ❖ You are stitching too fast
- ❖ Thread take-up level has not been threaded

BOBBIN IS BREAKING TOO EASILY
Bobbin may not be fully inserted into bobbin case, or has been incorrectly threaded. The bobbin has not been wound evenly or there may be lint in the bobbin case.

MACHINE IS SKIPPING STITCHES
Any one of the following may be the problem:
- ❖ The thread tension may be too tight
- ❖ The needle is bent or blunt
- ❖ The needle is the wrong size
- ❖ The needle and thread do not match
- ❖ The thread take-up lever has not been threaded

- ❖ Light pressure on pressure foot
- ❖ The needle is set incorrectly

STITCHES NOT FORMING PROPERLY
The thread may not be pulled into the thread sensor guide or the bobbin case has been threaded wrong. The spool cap may also be the wrong size for thread spool.

MAKING IRREGULAR STITCHES
Any of the following may be the problem:
- ❖ The needle may be the wrong size
- ❖ The threading may have been done incorrectly
- ❖ Loose upper thread tension
- ❖ You are pulling the fabric
- ❖ Light pressure on pressure foot
- ❖ You may have a loose pressure foot
- ❖ Bobbin wound unevenly

MY FABRIC IS PUCKERING UP, SHOULD I KISS IT?
The stitch length may be too long for the fabric, or the fabric is too sheer or soft. The problem can also be caused by using two different kinds of thread or if the tension is incorrect.

THREAD IS BUNCHING UP
The upper and lower threads are not drawn back under the pressure foot, or the feed dog is down and needs to be raised.

NEEDLE KEEPS BREAKING
Any of the following may be the problem:
- ❖ Using a thin needle for sewing a heavy weight fabric
- ❖ The needle may not have been full inserted into the needle bar
- ❖ The needle clamp screw is loose
- ❖ Using the wrong pressure foot
- ❖ Pressure foot too loose
- ❖ You are pulling on the fabric as you sew

LOUD NOISE IS HEARD
Dust has probably accumulated in the feed dog.

KNOCKING NOISE & JAM
There is lint in hook or the thread is caught in the shuffle.

MACHINE NOT FEEDING ITSELF
Any of the following may be the problem:
- ❖ The stitch length may have been set to zero
- ❖ The presser foot pressure is probably too low
- ❖ The feed dogs are lowered
- ❖ The threads may be knotted under the fabric

TROUBLE THREADING THE NEEDLE
The needle is probably not in its highest position.
Turn the hand-wheel until needle reaches its highest position.

NEEDLE THREADER WILL NOT RETURN HOME
The needle threader has been designed not to turn in order to protect it if the needle is not up. The needle just needs to be properly inserted.

NEEDLE THREADER NOT RETURNED AND MACHINE STOPPED
The sewing machine may have been accidentally started while threading hook was still in the needle eye. Slightly turn the handle clockwise and remove the threader.

STATIC ELECTRICITY
If a pin or needle will not penetrate an article, try rubbing it in your hair before trying it again.

HOPE YOU DON'T HAVE A MAGNETIC PERSONALITY
Never place a magnet near a computerized sewing machine. Some machines may have a problem.

DENTAL FLOSS THAT MACHINE
Clean out the tension discs with dental floss. Just tie several knots in a length of dental floss and slowly run it through the discs.

CHAPTER 18

BEDROOM

BEDDING

FIBERS USED IN SHEETS

There are a number of different fibers used in the manufacture of sheets. The following are a few of the more popular ones:

> **Egyptian Cotton** – This is special cotton that has been grown in Egypt and feels softer than other cottons. It also will generate less lint and is stronger.
> **Pima Cotton** – This used to be called American-Egyptian and is high quality cotton developed from Egyptian cotton and is grown only in the southwestern United States. It is very strong and exceptionally soft and firm.
> **Modal** – This is a category of manufactured fibers that are known for their strength. The fabric does retain its shape very well.
> **Lyocell** – Manufactured fabric produced from trees. It is very strong and absorbent. It is soft and strong when wet and is similar to silk or suede. It has wrinkle-resistant qualities and can easily be draped.
> **Polyester** – The most common type is polyethylene terphalate (PET). This is a strong synthetic fiber that will resist shrinking, mildew, stretching, abrasion, and wrinkling. It will wash easily and dries very fast.

THE HIGHER, THE BETTER

Thread count is the number of horizontal and vertical threads in one square inch of fabric. The thread counts can range from 80-700. Most stores sell bedding from 180-320. The higher the thread count, the softer the fabric will feel. However the quality of the fabric is just as important as the thread count. Cotton sheets with a thread count of 180-200 are a good buy and will hold up well.

HOW SOFT I AM................

Down is the soft inner plumage of waterfowl such as ducks and geese. It contains many light, fluffy filaments that extend in all directions, without a feather's quill shaft. Has the ability to spring back to its original shape, which is known as lofting. One of the more important aspects of down over synthetics is that it has the ability to let moisture such as perspiration escape in a process known as wicking. It is also more comfortable in varying temperatures and climates than other materials.

I've got soft feathers.

DOOR

GETTING SPOOKY IN HERE

If the bedroom door won't stay shut when closed and opens when pushed even though it shuts tight, the frame may a little too wide for the door. You can fix the problem by unscrewing the strike plate and placing a thin piece of cardboard behind the plate, which will move it just enough to allow the door to remain solid and not open when pushed.

MATTRESSES

GENERAL INFORMATION:

Mattresses do need special care if you want to keep them in good condition. Try and give the mattresses an occasional airing out in front of an open window on their side without the bedding. The fresh air will pass through and ventilate the mattress, freshening them. You should also sprinkle some carpet deodorizer on the mattress and allow it to remain for 15 minutes before vacuuming it off.

MATTRESS REPLACEMENT

The average mattress, will last 8-10 years, however, this will depend on the quality of the mattress purchased and how much use it gets.

TURNING OVER

A new mattress should be turned every two weeks for the first four months and turned every two months after that. First turn the mattress head to foot then end over end. Do not use the handles to turn the mattress, they are only meant to be used for positioning the mattress.

BEST OF THE BEST

This is an individual choice and the person that is going to sleep on it should be the person choosing it. If you sleep with a person, both people should be comfortable.

NEW MATTRESS, NEW BOXSPRING

All mattress designers make their mattresses and box springs to fit each other and provide a certain level of support. It is not recommended to place a new mattress on an old box spring.

POPULAR SIZES

The most popular mattress is the queen-size. However there are many factors that should determine the size of the mattress such as medical problems, physical length, and weight.

FRAMING YOUR MATTRESS

The bed frame should allow the mattress to be able to breathe on all sides. Never place an all-natural mattress on a piece of wood. Slats or air holes are required.

A GOOD FOUNDATION IS A MUST

A standard foundation is a wooden boxed foundation that is covered with fabric. It has no springs and is the firmest and the most inexpensive (usually 7-inches thick). Commonly used with latex mattresses.

BOX SPRINGS

Box springs are more than 7-inches thick and are usually used with innerspring mattresses.

MY MATTRESS IS VENTILATED

You will normally only find ventilation holes on synthetic mattresses. All-natural mattresses will breathe all over and ventilation holes are not necessary.

DON'T DROP IT OFF A CLIFF
The best way to dispose of a mattress is to call the Salvation Army.

FIRMNESS IS IMPORTANT
The number of coils in an innerspring mattress determines the firmness. If the innerspring is firm it has 364, extra firm has 510 and super firm has 780. In a latex mattress it has an ILD rating. Medium is 25, firm is 31, and extra firm is rated at 35.

MATTRESS CARE

> ➤ You need to cover both the mattress and the box springs with fitted, padded dust covers. If possible use one that will not allow dust mites to penetrate. Best to use the type that is quilted on both sides.
> ➤ Occasionally air out the mattresses by removing all bedding and turning the mattress on its side, allowing the air to flow through. This type of ventilation will freshen-up the mattress.
> ➤ If the mattress has been soiled it is best to use a special fabric cleaner, which can be purchased at most of the better mattress stores.
> ➤ Powder the mattress with a thin layer of baking soda and allow it to remain for 15 minutes before vacuuming it off.

PILLOWS

WOOL-FILLED PILLOWS
Wool pillows are excellent. They maintain their springy resilience and will absorb moisture from the head.

KAPOK BODY PILLOWS
You will get a molded form pillow for good support. Kapok is a natural seed fiber from the rainforest.

BUCKWHEAT, NOT THE OLD KID STAR
They can help to alleviate a stiff neck by providing proper support of your neck and head. The pillow will mold and conform to your head and neck. It also allows air to circulate better.

CAN YOU WASH A DOWN PILLOW?
It is best not to do this at home. Take the pillow to a laundry and use a front load commercial washing machine with regular detergent (never use a machine with an agitator). If the pillow is very old it may not be safe to wash it.

It will take about 3 hours to dry two pillows in a commercial dryer on medium heat. Never place more than two pillows in a commercial dryer to avoid a fire.

CHAPTER 19

WORKBENCH

ADHESIVES

GENERAL INFORMATION:

Don't get stuck-up.

If you want the best joint possible it should be affixed with a combination adhesive and screws, nails, or other type of fastener.

Carpenter's Wood Glue

This is white, creamy glue sold in plastic bottles that is used to adhere furniture, craft, and woodworking projects. It will set up in about one hour and dries clear without staining. However, it is vulnerable to moisture. If you stain wood make sure that carpenter's glue is not present or it will leave a light-colored streak.

Cyanoacrylate (instant glue)

Does not have good flexibility but has excellent strength and will dry in a few seconds. Its resistance to heat and moisture is excellent but can bond to your skin instantly and is toxic and flammable. You can clean it up with acetone and it is best used on smooth surfaces such as glass, ceramics, plastics, and metal.

Epoxy

The only adhesive that has strength stronger than the material it bonds. It will resist almost anything from moisture to solvents. Best used in warm temperatures and make sure that you read the manufacturer's instructions before using. Mixing must be exact if you want the desired results.

Hot Glue Gun

The strength of the bond will depend on the surface it is used on. It dries in about one minute and has a fair resistance to heat and moisture. Use with caution since it will give a bad burn.

Heat will loosen the bond and it is best used on smooth and porous surfaces such as metal, masonry, glass, or fiberglass.

Latex Acrylic Panel Adhesive

The strength is very good with a drying time of about 24 hours. The resistance to heat and moisture is very good. It may irritate the skin and eyes and will clean up with soap and water as long as it is still wet. Best used on porous surfaces such as framing lumber, plywood paneling, wallboard, foam panels, and masonry.

Resorcinol & Formaldehyde

Normally mixed just prior to use, however they can still be used up to four hours afterwards. It must be used at temperatures over 70^{0}F. It is used to bond veneers or to bond plastic laminates to wood for tabletops and counters. Both surfaces should be coated thinly and allowed to dry a little before bonding them. Use in a well-ventilated area.

Silicone Sealant

Has a very flexible bond and good strength with a drying time of about 24 hours. Its resistance to heat and moisture is very good. It will irritate the skin and eyes and will clean up with acetone. It is best used on smooth and porous surfaces such as wood, porcelain, fiberglass, plastics, and glass.

Superglue

These are great for a quick tight bond but they should not be used on clear glass since ultraviolet light will break down the bonding agent. If the material is porous or has a vertical surface, use gel superglue.

Water-based Contact Cement

It has good strength and will bond instantly, drying in about 30 minutes. Its resistance to heat and moisture is very good but it will irritate the eyes and skin. You can clean it up with soap and water as long as it is still wet. It is used on porous surfaces such as plastic laminates, plywood, flooring, and cloth.

White Glue

Will provide you with a moderate to rigid bond but has poor resistance to heat. It cleans up with soap and water and can be used on porous surfaces such as wood (indoors), paper, and cloth.

ADHESIVE TIPS

HOLD ON TIGHT!

Too much adhesive may weaken the bond. The only exception to this rule is when you use epoxy. Make sure that you rough up the surface to be bonded before applying any adhesive. Use a thin coat in most instances and clamp securely. Be sure and remove any excess after clamping.

PUTT, PUTT

Carpenter's putty is an essential to have around if you're doing any wood repairs. It comes in different colors making it easier to patch different woods.

CLAMPS

FAVORITE HELPERS

C-Clamps

These are "C" shaped with an adjustable screw on one end and are great for holding objects on a work surface. They come in many different sizes and are inexpensive.

Spring Clamps

These have plastic tips and will protect the material. They are very strong and can be used in many different ways to secure objects.

Miter Clamps

These are mainly used to hold 45^0 angles together that need to be glued or nailed. They are commonly used to hold picture frames together.

CLEAR FINISHES

HOW TO PICK A CLEAR FINISH?

Natural Resin varnishes

These varnishes are very effective in resisting scratches and scuffmarks. Spar varnish can be used outdoors. To apply use a varnish brush or cheesecloth pad. The varnish will dry in about 24 hours unless the weather is humid then allow about 36 hours.

Resin Oil

This finish will soak into the grain as well as hardening it and will resist scratches. It is usually applied by hand, rubbing in 2-3 coats and needs about 10 hours to dry.

Polyurethane Varnish
Good varnish that will be mar-resistant, durable and will remain clear. Best to use a natural bristle brush, roller, or it can be sprayed on. Allow it to dry for 1-2 hours and leave about 12 hours between coats for the best results.

Two-Part Epoxy Varnish
Has very high resistance to scuff marks and mars and is excellent for flooring. It is best applied with a brush with the first coat drying in about 3 hours and the second coat in about 6-7 hours.

Shellac
Will be easily damaged by water and be put on either clear or pigmented. Best to use small brush that has a chiseled tip. Always thin with alcohol or other recommended solvent. It will dry in about 2-3 hours.

Lacquer
This varnish is fast drying and is excellent for furniture. It is best sprayed on in numerous thin coats and be sure and allow the last coat to dry for at least 50-60 hours. After it has dried, rub the finish with a fine steel wool or use a hard wax.

FASTENERS & CONNECTORS

GENERAL INFORMATION:
Fasteners and connectors are now being made for almost any job. They can be used to secure wood-to-wood, concrete to any surface, and brick. Most are approved by the Uniform Building Code requirements. Fasteners can save you money on labor, materials, and time when used properly.

TYPES OF FASTENERS & CONNECTORS:

- **Drywall Clips** – Used for wallboard or paneling.
- **Masonry Connectors** – Used as foundation anchors, brick wall ties, or floor jacks.
- **Nail Plates & Plate Straps** – These are used as mending plates or for light-duty wood-to-wood splices and fence brackets. They help to simplify fence construction and will then allow for easy disassembly if necessary.
- **Post Anchors** – Supports a post from the ground up and eliminates deep post-holes. Prevents wood rot and termite damage.
- **Safety Plates** – Used to prevent accidental nailing into utility wires or pipes when they pass through the framing.
- **Sawhorse Brackets** – These will make a 2 X 4 or 2 X 6 into a supportive frame in just one easy step.

- **Stud Shoe** – Reinforces a joist stud or rafter after it has been drilled or notched during construction.

BASIC ANCHOR TIPS

The following are a few of the more common anchors that you should have available in your toolbox:

> Use the right anchor.

- ✓ **Plastic Anchor** – These are good for lightweight jobs, such as picture hanging or curtain rods. You will need to drill a hole for these, called a pilot hole.
- ✓ **Molly Bolt** – This is an anchor/screw combination and must match the thickness of the wall. Best for medium or heavy jobs, especially heavy mirrors or large pictures. Best to drill a pilot hole for the best results.
- ✓ **Toggle Bolt** – These are usually used for very heavy jobs, such as hanging shelves or hanging a bicycle from the ceiling. The object must be attached to the toggle bolt before you attach it to the wall or ceiling. Best to drill a pilot hole.

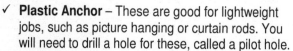

HAND TOOLS

GENERAL INFORMATION:

When it comes to hand tools, the average person who is not in a construction trade or has a background in repairs will have a problem choosing the right hand tool for the job. Since it would take a whole book to provide in-depth information we will only be able to assist you in choosing the right tool for the job.

THE BEST TOOLS FOR THE JOB

CHISELING

- **Socket Chisels** – Should always be used with a mallet, never a hammer. Always used to cut wood.
- **Tang Chisels** – Made for working with the weight of the hand only.

BE A GOOD CHISLER

Always start your blade digging into the wood just slightly inside your guideline mark and never cut too deep. Chisels are best used to chip and shave away using the beveled edge going into the work so that it constantly directs the chisel out of the wood giving you better control. Always keep the cutting edge directed away from your body and hands.

CUTTING

- **Backsaw** – Used with a miter box to cut a straight line across a piece of wood. Has a steel backing, which is used to keep it aligned.
- **Combination Saw** – Cuts both across and with the grain.
- **Coping Saw** – Follows an irregular, delicate, or intricate cut in wood. Has a thin, fine toothed, removable blade.
- **Crosscut Saw** – Used to make cuts across the grain with small offset teeth.
- **Hacksaw** – Used primarily to cut metals, plastic, and electrical conduit.

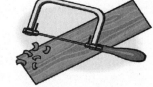

HERE A TOOTH, THERE A TOOTH

If you are cutting thin metal with a hacksaw or saber saw, be sure and choose a metal-cutting blade that has at least 3 teeth contacting the edge of the piece you are working on. If the blade has too few teeth it will catch the edge and dull the blade or even damage the piece you are working on.

- **Keyhole Saw** – Narrow tip blade saw used for cutting openings in drywall or paneling. Also, used for curved cuts.
- **Rip Saw** – Used to cut with the grain with large teeth.

I'LL GET HURT IN A TOOLBOX

Never store saws in a toolbox. The teeth will easily be damaged unless you use a plastic tooth guard.

EASY DOES IT

If you put a small amount of kerosene on the saw blade it will act as a lubricant and will make your work easier.

CIRCULAR SAW TIP When you are going to do a job using a circular saw, be sure you use the proper blade for the job. You need different blades for hardwood and softwood. You also need to know if you will be cutting across the grain or with the grain as this involves either ripping or crosscutting. When you purchase the blade for the job, be sure and tell the clerk what kind of job you plan to do.

PROTECT ME, PLEASE!

Saw blades need to be protected by coating them with paste wax or a light grade of machine oil.

WHOOOOA

Be sure and buy a model with a safety brake that will stop the blade from spinning when the trigger is released.

FILES & RASPS

Files are normally used for shaping and can be found in many shapes. They can be round, half-round, flat, square and triangular. Single-cut files have teeth that run in one direction and double-cut files have teeth that run in opposing directions. Double-cut will cut more quickly but will be courser.

PESKY WOOD SHAVINGS
Cleaning out wood shavings from files and rasps can be a real pain. However, just use a piece of masking tape and cover the length of the tool then press it firmly and pull off all the shavings.

- Use files with an attachable handle.
- Be sure and secure your work with a clamp or vise and at elbow height for general filing. Lower for heavier filing jobs.
- Always keep files very clean using a file brush after every use.
- Files should be stored in a rack or protective sheaths to keep them from becoming dull.

Rasps are different files in that they have teeth that are formed individually and not connected to one another. Files will cut smoother than rasps but when working with wood the file will work much slower and tend to clog frequently.

Great idea!

HAMMER

TENNIS ANYONE!
Woodwork is easily damaged when using a metal hammer to tap wood joints. To avoid doing damage, just cut open tennis ball with an "X" slit enough to get it over the striking face of the hammer.

PRACTICE YOUR AIM
You should be using a 12oz or 16oz hammer for the best results. Grasp the hammer with one hand toward the end of the handle and swing from the elbow. Make sure that you hit the nail head on or the nail will bend.

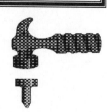

THE RIGHT DIRECTION

If you want to keep a wood hammer handle from breaking when removing a stubborn nail, just lever the handle to the right or left side of the nail instead of straight back.

NAILING WITHOUT SPLITTING WOOD

There are a few secrets when you are going to nail into a piece of wood and are concerned that the wood may split. Try drilling hole smaller than the nail for the nail to follow easily or rub a small amount of soap or wax on the nail before you try hammering it in.

POWER PLUS

To remove stubborn nails just place a small block of wood under the hammerhead to get added leverage. Make sure that the block is big enough to distribute the pressure from the hammerhead.

CHECK OUT THE GRAIN

When purchasing a hammer, check out the grain on the bottom of the handle. The grain should be running in the same direction as the head, if it is running perpendicular to the head it is not as strong and is more likely to break or come loose.

PLANES

These are used for removing thin layers of wood, trimming, and smoothing straight edges. They can also be used to add a groove.

- **Block Plane** – Usually about 6" long and used for small jobs that require smoothing and fitting.
- **Grooving Plane** – Capable of cutting a long slot.
- **Jack Plane** – This plane is usually around 15" long and used to smooth rough surfaces with a 2" blade.
- **Rabbit Plane** – Capable of cutting recessed grooves along and edge.
- **Scrub Plane** – This will provide a hand-hewn effect and will work faster for rough cuts.
- **Smooth Plane** – Smaller plane usually around 8" long with a 13/4 blade. Used to smooth small rough surfaces.
- **Trimming Plane** – This type of plane is used for more delicate work and is usually 3½" in length and only has a single blade.

PLIERS

There are several types of pliers and they all have a specific job:

- **Fence Pliers** – Designed to pull and cut out staples from fences as well as having a hammer head.
- **Locking Pliers** – Adjustable, vise-locking pliers that allow you to have both hands free.
- **Long-Nose Pliers** – Have a pointed nose that is used for reaching hard to get at spots.
- **Slip-Joint Pliers** – These are usually a tongue and groove design. These pliers give you the convenience of an adjustable joint, which can be opened to the specific size needed.
- **Solid-Joint Pliers** – This type is not adjustable and has a rivet or pin attached to the joint.
- **Standard Slip-Joint Pliers** – For general use around the home and has adjustable jaw and can cut wire.

SAVE THAT OLD INNER TUBE
Best to save any old inner tube, leather belt, or gloves to use as a liner for your pliers when you need to protect the finish of a surface from the pliers' teeth.

SCREWDRIVERS

There are many types of screwdrivers for every type of job. The quality of the screwdriver is very important. The following will provide information on the good quality and the poor quality screwdriver.

Good Quality
- Look for quality metal, a good finish, and the amount of grinding on the tip.
- Make sure that the handle is of good quality and the bar attachment goes all the way through.

Poor Quality
- If the end starts chipping away.
- The tip is not flared which will make it fall out of the slot easier.
- Blade not being attached properly to the handle and work its way out easily.

MAKE SURE IT FITS
When you shop for a screwdriver hold it in your hand and make sure that it fits and is comfortable. A secure grip is very important.

WRENCH

You should have two sizes of adjustable wrenches in your toolbox. Purchase a small and a medium one so that you will have one for every size nut and bolt.

LADDERS

BY THE NUMBERS

Most ladders have a Roman numeral on one of the side rails indicating the strength of the ladder, which is the weight that each rung can bear safely. Type III household-grade ladders are rated at 200 pounds, type II are commercial-grade and rated at 225 pounds, and type I is industrial-grade and rated at 250 pounds. The best type that is recommended for home use is a type II.

MEASURING

CAN'T FIND THE YARDSTICK?

If you always have trouble finding the yardstick just keep a yard long piece of string in your pocket. A dollar bill is about 6-inches long.

POWER CORDS

Bent Prongs

They can usually be straightened but you should replace the plug if the prongs are loose.

Cracked Plug Housing

Replace. Do not patch or tape.

Discolored or Pitted Prongs

Possibly could be a short circuit so check the wiring housing or appliance and replace plug if there are no other signs of a problem.

Exposed Wire at Plug

Just rewire the plug.

Frayed Cable

Cut the cable above the fray and then replace the plug.

Nicked Cable

Be sure and bend the cable and look for cracks or cuts and replace if they are found.

No Ground Prong

If the ground prong is broken off or missing, the plug needs to be replaced.

Worn Out Insulation

The wires will eventually become exposed. Cut away the worn out cable and replace the plug. If you need a certain length you may need a new cable.

POWER TOOLS

CUTTING & DRILLING

Always choose the proper saw blade for the type of material you are going to cut. Also be sure to support the board properly using sawhorses to support the board from both ends allowing room for the saw.

- **Band Saw** – Useful when more creative cuts are needed such as curves and precision cuts.
- **Circular Saw** – One of the most common saws, consisting of a replaceable blade and a blade guard which is spring loaded to move out of the way when you are sawing. Always set the cutting depth 1/8th"more than the thickness of the board. You can avoid binding if you keep the sole plate flat on the surface of the wood.
- **Jig Saw** – Used to make curving lines or very detailed cuts. If you want to start a cut from the inside of a piece of wood, drill a hole and insert the saw blade.
- **Radial Arm Saw** – Same as a table saw but capable of being used on heavier stock.
- **Reciprocating Saw** – Use to cut openings in existing walls. Can rough cut green wood, metal, linoleum, and plastic.
- **Table Saw** – Capable of crosscut rip, miter, groove and bevel. Can make moldings and sand stock.

CUTTING & DRILLING TIPS:

✓ If you are going to rip cut, use a rip guide or tack down a straightedge and use it as a cutting guide.
✓ If you are going to drill into metal, be sure and squirt a small amount of lightweight oil on the drill bit and even into the hole to tool the bit.
✓ Try pre-drilling a "pilot hole" with a smaller drill bit when nailing into hardwood as well as screwing into all other types of wood, especially if you are working with wood that will split easily.
✓ Be sure and unplug power tools when making adjustments or changing accessories.
✓ If you keep your tool adjustment keys taped to the cord near the plug end, it will remind you to unplug the tool.
✓ Always be sure that your tools are properly grounded.

268

NO MORE DRILL CORDS

If you purchase the right drill you can get plenty of power to do almost any job. Be sure and purchase one that is either an **18-volt or 24-volt model**.

These models will feature a torque control and eliminate the stripping of screws.

HEADS-UP

If you are going to drill above your head, be sure and place a Styrofoam cup on the drill bit (cut it if necessary, depending on the length of the bit). The debris will then fall into the cup instead of your eyes, hair or clothing.

WOODWORKING WIZARD

An **orbital sander** is an indispensable tool. The sanding pad rotates in small circles at thousands of revolutions every minute. It is more of a finishing tool. You can also use it to sand rough paint on exterior siding.

PNEUMATIC TOOLS

These tools contain air and are attached to an air compressor that runs them. This term covers a variety of tools that are available and are easy to use. There are, however, a number of common mistakes people make and tricks they should know, such as:

➤ A major problem is not reading the instructions that accompany a pneumatic tool.
➤ Not using the right length or gauge of extension cord. The longer the extension cord, the less power and lower efficiency of the tool.
➤ Always use an extension air hose rather than a cord for long distances.
➤ Use the correct pressure for the job.
➤ The oil must be changed every 250 hours.
➤ Be sure and locate the air compressor on a dry, clean, level area.
➤ Always keep the compressor properly lubricated.
➤ Always wear eye protection.
➤ Make sure that the pressure has been completely relived before changing tools.
➤ Never point the blowgun toward your eyes.
➤ Test safety relief valve regularly.
➤ Open the tank valve after every use.
➤ Make sure that there is a belt guard in place.

ATTACHMENTS INCLUDE:

Blow Gun	Nail Gun	Sandblaster
Air Stapler	Air Sander	Spray Gun
Caulking Gun	Air Ratchet Wrench	Air Hammer
Air Drill	Impact Wrench	

TOOL BELT

WORK LIKE A PRO

Buy a good quality tool belt since you will have it for many years and you will find that you cannot do without it. It will free up your hands and keep the tools you need for a specific job organized. It is actually safer to use one than not to use one since people may fall over one of your tools.

TOOLBOX

GENERAL INFORMATION:

Carrying heavy tools around can be very difficult, especially at older ages. You need to choose a box that will organize your tools and only carry what you really need. Really big tools should be carried separately and not be in too big a toolbox, making it heavy.

THE PROFESSIONAL MUDDLE

Professional workers normally purchase heavy metal boxes since they tend to throw them into the back of pickups and need something durable and strong. Try using a lightweight plastic box, which is perfect for the home handyman. Find a box with a removable tray and one that has compartments like sliding drawers so that you can store small items. Keep your larger tools in the bottom.

FISHING FOR A BOX

An old fishing tackle box makes and excellent toolbox for the beginner. Most have locking lids on small plastic boxes making it easy to find what you are looking for without tearing the whole box apart. Even the new ones are inexpensive and great organizers.

WOOD

COMMON GRADES OF WOOD

Clear - This grade of wood is an excellent grade and has no knots.

Select/Select Structural – Very high quality wood and will be broken down into Numbers 1-3 or grades A-D. The lower grades will have more knots.

Number 2 Common – Has tight knots but no major blemishes and is good for shelving.

Number 3 Common – It may have some loose knots and may be blemished or have some damage.

Construction or Standard – This is the type of wood used for general framing. Has good strength.

Utility – An economy grade that is usually used for rough framing.

HOW TO SELECT SOFT WOOD & HARDWOOD

Selecting Softwood

Cedar or Cypress

Wood is similar to redwood but only the darker color wood is rot resistant. Weak and brittle but will resist warping and has a pleasant smell. It is commonly used for siding, paneling, rough trim, roof shingles, and decks.

Fir

A very heavy, strong wood that will hold nails well. Has good resistance to warping and shrinkage, but it is somewhat difficult to cut. Used for framing studs, posts, and beams as well as flooring and sub-flooring.

Pine

From eastern, northern and western trees! Has a very light, soft, feel but has weak resistance to warping and has a tendency to shrink. Very easy to cut! Used for paneling, trim molding, flooring, and cabinets.

Redwood

Very durable and is resistant to rot and insects if you get the darker-colored heartwood variety. Light, soft, and not as strong as fir or Southern pine, however, it does have the tendency to split and is easy to cut. Used for exterior posts, beams, fencing, decks, siding, and paneling.

Southern Pine

Very hard wood, stiff, and has excellent strength. Tends to hold nails well but has a tendency to crack, splinter, warp, and cuts with ease. Used mainly for flooring and sub-flooring.

Spruce

Lightweight and soft, but is fairly strong, resistant to splitting and warping. Very easy to work with! Used mainly for framing, flooring, sub-flooring and trim (molding).

Treated Lumber

Several types can be treated especially fir and Southern pine. The green and brown color will fade in time making the wood a grayish color. Very resistant to rot and insects! Used commonly for bottom framing plates that rest on concrete. Also used on other framing that will come into contact with water, decks, and some types of fencing.

SAVING DOUGH

Softwood comes from trees that grow faster and will be less expensive. If you are not using the wood for major structural components such as floor and ceiling joists, you might want to save the money and purchase the softwoods. You may only find a few varieties of softwood at most retailers.

Selecting Hardwood

Birch

Very hard and strong-grained: resistant to shrinking and warping. The color is similar to maple and is sometimes used as a cheap replacement. It is hard to cut but takes a great finish. Used for painted cabinets, paneling, and furniture.

Mahogany

Durable hardwood that is fine-grained and resistant to shrinkage, warping, and swelling. It finishes well and is easy to cut. Do not get quality mahogany confused with the cheaper grade called "lauan mahogany." Used for fine furniture, cabinets, and veneers.

Maple

One of the hardest woods: pieces with wavy grain or with bird's eye are the best. The colors will range from reddish to brownish-white. The wood will finish well but is difficult to cut. Used for flooring, especially bowling alleys and basketball courts, butcher-block counters, and molding.

**Poplar Black
(Populus Nigra)**

Poplar

One of the softer hardwoods: has a fine grain with colors from white to yellowish-brown. It is easy to cut and easy to paint. Used for painted furniture, cabinet, trim, and used to replace more expensive hardwoods.

Red Oak

Hard, strong wood with a very pronounced straight grain! It resists warping but has the tendency to shrink if not dried well. The color is reddish, cuts easily and finishes well. It is used for flooring, cabinets, furniture, molding, and stair rails.

Walnut

One of the better hardwoods! It is heavy, strong and has a straight grain. It resists shrinking, warping and is found in light to dark brown colors. Finishes well and cut fairly easily. Used for fine furniture, cabinets, paneling, inlays and veneers.

White Oak

Opened grain, hard and a strong wood but the grain is not as pronounced as red oak. It resists shrinking and warping and has a pretty golden color. Finishes well but is somewhat hard to cut. It is preferred over red oak for flooring because it has less variation in color. Also used for molding, furniture, cabinets, and stair railing.

BUY THE BEST

Try to purchase "real" hardwood products if you are after the best quality. Many wood products that advertise some of the hardwoods are only using the hardwood veneers. Hardwood flooring especially is the best flooring you can put in your home. Select hardwoods that only have minor defects on one side only or no defects at all.

CHAPTER 20

USES FOR VINEGAR

CLEANING USES

Remove Water Rings
Mix vinegar and olive oil in a one-to-one ratio and apply with a soft cloth using slight pressure in a circular motion.

Polish Leather Furniture
Boil 2 cups of linseed oil for 1-minute then allow it to cool before stirring in 1 cup of white vinegar. Apply with a soft cloth then allow it to stand for 1-2 minutes and then rub off gently.

Remove Carpet Stains
Only works well if the stain is fresh. Combine 1 part of white vinegar to 3 parts of water and allow it to remain on the stain for 3-4 minutes. Using a sponge, rub the area gently from the center out then dry with a clean soft cloth. Try an area that is out of the way to be sure that the carpet is colorfast.

SPECIAL GUIDELINES FOR CARPET STAIN REMOVAL
✓ Always use a spot remover in an inconspicuous location first.
✓ Scrape away any residues with a blunt knife before starting.
✓ Never use a hard-bristle brush on a stain, soft only.
✓ Blot up any liquid until the paper towel used is dry.
✓ Vacuum after all liquid is gone to remove any residues.
✓ Try cleaning the area with clear water before using a spot remover.
✓ Never over-wet the area.
✓ If you get fresh mud on the carpet, allow it to dry before vacuuming it off.
✓ Club soda works great on fresh stains. The active ingredient is carbonic acid that produces the carbonation. Sop up any liquid first!

Chewing Gum Remover
White vinegar is capable of dissolving and softening chewing gum from a number of fabrics and carpeting.

Decal Remover
Apply warm vinegar on a sponge and allow it to stand for a few minutes then wipe with a soft dry cloth.

Mildew Remover
For severe buildup of mildew, use white vinegar full strength. For all other mildew buildup, use a solution of vinegar and water.

Plastic Upholstery Cleaner
Combine vinegar and water one to one and wipe the furniture with a dampened soft cloth. Follow with a dry cloth to buff.

Metal Cleaner
Use a small amount of vinegar, baking soda, or salt to prepare a paste and use the paste to clean bronze, copper, or brass pots or utensils.

KEEP BRASS SHINNING
After you polish your brass, try coating it with a small amount of wood finishing oil like tung oil. The shine will last at least 3 times longer. To clean the oil off the brass just use a small amount of paint thinner.

Clean Aluminum Pot Stains
Black stains on aluminum pots can be removed by boiling white vinegar in the pot up to the area of the stain. For large pots boil the vinegar in a small pot and pour it on the stain.

Wash Windows
Mix one-part water to three-parts of white vinegar. Use a coffee filter or piece of newspaper to clean the window.

Grease Cutter
Place a capful of vinegar in the dishwasher to cut grease.

Crystal Clear Glassware
If you want your crystal to sparkle, just rinse them in a solution of: one part white vinegar to three parts warm water.

Remove Lime Residue
Coffee pots, tea kettles, and irons are notorious for hard water residue buildup. When they get really bad, fill them with white vinegar and run them through a cycle.

Drain Cleaner I
Boil 2 cups of vinegar and pour it down the drain a small amount at a time. Allow the vinegar to remain in the drain for about 5-10 minutes before pouring a pot of very hot water down the drain. The alternative is to use ½ cup of baking soda poured into the drain followed by ½ cup of warm vinegar, cover the drain and allow it to stand for 5-10 minutes before running cold water down the drain.

Drain Cleaner II
Drop 3-4 Alka-Seltzer® tablets down the drain, the pour a bottle of white vinegar down. After 3-5 minutes run hot water down.

Clean Shower Head
Remove the head and place it in a container that will allow you to cover the head with vinegar. Allow soaking overnight, rinse and replace.

Weed Killer
Pour white vinegar on weeds in sidewalk or driveway cracks and they will be killed.

Pet, Flea Killer
Add 1 teaspoon of cider vinegar to every quart of water. Fleas will not go near your pet.

Cement Remover
When you are working with concrete or cement try cleaning your hands with vinegar, works great.

Ant Remover
If you are having a problem with ants just wipe your counters off with a solution prepared from equal parts of vinegar and water. Crawling insects hate vinegar.

Remove Scorch Marks
If you rub a scorched mark with a clean soft cloth that has been lightly dampened with vinegar it may remove a scorch mark if it not too badly imbedded.

Brighten Clothes
If you add 1½ cups of white vinegar to your rinse water it will brighten up the colors. If you are dying a fabric add 1 cup of vinegar to the final rinse to set the color.

Remove Crayon Stains
Moisten a toothbrush with white vinegar and rub the area lightly until the crayon is removed.

Eliminate Deodorant Stains
Perspiration stains can be removed by rubbing the area with vinegar before laundering.

Ink Stain Remover
Vinegar will remove most ink stains if they are fresh.

Rust Remover
To remove rust just moisten the fabric with white vinegar then rub the area lightly with salt. Place the garment in the sun to dry then launder.

MEDICINAL USES FOR VINEGAR

Dandruff
Massage white vinegar into the scalp 3-4 times per week then shampoo.

Nail Polish Saver
To make nail polish last longer, just soak the fingernails in a solution of 2 teaspoons of white vinegar and ½ cup of warm water for 1-2 minutes before applying the polish.

Sunburn Reliever
Place a piece of cloth that has been lightly dampened with apple cider vinegar on the burn. Replace every 20-30 minutes.

Athletes Foot
Rinse your feet 3-4 times per day in apple cider vinegar.

Morning Sickness
When morning sickness occurs just combine 1 teaspoon of apple cider vinegar in a glass of water and drink it.

Indigestion
To relieve indigestion place 2 teaspoons of apple cider vinegar into a glass of water and drink during a meal.

A BUNION SANDWICH

In a small bowl soak 2 slices of white bread and 2 slices of red onion in 1 cup of vinegar for 24 hours. Place the bread on the corn (bunion) and place a slice of onion on top. Wrap with a bandage and allow it to remain overnight.

AROUND THE KITCHEN WITH VINEGAR

Storing Pimientos

If you want to store pimiento peppers after opening a can or jar place them into a very small bowl, cover them with vinegar and refrigerate. They will last for 2-3 weeks.

Keeping Ginger Fresh

Prepare a clean jar filled with balsamic vinegar and add the grated ginger, seal tight, and refrigerate.

Flavor Enhancer

When preparing soup or tomato sauce, add one or two tablespoons of vinegar to the soup or sauce during the last 5 minutes of cooking time. This will really enhance their flavor.

Over-Salted Foods

Add 1 teaspoon of vinegar and 1 teaspoon of sugar then reheat the dish or sauce.

Mold Eliminator

Always remember to wipe down the outside of canning jars with vinegar to eliminate the possibility of mold growing.

Vegetable and Fruit Wash

Mix 2½ tablespoons of vinegar in 1 gallon of water and use the mixture to wash the outsides of fruits and vegetables before peeling or slicing into them.

Stops Food Discoloring

If you add 1-2 teaspoons of vinegar to the water you are boiling potatoes in, they will not discolor for a longer period.

Great Mashed Potato Trick

Once you have mashed the potatoes and added the hot milk try adding a teaspoon of vinegar and beat a little bit more. It will fluff them up and they will hold their shape.

Firm Gelatin

In warmer weather gelatin tends to lose its shape. Just add 1 teaspoon of vinegar to the gelatin to keep it firm.

BETTER WEAR DARK SHADES

If you would like the crust on your fresh baked bread to have a great sheen just brush the top of the bread with vinegar about 5 minutes before the bread has finished baking. Remove the bread before brushing on the vinegar, as the oven can get very cramped.

ALL CRACKED UP OVER EGGS

To keep the whites where they belong when an egg cracks during boiling just add some vinegar to the boiling water.

VINEGAR, RISING TO THE OCCASION

Next time you steam vegetables, try adding 2 teaspoons of vinegar to the boiling water. It will prevent unwanted odors and stabilize the color of the vegetables.

WELL PICKLE MY EGGS

Pickled eggs are found in every English pub and will be sitting in a big jar of malt vinegar and spices.

FISH MASSAGE

Before you try and scale a fish, give the fish a vinegar massage and the scales will come off easier as well as keeping your hands from smelling fishy.

I'm ready for my massage.

CHAPTER 21

USES FOR BAKING SODA

WHAT IS BAKING SODA?

Baking soda is actually bicarbonate of soda, which is derived from the manufacture of common washing soda also known as "sal soda." Baking soda is composed of carbon and oxygen molecules, which combine to form carbon dioxide gas. If batter has a sufficient acidic nature then only baking soda is needed to produce carbon dioxide. If the batter does not have sufficient acid then baking powder, which carries both acid and alkali, is needed. All baking soda in North America is mined from the mineral Trona, which is found in Green River, Wyoming.

The large deposit was discovered in the 1930's. Trona is actually composed of sodium bicarbonate and sodium carbonate, a very close relative. The ore is mined from deep mines, crushed, rinsed, and heated to produce sodium carbonate. The sodium carbonate is then dissolved in water and carbon dioxide is forced through the solution releasing the sodium bicarbonate crystals, which is washed, then dried, and packaged as baking soda.

When baking soda is added to a recipe it has an immediate rising action with the release of the gas, which means that your oven must be preheated and your pans greased before you even combine the ingredients. Baking soda should be added to dry ingredients first and the wet ingredients just before placing the food into the oven. Baking soda will last for approximately 6 months if stored in an airtight container and in a cool, dry location.

If you are not sure of the activity level of baking soda, try placing ¼ teaspoon in about 2 teaspoons of white vinegar, if carbon dioxide bubbles appear it is still active. Sodium bicarbonate is produced in the human body to assist in maintaining the acidity (pH) level of the blood as well as being found in saliva.

It will neutralize plaque acids, which might otherwise dissolve our teeth. Another action in the body is to neutralize stomach acid so that we don't get ulcers, as well as assisting in the breathing process by transporting carbon dioxide from the tissues to the lungs for disposal.

IN THE KITCHEN

FLUFFY OMELET
If you want the fluffiest omelet ever just add ½ teaspoon baking soda for every 3 eggs.

NICE SMELLING FISH
If you soak raw fish for about ½ hour in 2 tablespoons of baking soda in 1-quart of water you will not have a fishy taste. Make sure that you rinse well and pat dry before cooking.

MASHED POTATO MAGIC
To really fluff up those mashed potatoes the way grandma did, just add a pinch of baking soda to them while you are mashing.

HOW CLEAN I AM
Add a small amount of baking soda to the water that you clean the insides and outsides of chicken in. Rinse with clean cold water and there will be no residue to worry about.

POTATO PANCAKE INDIGESTION CURE
Be sure and add 1 teaspoon of baking soda to the batter next time you make potato pancakes. Some people cannot tolerate the pancakes and tend to get indigestion.

VEGGIE CLEANER
You can clean dirt and other residues off fruit and vegetables by sprinkling baking soda on a wet sponge and scrubbing them then rinse well with water.

LOWER COFFEE ACID CONTENT
If you wish to reduce the acid level in coffee just add a pinch of baking soda to a cup of regular coffee. The taste will not be affected.

HOW CLEAR I AM
If you add just a pinch of baking soda to a pot of steeping tea, the tea will not be cloudy. This will work for iced tea as well.

MAKE DISHWASHER DETERGENT

You can make your own dishwashing detergent by mixing 2 tablespoons of baking soda with 2 tablespoons of borax.

CLEANING AWAY MINERAL DEPOSITS

To get rid of mineral deposits from tea pots and coffee pots, just bring a solution of 1 cup of vinegar and 4 tablespoons of baking soda to a boil in them and allow it to simmer for a few minutes.

AVOID A SMELLY BOTTOM

If you sprinkle the bottom tray of your toaster with a teaspoon of baking soda it will eliminate any burnt smell from drippings and crumbs.

BARBECUE GRILL CLEANER

You can easily de-grease the grill on the barbecue by applying a paste of baking soda and water with a wire brush. Allow the solution to remain for 15 minutes before wiping it clean. The fire will burn away any residue that remains before you add food to the grill.

OVERNIGHT GRILL CLEANER

Place the grill in a large plastic garbage can and cover it with an industrial strength detergent. Fill the garbage can with water and allow it to soak overnight. This will remove all the baked on grunge and dirt then just hose it off.

A SHINY BOTTOM

If you want your copper pots to look like new again just sprinkle them with baking soda then pour white vinegar over them. Allow the pots to stand for 15 minutes before rinsing them. If you prefer, you can use baking soda and ½ a lemon to scrub them to a shiny finish. Rinse well and dry before use.

RUST REMOVER

If you prepare a paste composed of 1 tablespoon of baking soda and 1 teaspoon of water you will be able to remove rust from a metal chair or table leg. Wipe the paste on to the area then scrub lightly with a piece of aluminum foil. Clean up with paper towel.

IN THE BATHROOM

GERM ALERT! CALL OUT THE HEAVY ARTILLERY

The first thing to remember is that germs love moisture. If you keep surfaces dry it will reduce the incidence of bacteria getting a foothold and causing odors and unhealthy conditions. Disinfectants will kill bacteria and almost all molds, but only for a short period of time. Therefore it is necessary to clean the surfaces that are more susceptible to contamination more frequently than most other areas of your home.

BATHROOM DISINFECTANT CLEANER
The following ingredients will be needed:

1	Quart of very hot tap water
1 1/3	Cup of powdered household laundry detergent
1 1/3	Cup of pine oil (Pinesol™ will do fine)
1	Half-gallon plastic container

Place the water and detergent in the ½ gallon plastic container and mix until the detergent is fully dissolved. Skim off any foam that develops and then gradually add the Pinesol™ or pine oil as you continue stirring. To use the solution add 1 part disinfectant to 1-part warm water. For toilets, use full strength. Store in well-sealed container and as with all chemicals store away from children.

SCUM AND MILDEW BUILDUP, ACTIVATE THE SALT
Shower curtains will develop a layer of mildew and scum, especially over the course of a year. Most curtains can be washed in the washing machine, which should do the job. However you may wish to use the following formula, or at least soak the curtains in the bathtub in a strong solution of salt water, before you hang them up after they get out of the washing machine. The salt bath should only be needed about once a year.

SHOWER CURTAIN CLEANER
The following ingredients will be needed:

½	Cup of soap flakes
½	Cup of baking soda (fresh)
1	Cup of white vinegar
	Mineral oil

Place warm water in the washing machine and add 2 large towels and the shower curtains. Add the soap flakes and baking soda and run the wash cycle.

Add the vinegar and a few drops of mineral oil to soften the curtains in the rinse water.

MAKING TILE CLEANER
The following mixture can be used with a brush or sponge:
Mix together:

¼	**Cup baking soda**
½	**Cup white vinegar**
1	**Cup household ammonia**
2	**Gallons of warm water**

A SLIPPIN & A SLIDIN
Try sprinkling baking soda in the bathtub then place 2 sponges or washcloths on the bottom and let your feet clean the tub. Only for the very agile!

CLEAN UP YOUR POTTY
If you sprinkle ½ box of baking soda in the toilet tank then allow it to remain overnight it will clean the tank and the bowl.

BATHROOM FIXTURE CLEANER
The following ingredients will be needed:

½	**Cup of white vinegar**
1	**Cup of clear household ammonia**
¼	**Cup of baking soda (fresh)**
1	**Gallon of warm tap water**

Place all the ingredients in a small bucket and mix well. Pour into a number of smaller jars for storage. Place a small amount into a spray bottle and use on fixtures and soap scum. Wipe clean with a warm soft cloth.

DETECTING SEWER GAS
The following ingredients will be needed:

2	**Ounces of lead acetate**
1	**Pint of distilled water or rainwater**

Place the ingredients into a container and mix well, then place a piece of unglazed white paper into the solution. Remove the paper immediately and allow it to dry. If the odor you smell is caused by a sewer gas leak the paper will turn a dark color.

THERE'S A STRANGE SMELL COMING FROM THE BATHROOM

 If you have a septic tank, you are probably familiar with a strange smell occasionally and know to have it pumped or to add special bacteria. However, if you are not on a septic tank and you smell a strange odor it may be from "sewer gas," which contains methane. The odor is usually associated with sulfur and you should call your gas company or a plumber as soon as possible. Plumbers have special gas detectors and can locate the problem and correct it.

INEXPENSIVE AIR FRESHENER

Mix equal parts of your favorite bath salts with equal parts of baking soda to prepare a room freshener.

GENERAL BATHROOM CLEANER

The following ingredients will be needed:

1	**Pound of baking soda (fresh)**
4	**Tablespoons of liquid hand soap**
1	**Cup of warm tap water**

Place all the ingredients in a spray bottle and shake to mix. This formula is not as harsh as the one with ammonia. It is also safer around children.

AROUND THE HOME

SPARKLING WINDOWS

To clean a dirty window, just use a wet sponge sprinkled with a small amount of baking soda. Rinse the window with a clean sponge and dry well.

WATER SPOTS FROM WOOD FLOORS

Water spots can be removed from wood floors by applying a baking soda solution on a damp washcloth. Don't allow the wood to get very wet and dry well afterwards.

INEXPENSIVE CARPET MAINTENANCE

Best to sprinkle baking soda mixture on your carpet monthly to keep the carpet deodorized. Just sprinkle it on and allow it to remain overnight. Use a brush to rub it into the carpet then vacuum it up the next morning. The deodorizer is prepared from:

½   **Cup baking soda**
½   **Cup cornstarch**
10   **Drops of your favorite essential oil**

ICE REMOVER

You won't need cat litter or rock salt, just use baking soda to de-ice the steps or walkway. It will provide traction and will melt away the ice. It is safe and will not harm the outside surfaces, shoes, or any indoor surfaces if you track it inside. You can mix it with sand for even better traction.

REMOVE PLASTIC TABLECLOTH ODOR

Plastic tablecloths tend to have an odor all their own and it is not very appealing. To remove the odor, soak the tablecloth in a solution of baking soda and water overnight to remove the smell.

FIGHT STINKY SHOES

If you sprinkle baking soda in shoes that have an offensive smell and allow it to remain overnight, the smell will be gone by morning. Just tap out the baking soda.

INEXPENSIVE TOILET BOWL CLEANER

The following ingredients will be needed:

1   **Cup of Castile soap (liquid)**
¼   **Cup of borax**
¼   **Cup of baking soda**

Place all the ingredients into a container and mix well. Add a small amount of very warm water if you have a problem blending the ingredients. Pour into toilet and scrub with a brush.

SOME LAUNDRY TIPS

WHY BUY FABRIC SOFTENERS?
You can save money by not buying fabric softeners and just add ½ cup of baking soda to your rinse cycle.

HOW BRIGHT I AM............
You can boost the whitening power of your bleach and use less bleach. If you normally use 1 cup of liquid chlorine bleach, you will use only half that amount if you add ½ cup of baking soda to top loaders and ¼ cup of baking soda to front loaders. In fact, the whites will get even whiter.

PERSPIRATION BEGONE
Just make a paste of baking soda and water and rub into the area before you wash the garment. If the stain is stubborn, just allow the paste to remain in place for 2-3 hours before washing.

IRON CLEANER
You can clean starch buildup from the bottom of an iron by rubbing it with a paste prepared from baking soda and water. Be sure that the iron is cool before doing the cleaning.

IRONING TIPS
If you need to remove melted plastic or fabric residues heat the iron on low temperature until the foreign material softens and scrape it off with a piece of wood. Baking soda and water made into a paste will also work well. If a steam iron clogs from lint, just fill the iron and allow it to steam until it runs out.

REMOVING IRONING SCORCHES
The following ingredients will be needed:

½	**Cup of hydrogen peroxide (3% solution)**
½	**Cup of cool tap water**

Place the ingredients into a small bowl and mix then allow the scorched area of the garment to soak in the solution for about 10 minutes. Rinse the garment in cold water. Works better with natural fibers than it does for synthetics.

FLOSS AWAY
An old dentist's trick to remove more plaque is to dampen a piece of dental floss in baking soda before using it.

A CLEAN TOOTHBRUSH IS A HEALTHY BRUSH
If you place your toothbrush in a solution of baking soda and warm water overnight the bristles will be sparkling clean.

SPIT POLISH
To remove any marks and to get a better shine on a cleaner shoe, try using a paste of baking soda and water to clean the shoes. This will not damage leather shoes.

GROOMING TIPS

UNDER ARM MAGIC
Sprinkle baking soda under your arms for a natural deodorant. You won't have to worry about some of the ingredients that are in the over-the-counter products.

HOMEMADE TOOTHPASTE
The following ingredients will be needed:

1	**Tablespoons of bicarbonate of soda**
1	**Tablespoon of table salt**
¼	**Cup of cold tap water**
3	**Teaspoons of glycerin (vegetable source from pharmacy)**

Place the bicarbonate of soda, salt, water and glycerin in a small bowl and mix until it is a thick paste. Add additional water if need. A few drops of peppermint oil can be added to improve the flavor then store in a sealed container.

CHAPTER 22

GETTING OUT THE STAINS

RULES FOR STAIN REMOVAL

- Never rub too hard to remove a stain since this will cause damage to the fabric, which can never be repaired.
- Never wash any fabric before attempting to remove the stain. Washing in a detergent may actually set the stain and make it impossible to remove later.
- Stains on washable fabrics should be treated as soon as possible.
- Remember fresh stains will come out more easily than old ones.
- Non-washable items that normally go to the cleaners should be taken to the cleaners as soon as possible. Identify the stain for the dry cleaner. If you know what the stain is be sure and tell them.

MILDEW AWAY
Just moisten the mildew area with salt and lemon juice and allow it to sit in the sunlight to bleach out the stain.

POURING SALT ON AN OPEN SPILL

If you ever spill red wine on your carpet, try pouring salt on the area as soon as possible and watch the wine being absorbed almost instantly, then wait until it dries, and vacuum it up. Salt tends to provide a special capillary action that will attract most liquids.

HELP! I CAN'T SEE MY STAIN
When trying to remove stains at home, make sure you do it on a clean, well-lighted work surface. Always use fresh clean rags or a towel.

STOP COLOR RUN-OFF WITH NEW CLOTHING
To eliminate the possibility of color run-off with new clothes presoak the garment in cool water with a small amount of white vinegar.

RUST REMOVAL
Rust stains can be removed by wetting the areas with lemon juice, then sprinkle with a small amount of salt and allow to sit in direct sunlight for 30-45 minutes.

WELL, CLEAN MY CHROME
Automotive chrome cleaner will clean many kitchen appliances.

BACK-UP CHROME CLEANER
To shine chrome fixture try rubbing them with newspaper while they are still damp. Baby oil and a soft cloth works well! Aluminum foil will also do the job.

YUK! MAKE SURE IT'S CHILLED
Bloodstains may be cleaned with cold club soda.

VINEGAR WILL WORK TOO!
A scorch can be removed by rubbing a raw onion on the scorched area and allowing the onion juice to soak in thoroughly for at least 2-3 hours before washing.

A WORD TO THE WISE
If you are going to use a commercial stain removal substance make sure to follow directions carefully.

TESTING, ONE, TWO
Always test a stain remover on an area of the fabric that will not show to be sure of the colorfastness of the fabric. Allow the product to stand on the area for at least 3-5 minutes before rinsing off. If there are any changes in the fabric color, do not use.

HIDE THAT SPOT
When treating a spot, it should be placed face down on paper towel. Then apply the stain remover to the underside of the garment, allowing the stain to be forced to the surface and not back through the fabric. The paper towel should be replaced a number of times if it is a tough stain to remove.

WHERE ART THOU COLOR

If you are going to use a bleach product, never use it on a colored garment. It is necessary to bleach the whole garment to avoid uneven color removal. If there is a change in color it will at least be uniform.

RESIDUES BEGONE

As soon as the stain is removed, launder immediately with your favorite laundry detergent. This will also remove the residues from the stain remover.

STAIN REMOVAL PRODUCTS

Prompt treatment is the key to stain removal, and it would be wise to have the supplies on hand at all times. The following is a list of some of the more common ingredients needed for most stain removal, however, more natural stain and general cleaning preparations are recommended.

BLEACHES	MISCELLANEOUS REMOVERS
Chlorine bleach	Ammonia
Fabric color remover	Rust stain remover
Non-chlorine, all fabric, bleach	White vinegar

DETERGENTS	SOLVENTS
Enzyme detergent	Dry cleaner spot remover
Enzyme pre-soaker	Nail polish remover
Liquid detergent	Rubbing alcohol
	Turpentine

SOAPS	SUPPLIES
Laundry detergent	Clean, white cloths
White bar soap	Paper towels

Any of the above products that cannot be found at the supermarket will be found at any drug store.

CAUTION

Some stain removal materials are flammable, while others are poison or toxic. Store them safely and use with care.

BEWARE! CHEMICAL ALERT

Keep stain removal supplies out of reach of children. They should be stored in closed containers with childproof lids and in a cool, dry location away from any food products.

LEMON TREE, VERY PRETTY............
Lemon extract will remove black scuff marks left from shoes and luggage.

HARD ONE TO GET OUT
Stains from ballpoint pens can be removed with hair spray or milk.

READING THE WRITING
Read the labels on cleaning products and follow directions. Heed all label warnings and always try to store them in their original containers.

CONTAINER SMARTS
Empty and wash all containers immediately after using them. It is best to store stain removal supplies in glass or un-chipped porcelain containers. Solvents will ruin plastic containers. Rusty containers should never be used.

Be careful never allow chemicals near your face and especially your eyes. Wash any spilled chemicals off your hands as soon as possible.

WEAR A GAS MASK
Use chemicals that give off vapors in a well-ventilated location, preferably outside. Try not to breathe the vapors.

POOOOF
Never use a solvent near an open fire or an electrical outlet.

YUM, YUM, FABRIC
Never add solvents directly into the washing machine. Always allow a solvent-treated fabric dry before washing or placing it into the dryer. A WITCH'S BREW
Never mix stain removal materials with each other, especially ammonia and chlorine bleach. If it's necessary to use both, make sure
one is thoroughly rinsed out before adding the other.

RECIPES FOR SAFE CLEANING PRODUCTS

The following recipes are safe when mixed in the quantities indicated below. The mixing of other household chemicals may be dangerous.

- **All-Purpose Household Cleaner**
  Add 1 teaspoon of any liquid soap and 1 teaspoon of trisodium phosphate (TSP) to 1 quart of warm water.

  This is a very effective cleaner for many cleaning jobs including countertops and walls. Try an area of the wall that will not show before using in case your walls are painted with a poor quality water-based flat paint.
- **Chlorine Bleach**
  Best to use hydrogen peroxide-based bleach.
- **Degreaser (engines, etc.)**
  It is best to use a water-based cleaner that is well diluted instead of kerosene, turpentine, or a commercial engine degreaser. These are available in parts stores and the label should read "nonflammable," "non-toxic," or "store at temperatures above freezing." These will be water-based products and will do the job.
- **Degreaser (kitchen, grill)**
  Add 2 tablespoons of TSP to 1 gallon of hot water or use a non-chlorinated scouring cleanser with a scouring or steel wool pad.
- **Fabric Softener**
  Fabrics produced from natural fibers do not need fabric softeners, only synthetics.
- **Floor Cleaner**
  Vinyl floors use ½ cup of white vinegar to 1 gallon of warm water.
  Wood floors may be damp mopped with a mild liquid soap.
- **Furniture Polish**
  Mineral oil may be used but most wood surfaces may be cleaned with a damp cloth.
- **Oven Cleaner**
  Mix 2 tablespoons of baking soda or TSP in 1 gallon of warm water and scrub with a very fine steel wool pad (0000). Rubber gloves should be worn and the area rinsed well. For difficult baked-on areas, try scrubbing with a pumice stone.

If the above fails, try using an oven cleaner that states "no caustic fumes" on the label.

- **Glass Cleaner**
  Use 2-3 cups spray bottle with ½ teaspoon of liquid soap, 3 tablespoons of white vinegar and 2 cups of water. If the windows are very dirty, try using more liquid soap.

- **Laundry Detergent**
  Use laundry soap in place of the detergents. Washing soda may be used in place of a softener. An alternate would be to use detergents with no added bleaches or softeners. Bleach should be used in moderation when needed.

- **Mildew Remover**
  Scrub the area with baking soda or if very stubborn with TSP.

- **Scouring Powder**
  Baking soda will work well in most instances.

- **Toilet Bowl Cleaner**
  Use a non-chlorinated scouring powder and a stiff brush. To remove hard water deposits, pour white vinegar or a commercial citric acid-based toilet bowl cleaner into the toilet and allow it to sit for several hours or overnight before scrubbing.

NOTE: Washing soda and TSP are caustic and should be kept out of the reach of children.

Always get the stain out before washing.

FABRIC ADVICE
It is best to know the fiber content in clothing items. If sewn in labels are to be removed a note should be made as to which item it was removed from. Any durable press or polyester fabric such as Dacron holds soil very well and especially stains. A dry cleaning solvent will work the best. If the stain remains after the first treatment, try once more. If the fabric has been washed or has been placed in a dryer, the stain may never come out.

- Never use chlorine bleach on silk, wool, or Spandex.
- Never remove a stain from leather: take it to dry cleaners to send to an expert.

STAIN REMOVAL FROM WASHABLE FABRICS

A number of stains can be removed right in your washing machine. Laundry detergents that state that they contain enzymes will provide the best cleaning and stain removal.

Enzyme presoak products provide extra cleaning and stain removal for fabrics that may have a more difficult stain. An enzyme detergent or enzyme presoak product should be able to remove the following common stains:

Blood	Gravy	Body soils	Egg
Fruits	Milk	Chocolate	Grass
Cream soups	Baby formula	Puddings	Vegetables
Baby foods	Ice cream	Most food soils	

I WONDER WHERE THE YELLOW WENT

Yellowed fabrics can be restored and even old unknown stains may be removed by first soaking in an enzyme presoak product (Proctor & Gamble has excellent ones) such as Biz and then laundering.

CAN'T PERFORM MAGIC

Remember, even the best enzyme detergent or enzyme presoak product is not capable of removing all types of stains.

A number of grease soils and highly colored stains may require special pretreatment before laundering. Since many stains require a variety of different soil removal treatments and techniques, it is important to identify a stain before trying to remove it. A number of stains may actually be set if the wrong method is used.

STAINS & THEIR REMOVAL METHODS

Beverage

Sponge the area with cold water or soak then sponge again. Launder with oxygen bleach and the hottest water that is safe for the fabric.

Blood

Soak the fabric in cold water as soon as possible. If the stain persists, soak in warm water with a presoak product before laundering. Try club soda.

Candle Wax

The surface wax should be removed with a dull knife. The item should then be placed stain face down on paper towels and then sponge the remaining stain with dry cleaning solvent. Allow it to dry and then launder. If traces of color from the wax remain: try soaking it in Biz®

or oxygen bleach before laundering again. If the color is still present, try laundering again using chlorine bleach if the fabric is chlorine bleach safe.

Catsup\Tomato Products
Remove excess with a dull knife, then soak in cold water then launder using the hottest water the fabric will stand.

Chewing Gum/Adhesive Tape/Rubber Cement
First: apply ice to the stain to harden it. Remove excess stain material with a dull knife. Place the item face down on paper towels and sponge with a dry cleaning solvent.

Chocolate\Cocoa
Soak in cold water then launder with oxygen bleach using the hottest water the fabric will stand.

Coffee/Tea
It is best to soak in Biz® or oxygen bleach using the hottest water that is safe for the stained fabric then launder. If the stain persists, try laundering again using chlorine bleach if it is safe to do so.

Cosmetics
Dampen stain and rub gently with a white bar soap, then rinse well and launder.

Crayon
If there are only a few spots they can be treated the same as candle wax. If there are many items that are stained, first wash the items with hot water and laundry soap (e.g. Ivory Snow®) and 1 cup of baking soda. If the spots remain, have the clothes dry cleaned.

Deodorants and Anti-Perspirants
Apply white vinegar, then rub and rinse. If the stain remains, try saturating the area with rubbing alcohol, rinse then soak in Biz or an oxygen bleach and launder. If the stain remains wash in chlorine bleach if safe for fabric.

Dye Transfer
If you have white fabrics that have picked up dye from a colored garment that "bled," try restoring the white by using a fabric color remover. Launder if any of the dye remains using chlorine bleach, if it is safe for the fabric.

Egg/Meat Juice
Remove excess with a dull knife then soak in cold water. Launder in oxygen bleach in very hot water.

Fabric Softeners
These stains usually result from accidental spills and can be removed by rubbing the area with a piece of cloth moistened with bar soap then launder.

Formula
Soak in warm water then launder with oxygen bleach and the hottest water that is safe for the fabric.

Fruit\Fruit Juices
Soak in cold water before laundering.

Grass
The green area should be sponged with denatured alcohol before washing in very hot water and oxygen bleach.

Grease Stains
The stained area should be placed face down on paper towels. Dry cleaning solvent should be placed on the backside of the stain and then brushed from the center of the stain to the outer edges using a clean white cloth.

Moisten the stain with warm water and rub with bar soap or a mild liquid detergent, then rinse and launder.

Gum
Rub with ice and carefully remove the gum with a dull knife before laundering.

Ink Stains
For removal of ballpoint stains, place the stain face down on paper towels and sponge the back of the stain with dry cleaning solvent. If there is some ink left, try rubbing the area with a moistened bar soap, rinse, and then launder. For any other type of ink stains just try and remove the stain with a dampened cloth and bar soap, rinse, and soak in Biz or oxygen bleach using very hot water. If the stain won't come out, try using chlorine bleach, if the fabric is safe. Some permanent ink may never be removed.

Ink, Felt Tip
Rub the area with Fantastic or Mr. Clean, rinse, and repeat if necessary. It may be impossible to remove.

Iodine
Rinse the fabric from the underside with cool water, then soak in a solution of fabric color remover, rinse and then launder.

Lipstick

The stain should be placed face down on paper towels and then sponged with dry cleaning solvent replacing the paper towels frequently while the color is being removed. Moisten the stain with cool water and then rub with bar soap, rinse, and launder.

Mildew

Fabric should be laundered using chlorine bleach if it is safe for the fabric. If not, try soaking it in oxygen bleach and then launder.

Milk

The fabric should be rinsed in cold water as soon as possible, and then washed in cold water using a liquid detergent.

Mustard

Moisten stain with cool water then rub with bar soap, rinse and launder using chlorine bleach, if it is safe for the fabric. If not, soak in Biz or an oxygen detergent using very hot water then launder. It may take several treatments to remove all of the stain.

Nail Polish

The fabric stain should be placed face down on paper towels then sponge the back of the stain frequently and repeat until the stain disappears then launder. Never use nail polish remover on fabric, best to have them dry cleaned.

Paint

Try to treat the stain while it is still wet. Latex, acrylic, and water, based paints cannot be removed once they have dried. While they are wet: rinse in warm water to flush the paint out then launder. Oil-based paints can be removed with solvent that is recommended on the paint can. If it does not give this information, try using turpentine, then rinse and rub with bar soap, then launder.

Perspiration

Moisten the stain and rub with bar soap. Be gentle as perspiration may weaken some fibers, especially silk. Most fabrics should be presoaked in Biz or an enzyme detergent and then laundered in hot water and chlorine bleach, if the fabric is safe.

Another method is to mix 4 tablespoons of salt to 1 quart of hot water and sponge on the fabric until the stain disappears.

Perfume (Same as Beverages)

Rust
Never use chlorine bleach on rust, apply a rust stain remover, rinse then launder. You can also use a fabric color remover and then launder or if the stain is really stubborn, try using 1 ounce of oxalic acid crystals (or straight warm rhubarb juice) dissolved in 1 gallon of water, mixed in a plastic container, then rinse and launder.

Scorch
Soak the fabric in a strong solution of Biz and oxygen bleach using very hot water if safe for the fabric, then launder. If the scorch remains, it will be necessary to repeat the procedure using chlorine bleach, if the fabric will take it.

Shoe Polish
Try applying a mixture of 1 part rubbing alcohol and 2 parts of water for colored fabrics and only the straight alcohol for whites.

Suede
Rain spots can be removed by lightly rubbing the area with an emery board. If there are grease spots, try using white vinegar or club soda then blot out the stain. Afterwards brush with a suede brush.

Tar
The area should be rubbed with kerosene until all the tar is dissolved then wash as usual. Test a small area first to be sure it is color fast.

Tobacco
Moisten the stain and rub with bar soap rinse and then launder. If the stain persists, try soaking it in Biz or an oxygen detergent, then launder. As a last resort use chlorine bleach if the fabric is safe.

Urine, Vomit, Mucous
Soak the fabric in Biz or an enzyme detergent: launder using chlorine bleach, if safe for the fabric. If not, use oxygen bleach with detergent.

Wine/Soft Drinks
Soak the fabric with Biz or oxygen bleach using very hot water then launder. Use chlorine bleach if needed and if the fabric is safe.

NATURAL METHODS OF STAIN REMOVAL

TOTALLY THRIFTY
If you wish to use less detergent and save money, try using slivers of old soaps placed in a sock with the neck tied. Place the sock into the washer and you will use less detergent.

Works great, for most jeans.

SETTING IT PERMANENTLY
To colorfast a possible problem garment: try soaking the colored garment in cold saltwater for 30 minutes before laundering.

DON'T GET STUNG
After washing a piece of clothing with a zipper that has given you problems, try rubbing beeswax on the zipper to resolve the problem and remove any grime that has accumulated.

BEGONE OLD SOAP
When washing clothes, to be sure that all the soap has been removed, try adding 1 cup of white vinegar to the rinse cycle. The vinegar will dissolve the alkalinity in detergents as well as giving the clothes a pleasant fragrance.

THE OLD BUBBLE MACHINE
Placing too much soap in the washing machine can cause problems. If this happens, just pour 2 tablespoons of white vinegar or a capful of fabric softener into the machine to neutralize some of the soap.

THE GREEN, GREEN GRASS OF HOME
Grass stains will be easily removed with toothpaste, scrub in with a toothbrush before washing. Another method is to rub the stain with molasses and allow it to stand overnight then wash with regular dish soap by itself. If all else fails, try methyl alcohol, but be sure the color is set, best to try an area that won't show first.

300

GREASELESS
Spic and Span placed in the washer is a great grease remover, 1/4 cup is all that is needed.

WRINKLE REMOVER
To avoid ironing many different types of clothes, just remove them from the dryer the second it stops and fold or hang up immediately.

CATCH THAT COLOR
Washing colored material for the first time may be risky unless you wash it in Epsom salts. One gallon of water to 1 teaspoon is all that is needed. The material will not run.

THE DISAPPEARING ACT
An excellent spot remover can be made using 2 parts of water to 1 part rubbing alcohol.

A DIRTY JOB
To remove difficult dirt, such as collars, mix 1/3 cup of water with 1/3 cup of liquid detergent and 1/3 cup of ammonia. Place the ingredients in a spray bottle. Rubbing shampoo into the area may also work.

LINT MAGNET
To keep corduroy garments from retaining lint, turn them inside out when washing.

HAIRBALLS
To avoid hairballs on acrylic sweaters, turn them inside out when washing them.

ONE OF THE TOUGHEST
Iodine stains can be removed using a mixture of baking soda and water. Allow it to remain on for about 30 minutes rub with mild action.

USE ONLY THE UNSALTED
Butter or margarine will remove tar from clothing, just rub until it's gone. The butter is easily removed with any type of spray and wash product.

INKA-KA-DINKA-DOO
Rubbing alcohol or hair spray may remove a number of ink pen stains.

BEWARE OF A TIGHT FIT
If you wash slipcovers, be sure and replace them when they are still damp. They will fit better and will not need to be ironed.

BLOWDRYING
If sweater cuffs are stretched, dip them in hot water and dry with a hairdryer.

A SPOT OF TEA, PERHAPS
Tea stains on tablecloths can be removed with glycerin, try letting it sit overnight in the solution before washing.

INTO THE FREEZER
Candle wax on tablecloths can be removed by freezing with ice cubes.

YUK
Lace doilies should be hand washed in sour milk for the best results.

HOLD THE SHAVING CREAM
If you have a problem with small burrs on sweaters, try using a disposable razor to remove them.

EASY DOES IT
If you are washing a wool garment, be careful not to pull on it. Wool is very weak when wet. Lay the garment on a towel and roll it up and squeeze the excess water out.

NEUTRALIZER
If you have a difficult bloodstain, try making a paste of meat tenderizer and cold water. Sponge on the area and allow it to stand for 20-30 minutes. Rinse in cold water, then wash. Hydrogen peroxide may also work.

BATHING STUFFED ANIMALS
To clean stuffed animals that cannot be placed in the washer, just place them in a cloth bag and add baking soda, then shake.

POWDER ME
White flour will clean white gloves, just rub.

A SLIPPERY SUBJECT
Lipstick stains will clean out of clothes by using Vaseline.

A REVIVAL

If you shrink a woolen garment: try soaking it in a hair cream rinse. This will usually make them easy to stretch back into the original size. Another method is to dissolve 1 ounce of Borax in 1 teaspoon of hot water then add it to 1 gallon of warm water. Place the garment in, stretch back to shape, then rinse it in 1 gallon of warm water with 2 tablespoons of white vinegar added.

BE STINGY, BE SMART

When you are doing a small wash load tear the fabric-softening sheet in half for the same results.

A SOLID FACT

To make your own spray starch, purchase 1 bottle of liquid starch concentrate and mix one part of liquid starch to 1 part of water, use a spray bottle.

BUTTON, BUTTON, WHO'S GOT THE BUTTON

If you lose buttons regularly on children's clothing try sewing them on with dental floss.

TRUE GRIT

If your iron is sticking, try running it over a piece of paper with sprinkled salt on it.

WELL, SEASONED CURTAINS

Water stained fabrics should be placed in salt water and soaked until the stain is gone.

BRING IN THE SUB

If you prefer not to use bleach try substituting 3 tablespoons of hydrogen peroxide to the wash load.

SAVE THE BUTTONS

Always remove buttons before discarding a garment. They may come in handy at a later date.

ATTRACTIVE SALT

Cleaning silk flowers is easy if you place them in a plastic bag with 2 tablespoons of salt and shake vigorously while holding on to the stems. Salt tends to attract the dust.

IRONING SMARTS

When ironing, always iron the fabrics that require a cool temperature first as the iron heats up.

DEW TELL

Mildew on shower curtains can be removed with a mixture of ½ cup bleach, ½ cup powdered detergent, and 1 gallon of water. To prolong the life of shower curtains add 1 cup of white vinegar to the final rinse.

MAKING COLORS FAST

To prevent jeans from fading (if you want to) soak the jeans in 1/2 cup of white vinegar and 2 quarts of water for 1 hour before you wash them for the first time.

JEAN SMARTS

Blue jeans should only be washed in cold water then placed in a moderate heat dryer for only 10 minutes. Then they should be placed on a wooden hanger to continue drying.

DOLLAR SAVER

If you would like to save dollars on dry cleaning of wool blankets try washing them in mild dishwasher soap on a very gentle cycle then air fluff to dry.

NO ONE WILL EVER KNOW

If you scorch a garment, try removing the scorch with cloth that has been dampened with vinegar. Only use a warm iron, not too hot. Cotton scorch marks tend to respond better to peroxide.

INSULATION

A sheet of aluminum foil placed underneath the ironing board cover will allow the heat to be retained for a longer period of time.

BUTTON, BUTTON....

Always remember to place a small amount of clear nail polish in the center of every button on a new garment. This seals the threads and they will last longer.

A SHOCKING SITUATION

A pipe cleaner dipped in white vinegar should be used to clean the holes in the iron after it is completely cool. Make sure it is unplugged.

IF YOU'RE IN A SPOT

Glass cleaner sometimes makes an excellent spot remover if you need something in a hurry. Make sure the fabric is colorfast.

BRIGHTEN-UP
If you want to whiten your whites, try adding a cup of dishwasher detergent to the washer. Even whitens sweat socks.

ANY PENCIL WILL DO
A sticky zipper will respond to a rubbing with a lead pencil. It does an excellent job of lubricating it.

A TEMPORARY SOLUTION
If a button comes off try reattaching it with the wire from a twist tie.

DON'T SUCK YOUR THUMB
If you use a thimble to sew or sort papers, try wetting your finger before you place the thimble on. This creates suction and holds the thimble on.

A SEALER
When you wash you sneakers, spray them with a spray starch to help them resist becoming soiled.

DIRTY BOTTOM
If the bottom of the iron gets dirty, just clean it with a steel wool soap pad. If you want to make it shiny again, just run a piece of waxed paper over it.

RUSTADE
Rust marks on clothing can be removed with lemon juice and a small amount of salt, easily rubbed in and then allowed to sit in the sun for 2 hours.

AND AWAY WE GO
To dry the insides of shoes or sneakers, try placing the blower end of the vacuum hose inside.

A TRIPPER-UPPER
If you have problems with your shoelaces becoming undone just dampen them before tying them.

A WORD OF CAUTION
Silk clothing should be hand washed using cool water with Ivory liquid soap. When you rinse, try adding a small amount of lanolin to help preserve the material. Always drip dry, never place the garment in the dryer, and then iron using a soft piece of cloth over the garment.

CHAPTER 23

PAINTING

PAINTING (INTERIOR)

GENERAL INFORMATION:

There is more to painting than just buying a can of paint and painting a wall! There are different types of paints for different surfaces. You need to know the difference between oil-based, water-based, acrylics, primers, etc. and when they should be used. The  equipment to paint with paints also varies depending on the project. The following are the bare minimum requirements for every painting project.

CAULKING

It is used to fill open crevices and cracks around doors and windows. Colored caulking is also available and makes for a great looking job.

BEAD A PROFESSIONAL LINE

Running a professional caulking bead is not as easy as the pros make it. You need to push the bead forward then pull it back. Be sure you are using the right caulking for the job and follow the manufacturer's instructions. Practice making shallow beads before starting to use it on the job and use your finger or plastic spoon to shape the bead.

TYPES OF CAULKING

Acrylic Latex
Easy to use indoor caulk and will last about 3-10 years.

Butyl Rubber
This is very durable for outdoor use, but it is difficult to clean up. The seal should last for about 10 years.

Silicone Acrylic
Easy to apply and clean up and will last for 20-30 years.

Urethane Foam
It is sold in aerosol cans with the foam expanding after release. Handy for filling hard to reach areas: best used around electrical outlets and new windows. Be sure and wear gloves when applying. Somewhat expensive!

- **Drop Cloths** – Plastic, to prevent spills from damaging areas. Purchase throwaway.
- **Masking Tape** – To protect non-painted areas and to hold down plastic drop cloths.

A NEW WAY TO MASK
A new product is now available for masking off windows instead of using masking tape. It is *acrylic latex* and is specially formulated to prime and seal wood trim around windows as well as masking off the glazing very quickly and efficiently. To use it, all you have to do is paint the thick, white paste onto the trim and lap it over the glass.

When the latex dries it forms a clear, thin sheet that will adhere solidly to the wood. However, the latex will peel off the glass very easily and leave a clean, unpainted surface.

- **Paint Tray** – Disposable liners for trays.
- **Patching Compound** – Premixed or powder form for repairing cracks and holes.
- **Sandpaper** – You may need coarse, medium, or fine grades.

CONVENIENCE
Keeping track of pieces of sandpaper is a real pain. However, just try keeping sandpaper on a clipboard and hang it on the wall for easy retrieval.

- **Screwdrivers** – Both Phillips and standard for removing wall plates and door hardware. Can be used to open a can if you don't have a pint can opener.
- **5-Gallon Mixing Bucket** – Good for stirring paint from multiple cans.
- **Wall Cleaner & Sponges** – To clean up dusty areas, cooking grease spots, soot or cigarette damage.

EVALUATE THE PAINTS
Select a quality paint manufacturer. Inexpensive or poor quality paints will produce a mediocre job.

COMPARING INTERIOR PAINTS & PRIMERS

Acoustic
Used on acoustic ceilings and tiles and will not affect their sound-reducing qualities. It can be applied by spraying or using a special type of roller. The color choices are very limited, you don't need a primer and it will clean up easily with water.

Alcohol-based primer
This is the best primer for almost any surface with the ability to kill almost any stain providing a slick surface. Needs to be thinned: will clean up well using denatured alcohol.

Alkyd
This best used for a rough surface and has excellent hiding power. It is best not to apply the paint over unprimed drywall surface since it will cause the surface to become rough. It will dry slower than latex and the odor is somewhat strong, causing it to be banned in some areas. To thin alkyd and for cleanup: best to use a solvent and be sure and coat unfinished surfaces with an alkyd primer.

Latex
This is the paint of choice for the majority of interior paint jobs. However, best not to use it over unprimed wood, metal, or wallpaper. The glossiness will vary from flat to high and will adhere to all surfaces with the exception of slick surfaces. Latex dries fast enough allowing you to apply two coats in one day but it is less durable than alkyd-  based paints. Cleanup is easy with just soap and water. Be sure and prepare new surfaces with a latex or alkyd primer for the best results.

Latex primer
Best used to prepare patched areas and on new drywall. It is inexpensive and dries very fast. Very easy to clean up using soap and water!

Metal
Commonly used over primed or bare metal surfaces. Rusty metal primer can be used to cover rust areas. The self-primers will adhere to bare surfaces but preparation will depend on the type and condition of the metal surface. Some can be thinned using only water, while others need solvent or mineral spirits. The primer will depend on the type of metal being covered.

Oil
These paints are rarely available anymore since they dry very slowly and will give off flammable fumes. The paint will not stand up as well as alkyds. It cleans up well with mineral spirits, low odor thinner, or turpentine.

Oil-based primer
One of the best all-purpose, oil-based primers, but it dries slowly and will give off fumes. Cleans up with mineral spirits!

One-coat
It works well as long as the surface is sealed and of similar color. Be sure that there is not a lot of patchwork that may need to be covered. These are latex or alkyd paints with the addition of pigments, which will increase their hiding power but makes them more expensive. Be careful thinning since it lessens the paint's ability to hide flaws. Will clean up easily with either water or solvent depending on whether its latex or alkyd.

Texture paint
Great at covering up imperfections and provides the look of stucco-finish plaster. Applying the paint is somewhat difficult and it is best to paint a section at a time, while keeping the desired effect consistent. Best not to thin since it defeats the purpose. Hard to stir and be sure and check the label for compatible primers.

DON'T BUY CHEAP STUFF
Purchase quality brushes. Inexpensive brushes will shed bristles and will take you twice as long to do the job.

PREPARE THE SURFACE FOR A GOOD JOB

Be sure and totally prep the room before starting with drop cloths and masking tape (if applicable). Different cleaning and prep methods need to be used depending on the type of paint you are going to use.

* ❖ Use blue painters tape around all edges, windowsills, and outlets.
* ❖ Place a drop cloth on the floor and be sure and tape it to the baseboards or floor.

HELP! I'M CHOKING

Read the label on every can of paint you buy since the manufacturers are always changing the paints. The drying times between coats may be different for different paint types. Be sure and read warning labels on paint cans. Chemicals are always changing. Paint fumes can be flammable. Don't smoke when painting and wear a respirator when working with solvent-based paints.

EVALUATING THE SURFACE

Rough vs. smooth surfaces will make a difference in the type of paint you choose. The following information will provide some valuable information regarding the type of different surfaces and how they need to be prepared.

Previously Painted Plaster

Start by washing the surface, rinse and dry, then sand the surface lightly and remove any debris. Be sure and fill any cracks with spackling compound then sand and de-gloss before applying primer if necessary. Use polyvinyl acrylic primer if painting over a dark surface or if it had strong colors.

Previously Painted Wallboard

Make sure that the surface is free of any dirt or grime then rinse with water and dry. Apply flat latex primer if you are painting over dark, strong colors.

Previously Painted Wood

Start by washing the surface, rinse and dry then sand the surface lightly and remove any debris. Wipe the surface down with a damp cloth and apply primer. The primer should be fast-drying oil-based or latex and only used on areas of bare wood.

Previously Varnished Wood

Start by washing the surface, rinse and dry, then sand the surface lightly and remove any debris. Sand the surface to de-gloss then wipe with a damp cloth and apply primer. Use fast-drying oil-based or latex primer.

Unfinished Wallboard

Vacuum with soft brush furniture attachment and apply a flat latex primer.

Unfinished Wood

Be sure and sand the surface and wipe down with a damp cloth to remove any grime or dirt. You need to apply a primer that is fast, drying oil-based or a latex primer.

Unpainted Plaster

Sand the surface if necessary and dust with a vacuum using a soft brush. Apply polyvinyl acrylic primer.

PREVIEW THE PAINT COLOR

Preview the paint color on a computer at the store. To test a color to see if you will like it, test it on a natural gray card and allow it to fully dry for 24 hours. Glossy paints will brighten up a room and give the room a warm feeling. Study the colors in natural light as well as artificial light. Be careful as some store lighting is designed to tint colors to make them look better.

BASIC INTERIOR PAINTING TECHNIQUES

> Slow strokes for a better job!

PAINTBRUSH

♦ Don't overload the brush! Only dip the brush to $1/3^{rd}$ of the bristle length then tap the bristles against the side of the can to remove the excess paint.

♦ Never dip the brush deep or you will overload the brush. Dragging the brush on the rim wears out the bristles.

♦ Cut in the edges using the narrow edge of the brush and press just hard enough to flex the bristles. Paint with long, slow strokes.

♦ Always paint from the dry area to the set area.

♦ Brush the wall corners using the wide edge of the brush.

♦ Paint all pen areas and be sure to cut in before the paint dries otherwise you will get lap marks.

♦ If you are going to paint large areas, apply the paint with 2-3 diagonal strokes. Hold the brush at a 45^0 angle and work the surface. Press only hard enough to flex the bristles. The paint should be distributed evenly with horizontal strokes.

♦ All the surfaces should be smoothed: by drawing the brush vertically from top to bottom of the painted area. Use light strokes and lift the brush away from the surface of each stroke. This method is best if you are using oil-based paints.

PAINT ROLLER

- Use a 5-gallon paint bucket with a paint screen, which will speed up painting of large areas. Load the paint roller right from the bucket and use a roller extension handle. Always keep the paint bucket on the floor and never on a ladder.
- Use a paint ray when painting small areas. Fill the paint tray reservoir then dip the roller fully into the reservoir. Lift the roller and roll it on the textured area of the tray, which will distribute the paint evenly on the roller nap. Make sure that the roller is not dripping when you lift it from the tray.
- Load the roller and make a sweep in the shape of a "W" that is about 4-inches long on the surface. On walls roll upward on the first stroke to avoid spilling paint. Best to use slow roller strokes, which will avoid splattering.
- For the second stroke, draw the roller straight down, starting at the top of the first sweep. Move the roller to the beginning of the diagonal then roll it vertically and complete the uploading. If the roller begins to make noise, put more paint on it.
- Be sure and distribute the paint over the area using horizontal strokes. Smooth off the area by moving the roller in a vertical direction from top to bottom of the painted area. Then lift the roller and return it to the top of the area after you make each stroke.

A FLUFFER-UPPER

If you want to fluff up your paint roller, even if it's soggy, just rinse it and cut the handle off an inexpensive roller frame. Make sure to leave enough stem to fit it into a drill. Attach the wet roller, chuck assembly into the drill and spin the roller inside of a big brown grocery bag until it's dry.

CEILINGS & WALLS

- Paint the wall and ceilings in small areas if you are looking for a smooth finish. After you roll a section, use a paintbrush and immediately cut in the edge before you continue on.
- If the rolled areas are left to dry before the edges are painted, visible marks will be left on the finished surface where you ended rolling out the paint.
- Always paint a ceiling first when painting a room.

- Plan the job so that you will always be facing the light. It will be easier to spot areas that you may have missed.
- If you are going to paint acoustical tiles, check with a professional where you purchase your paint before you start.
- Keep roller speed slow to avoid splattering.
- Mask off or remove drapes and any other window coverings.
- Pressurized power rollers and pads are great!
- Use a hand roller extension to make the job easier.

MY EXTERIOR IS PEELING

Surface was nor scraped and cleaned properly before painting. Sand, scrape, prime, then repaint.

I'VE GOT A BLISTER

Moisture or solvent trapped under paint. Scrape, fill depression, sand, prime, and repaint.

WRINKLE, WRINKLE, DRIP, DRIP

The paint was probably applied too thick and the surface will have to be sanded smooth and repainted.

FOUNDATION PEELING

You have alkali compounds on the foundation and will need to scrape, apply alkali neutralizer and repaint.

MY WOOD KNOTS ARE BLEEDING

Wood resin is seeping out. You will have to sand, apply stain killer, and then repaint.

I DON'T LIKE ROLLER MARKS

They are probably from not using the proper roller cover or too a grade of paint. Quality rollers also make a big difference. Paint buildup on the ends of the roller may cause the problem. Make sure you spread the paint in a zigzag pattern, like an **"M"** or **"W."** Fill in the zigzag pattern with even, parallel strokes.

I'M GETTING KRINKLED

The paint is being applied too thickly and possibly the weather is too hot. You will need to remove the paint and sand the substrate if necessary. You may also be trying to use poor quality paint and are having trouble covering.

CRACKING & FLAKING IS NOT PRETTY

The splitting of dry paint is usually caused by poor quality paint, over-thinning the paint, or poor surface preparation. Best to re-do the job after you scrape off and/or sand off the surface and do a better preparation job.

TOOTHPASTE & ASPRIN

If you want to quick fix, a small hole in a white wall, just mix white toothpaste with a small amount of water or crush up a moistened crushed aspirin.

VINEGAR TO THE RESCUE

When you paint, brushes will harden over time. Try softening them by soaking them in full strength white vinegar then cleaning with a comb or they can be stored in a small amount of vegetable oil.

LITTLE BOTTLE DOES THE TRICK

Empty nail polish bottles make excellent holders for touch-up paints.

TOPY TURVY

To reduce the amount of evaporation and seal the paint can better, try turning the can upside down with the lid secured for a few seconds then turn it right side up again. This will coat the inside of the top surface with a thin film and help to seal the lid better or just store the paint can upside down and it won't form a skin.

UP, UP, AND AWAY

Try placing a blown-up balloon the size of the space in the can. It will reduce the air in the can and keep the paint fresher longer.

RUBBER BAND TRICK

If you place a thick rubber band across the middle of the top of a paint can you will be able to clean the excess paint from the brush.

MIXING FLOUR AND PAINT...YUK
If you are painting old woodwork that has small holes that need patching, try filling the holes with flour and some of the paint, it will harden and will not be noticeable.

CLOSE THE PORES
Using a hand moisturizer or creamy hand lotion when painting or doing other dirty chores will prevent dirt and paint from seeping into your skin's pores making personal cleanup easier. Thin rubber gloves work great and are disposable.

SMILE!
A method of cleaning dentures that works as well as the expensive spreads is to just soak them overnight in white vinegar.

A CLEAN RIM IS A HEALTHY RIM
If you place masking tape on the rim of your paint can before pouring the paint out, you can remove the tape later and the rim will be clean.

SUPER IDEA FROM PROFESSIONAL PAINTER

If you have lumps in your paint can, try cutting a piece of screen the size of the can and allowing it to settle to the bottom, it will carry the lumps to the bottom.

EYE PROTECTION
When painting ceilings try wearing a pair of old plastic goggles.

GET IT RIGHT, THE FIRST TIME!

Water, latex-based paints
The area to be painted must be pre-primed or painted over the previously painted water-based paint. This paint will clean up easily with soap and water and you can store a partially used can of paint.

Latex, oil-based paints
Area should be primed before painting or painted over previously painted oil-based paint. You must use mineral spirits to clean up. Has longer drying time and odor.

Acrylics

Used mainly as a base or primer. If water-based latex won't adhere, use acrylic first. Problem surfaces that require primers are drywall and lathe and plaster walls.

Primers

Use primers on all non-porous materials.

OIL OR LATEX

Oil-based paints are usually preferred especially for a child's room since they will last longer and be easier to clean up. They are more expensive but well worth the extra money.

METHODS OF PAINTING OLD DRYWALL

If you want a smooth finish on old drywall, ceilings, or walls it would be best to follow these methods.

✓ First scrape off any of the old texture or loose paint using a 6-inch putty knife.

✓ Never try and remove old nails that show through. It is best to drive a new nail beside it, which will secure the existing nail in place. You can dimple the drywall with a hammer if necessary.

✓ Use a 6-inch drywall knife and fill the holes and dimples with drywall compound. Tape and repair all cracks and any open joints then allow the compound to fully dry.

✓ Apply a thin coat of drywall compound across the entire ceiling or wall surface using a 12-inch drywall knife then allow the area to dry fully.

✓ Lightly sand off the surface using 100-grit sandpaper then touch any areas with drywall compound as needed. Allow the area to dry!

✓ Sand the surface with 120-grit sandpaper then using a roller with a ¼-inch nap, apply a quality latex paint and allow it to dry.

✓ Lightly sand the entire surface and touch up any bad areas that may still appear then cover them with drywall compound and allow it to dry.

✓ Complete the job by covering the surface with one or two coats of paint.

GOOD COLOR, BAD COLOR

Rooms should be painted with light or brighter colors. The darker the color the more the negative impact will be on the inhabitants. Dark colors may bring on negative emotions while bright or light colors have a positive effect. Children's rooms should always have bright colors such as yellow, which is especially popular making the room appear, sunny.

STABILIZING COLOR
If you add 7-10 drops of black paint to each quart of white paint, the paint will not yellow.

A CHILLY ROLLER SOLUTION
If you are going to use your roller and did not finish the job, just wrap the whole roller with the paint on it in a plastic bag sealed up well and place it into the refrigerator until the next day.

A LITTLE DAB WILL DO YA
Enamel or oil paint can easily be removed from your hands with paste floor wax then washing with soap and water.

A REAL GOOD TOPPER
To prevent a skin forming on top of the paint try placing a piece of waxed paper the size of the opening on top of the paint.

HOW SOFT I AM
After you clean out a paintbrush rub a few drops of vegetable oil into the bristles to keep them soft.

LAZY WAY OUT
If you don't feel like cleaning a roller place it in a plastic bag and place in the freezer. This will keep it moist and usable for a few days.

CAN STILL GET TO THE KIDS
If you need to paint steps, try painting every other step, when those are dry go back and paint the rest. This will allow you continued access to the upstairs.

GREAT IDEA
When painting anything, make sure you dip a 3 X 5, index card into the paint to make it easier to match it at a later date if needed.

SMART PAINTING

If you are going to paint cabinet doors, try rubbing a small amount of Vaseline on the hinges. That will make removing the paint easier.

THE RIGHT ORDER
Paint windows and trim using a 1½-inch tapered brush and do the crossbars first then the frames and end up with the sills.

SIZE MATTERS
If you are painting walls use a 3"-5" wide brush.

A REAL WINNER
If you are sure you will use up all the paint in a can, try punching a few holes near the rim you are removing the paint from. The paint that is wiped off the brush will go back into the can.

CEILING STAINS BEGONE
Water stains on a ceiling can be unsightly and can be eliminated most of the time by just blotting the area with a small amount of chlorine bleach. Older spots need a little more attention.

TENNIS ANYONE
If you are going to paint a ceiling, try cutting a tennis ball in half and placing half on the brush to catch the drips.

CHOOSING THE RIGHT PAINT BRUSH

Paint brush bristles are set in a base of solid resin to hold them together and will be either natural bristles (best is hog) or a synthetic fiber. The best brushes have bristles that taper from a thick base to a narrow tip. The narrow tip gives the brush flexibility and is a sign of a quality brush. The best brushes have longer bristles so that they will hold more paint.

Unfinished wood handles are best and will not slip out of your hand. If you are going to paint with an oil-based paint try and find a good hog-hair brush.

Natural-bristle brushes should not be used for water-based (latex) paints since the bristles will absorb water and swell up. Use nylon or polyester bristle brushes with water-based paints.

ROLLER INFO

For semi-gloss and glossy finishes use a roller with less than a ¼ inch nap. When you are applying flat paints on a medium-smooth surface use a roller that is 3/8" to 1" thick.

PAINTING A POPCORN CEILING

If you have more than one room to do, it is best to rent an airless sprayer and get it over with. If you only have one room use a roller with a 1 ¾" nap and thin the paint with a pint of the appropriate thinner. The first coat does not have to cover but it will strengthen the popcorn material so that it will be easier to place the second coat on.

PREPARATION TIPS BEFORE PAINTING

- Be sure and thoroughly clean the surface.
- Repair any damage to the wall, such as nail holes or cracks, with spackling then sand off and allow to fully dry.
- Always follow manufacturer's instructions on the can.
- Mask off areas that may be a problem with masking tape.

TAKING CARE OF YOUR BRUSHES

- Clean the brush as soon as you finish the job.
- Always remove any loose bristles by tapping against a hard surface.
- Remove all excess paint.
- Wrap bristles in paper to store so that dust will not settle on them.
- Don't use paintbrushes for any other liquid chemical that it was not specifically made for.
- Always allow the brushes to dry fully between uses. Never use a wet brush.

SOFTEN, HARD PAINT BRUSHES

The following ingredients will be needed:

½	Gallon of cool tap water
1	Cup of baking soda (fresh)
¼	Cup of white vinegar

Place the ingredients into a medium pot and mix well, then place the brushes in and boil them until they become soft.

BRUSH WILL LAST LONGER

If you soak a new oil paintbrush in a solution of linseed oil for about 24 hours before you use it, the brush will last longer and be much easier to clean up. If you prefer you could just soak the brush in a small container of water with a capful of fabric softener in it.

TOOL & PAINT BRUSH CLEANER-UPPER
The following ingredients will be needed:

- 1 ½   Cup of baking soda (fresh)
- ½   Cup of white vinegar
- 3   Tablespoons of rubbing alcohol
- 1   Gallon of cool tap water

Place all the ingredients into a bucket and mix well. It works great on tools and paintbrushes, and always store away from children.

COUGH, COUGH, HACK, HACK
When paint cans state, "adequate ventilation" it means just that. The number of people that end up in emergency rooms every year from breathing in paint fumes is probably in the hundreds. Vapor buildup indoors is a real problem if you can't get enough air moving in the room to keep the fumes down. Be sure and wear a "dual-cartridge" mask if you feel that there is not adequate ventilation.

PAINTING (EXTERIOR)

Exterior paints are usually more expensive than interior paints since they contain more resins and ingredients to make them last for a longer period of time. Most also contain more pigments giving them a deeper and richer color. The exterior paints can be purchased in two varieties similar to interior paints: water-based or oil-based paints.

COMPARING EXTERIOR PAINTS & PRIMERS

Acrylic latex
The best quality latex paints will contain 100% acrylic resins since vinyl are not as durable. The latex will dry faster and is capable of covering almost any building material, which even includes masonry and primed metals.

Alkyd paint
The most common type of solvent-thinned paint! It contains almost all of the properties of oil-based paints but it will dry more rapidly and have excellent hiding ability. It has a thick consistency, which makes it somewhat difficult to apply, but it will level smoother than latex.

Marine
Produced especially for boats, provides a durable finish on both wood and metal trim. It is very expensive and not appropriate for large areas. Its gooey consistency makes it somewhat difficult to work with.

Masonry
This type of paint includes latex, Portland cement, alkyd, and rubber with some actually serving as their own primers. You need to seal masonry with a clear primer. Easy to apply paint!

Metal
The solvent or water-thinned types include priming ingredients that are rust-resisting helping to cover small bare spots. Be sure and prime all bare metal using rusty-metal primer to seal the rusty spots. You can use a brush, spray, or roller to produce a broad range of finishes.

Oil
Oil paint takes about 12-48 hours to dry and has a strong odor as well as making cleanup somewhat difficult. It has excellent durability but the drying time sometimes causes problems with bugs and dust sticking to it as well as rain.

Porch & Deck
The most durable are alkyd and polyurethane types since they produce a hard, washable surface. However, some of the types are formulated for concrete surfaces and preparation methods will vary. The colors are also limited. It is relatively easy to apply since you just pour it out on the floor and work it outward using a long-handled roller.

Primers
New wood or metal should be primed according to the paint manufacturer's instructions to kill any stains or if you are going to apply latex paint over any existing solvent-based paint. The most effective is alcohol-based primer but solvent and latex types will work as well. Remember porous surfaces will soak up a lot of primer.

Stains

Both solvent and latex paints will provide transparent, semi-transparent, or opaque finishes when used on natural wood siding and trim.

Some of the stains may include a preservative and even offer a weathered look. They can be applied almost anyway that you are comfortable with such as spraying, rolling, or using a brush.

Vinyl latex
This paint is easy to cleanup, has good durability, and is fast drying. You can apply it over a damp surface and it is naturally mildew-proof but cannot be painted over a previous solvent-painted surface. Don't thin out latex and try and apply with one stroke using a brush or roller. Working it out too fast may cause thin spots.

MY HOUSE HAS SCALES
If the paint is cracking and it looks like the scales on the back of an alligator, it was probably caused by the application of a very hard coating, such as alkyd enamel, placed over a more flexible coating, such as latex primer. Remove the old paint and scrape the surface well then power wash the surface and sand it before painting again.

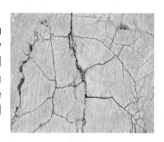

ROUGH SURFACE IS NOT GOOD
If the surface to be painted is rough and crinkly, the paint has formed a skin, which is caused by the paint being applied too thick or the paint was applied in too hot weather, or cool damp weather. It can also be caused by painting over a contaminated surface. Scrape and sand the substrate to remove the wrinkled coating.

BASIC EXTERIOR PAINTING PREPARATION TIPS

SURFACE PREPARATION
- ◆ Be sure and tie-back any bushes and limbs that may get in the way. Cover all plants and work area with plastic sheets or tarps. Make sure you turn off the air conditioner and any exhaust fans in the paint areas. Best to cover and seal the air conditioner unit and tape it down.
- ◆ All shutters should be removed as well as the hardware. Close all storm windows if they are still on or remove them. Make any repairs to the siding and trim that is necessary and be sure to fill any rotted or insect damaged areas with wood filler.

322

- This is the best time to re-glaze the windows in any area that needs it. Carefully remove any old putty with a putty knife or small chisel being careful not to break the window.
- Starting at the top of the wall, scrape any loose paint or debris from the siding and trim.
- Use a power sander to remove any paint particles and to smooth out any wood-filled areas. Be careful not to damage the siding since the sander cuts through paint very quickly. Make sure that the sander you use is not too powerful or it will leave swirl marks. Speed should be around 10,000 rpm.
- Use a brush or stiff broom to wash the siding and all the trim with a solution of TSP (trisodium phosphate) or even better a phosphate-free cleaner. If you have a pressure washer use it or rent one for a really clean job.

- Be sure and rinse the entire house with a garden hose until the water runs clear. If you used TSP then rinse the house twice to be sure that all the solution has been cleaned off.
- Allow the siding to dry thoroughly for about 2 days before painting.

PAINTING EXTERIOR WALLS

- Be sure and wait until the surface is completely dry and that there is no rain in the forecast.
- Always apply primer to any bare siding and make sure you allow the primer to dry thoroughly.
- You can use a brush, roller, or sprayer, whichever you prefer.
- If there are any masonry surfaces they must be primed for the best results, especially if water stains are present or if glossy paint is to be top coated.
- Remember cedar and redwood contains resins that will bleed through water-based paints. Be sure and use oil-based paint and primers on wood.
- Always paint the roof trim and soffits before the walls if they are going to be painted a different color. This will prevent any trim paint from dripping on the freshly painted walls.
- Use a corner roller or trim brush to paint the inside corners and around the trim.
- If you have clapboard or shingle siding, be sure and cut in the lip (bottom edge) of the siding before you paint the face.
- Whether you use a brush or a roller, always start at the top of the wall. Work as far as you can reach to your left and pull the roller or brush toward you. Finish the stroke right in front of you and repeat until the block of siding you can reach is painted then use the same method on the right

side.

- If using a brush, start each stroke to the right by feathering the brush. Feathering means placing the surface of the brush against the siding gradually, instead of abruptly. This will eliminate a definite start line and will make it easier to blend the next block of strokes into the present block.
- Next blend the two strokes together in front of you and work quickly. It is critical to blend the new stroke into the completed stroke while the paint is still wet to avoid overlap marks. Never stop painting in the middle of a section. Paint into the corner of the house so that the paint color is consistent.

SURFACE HAS A CRINKLY LOOK AND A SKIN
The paint was probably applied too thickly or was applied during very hot weather or the humidity was too high. Another cause is that the primer was not cured enough before it was painted over. Scrape and sand off the paint to remove the wrinkled surface and be sure and allow enough time for the primer to dry adequately before applying a coat of paint.

MY SKIN IS GETTING WRINKLED
Oil-based paints are hard to remove from your skin! Most people tend to use kerosene, mineral spirits, or paint thinner to remove the paint, but these products are hazardous to the skin, cause irritation, and can be absorbed into the body. Try using vegetable oil to remove oil-based paints safely without damaging the skin.

MY WAX IS BLEEDING
Wax bleed areas look similar to mildew areas but wax bleed area will bead water and mildew areas will not. These areas come from waxy substances in the reconstituted wood products used to make hardboard siding. They can be caused by failing to apply a proper primer to hardboard before applying the topcoat.

HOW BROWN I AM.............
Brown discolorations on the paint surface is usually due to the migration of tannins from the substrate through the paint film and usually comes from poor priming or not sealing the surface properly.

NOT HOLDING A GLOSSY LOOK

The loss of luster in a topcoat can be caused by direct sunlight, which degrades the binder and the pigment of paint. This causes the paint to "chalk" and lose its gloss. It is often caused by using an interior paint outdoors or a paint of lower quality.

324

Poor surface preparation can also cause this problem.

I'M TOO IMMATURE TO BE PAINTED
Masonry must be cured for a full year before being painted if you use vinyl acrylic latex paint. The lime in the masonry must have a chance to react with carbon dioxide from the air or it will attack the paint. At least allow the masonry to cure for 30-60 days before painting. If this is not possible then apply a high quality latex severe weather primer followed by premium latex house paint.

PAINT-SPRAYING TIPS

Paint-sprayer is usually best for a large surface area. The following are tips when using a sprayer to get a smoother, better appearing job.

- ✓ Make sure you always strain the paint before you place the paint in an airless paint sprayer. Occasionally even new paint may contain material that will clog the sprayer filter.
- ✓ Be sure and keep the sprayer in motion to avoid a buildup. You should always start the gun moving before pressing the trigger and be sure and release the trigger before stopping the gun at the end of a stroke.
- ✓ If you are using an oil-based paint make sure to clean out the sprayer with Martini Paint Solvent. Wipe out the canister first with a rag and then wash it good with solvent.
- ✓ Use lacquer thinner to clean the tip after using a water-based paint.
- ✓ Remember tips only last for 35-40 gallons and should be replaced after that.

I'M PEELING
This is caused by poor adhesion, seeping moisture through un-caulked joints, worn-out caulk, or leaks in the roof or walls. You need to identify where the moisture is coming from and correct the problem before re-painting.

REDDISH-BROWN STAINS THROUGH THE NAIL HEADS
Non-galvanized nails were used and they are rusting or if you used galvanized nails, they have been subjected to sanding or excessive weathering. If you use non-galvanized, they must be countersunk. Try filling the hole with a high quality, water-based all- acrylic or siliconized acrylic caulk.

NOW I'M FLAKING OFF

This usually appears as hairline cracks, then flakes or chips away. It is often caused by using a poor quality paint that has poor adhesion and flexibility.

It is also caused by over-thinning and spreading the paint too thin. This usually means cleaning off the old paint and re-painting the whole area.

I'M BLISTERING

This results from localized loss of adhesion and lifting of the paint away from the underlying surface. It can be caused by applying oil-based or alkyd paint over a damp surface. It can also be caused by moisture seeping into the home through the exterior walls. Scrape or sand the area and prime it with a quality latex or oil primer then re-paint.

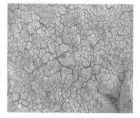

THERE ARE SPOTS EVERYWHERE!

These spots are mildew and they form on areas that are damp or areas that receive little or no sunlight. Lower quality paints will also cause this to happen more frequently or painting over a surface that has mildew already on it, which frequently happens. If you are not sure if it's mildew or not, try placing a small amount of household bleach on the area. If it bleaches away, it's mildew!

I'M FADING AWAY! HELP ME!

This can be caused by excessive lightening of the paint or paint on a southern exposure to the sun. It is usually caused by using poor quality paint or interior paint outside. If the paint is going to be exposed to a southern exposure, be sure and purchase a paint that has a UV protectant in it.

CHEAPSKATE!

The paint easily accumulates dirt and dust particles, which is usually caused by using poor quality paint as well as air pollution. Clean off the dirt with a scrub brush and mild detergent solution.

BEWARE OF BAD SURFACES

Most paint failures are caused by painting on hot, moist surfaces. Keep an eye on the sun and paint the shady side first then as the sun moves away from each side, go ahead and paint it. Painting in the sun will almost always cause a problem.

MOISTURE VS OIL-BASED PAINTS

Moisture will affect an oil-based paint so be sure and wait until all the dew is gone before painting an area. The moisture from latex paints will not be affected by the dew. If it rains it would be best to wait at least 24 hours before using oil-based paints for the best results.

NAIL HEADS & LATEX PAINT

All exposed nail heads need to be touched up with a primer or they may rust and cause stains. This is more important when painting with a latex paint.

ALL MIXED UP??????

Even though the paint is thoroughly mixed by machine when you purchase it, it would be best if you check it again before starting to use it. Best to pour half into another can then mix both halves with a wooden stirrer until all the pigment is well blended. Double-check it by pouring it back and forth a few times

PROTECT ME!

Your plants and shrubs need to be well protected from the paint. Be sure and cover them with a lightweight drop cloth.

NO SMELL PAINT

If you add 1 capful of vanilla extract to the paint can, it will reduce the odor considerably. The vanilla will not affect the consistency or color and will only affect the odor.

HOW TO ESTIMATE EXTERIOR PAINT NEEDS

❖ First determine the average height of the house. If the house has a flat roof, measure the distance from the foundation to the eaves. If the roof is pitched, add two feet.
❖ Next measure the distance around the house (around the foundation).
❖ Then multiply the average height by the distance around the foundation, which will equal the surface area.

❖ Divide the surface area by 500 (the average American gallon of paint covers 500 square feet). Your results will equal the number of gallons required for one coat on the house.
❖ For the trim, the average six to eight room house will require 1 gallon of paint.

HANG 'EM HIGH

After cleaning your brushes thoroughly and rinsing them well, be sure and hang them up to dry allowing all the excess water to fall out and the brush air dry.

GREAT SECRET

Since you may have to go back and do some touch-up or re-paint an area, it is best to save your brush. You can just save the brush without extensive clean-up if you are going to use the same paint by just wrapping the brush in plastic wrap and placing the brush in the refrigerator.

The right tools make a big difference

CHAPTER 24

TIPS FOR EMERGENCIES

PORTABLE ELECTRIC GENERATORS

MY HOUSE JUST FIZZLED OUT!
To avoid a serious problem, never connect a portable electric generator directly to the house wiring. This can be a deadly mistake to you as well as the neighborhood. The problem is called "back-feeding" and the pole transformer can then "set up" or increase the back-feed to many thousands of volts and can even kill a utility lineman who is making repairs a long distance from your home. This can cause extensive damage to your home as well as the utility equipment in your entire area.

The best suggestion if you need to connect it to your home is to have a licensed electrician come to your home and install a transfer switch, which will transfer power from the utility pole to your generator power.

HELP! I'M GETTING LOADED
Never operate too many appliances that exceed the output rating of the generator. Overloading it will cause serious damage to appliances and electronics. Only use a portable generator when they are really needed and only to power essential equipment or appliances.

THERE'S A FUNNY SMELL IN HERE OR IS THERE?
Portable generators use an internal combustion engine just like your car. The engine emits deadly carbon monoxide gas and should never be placed in the house or in a closed garage.
It should only be operated outdoors or in a well-ventilated area. Be sure that the exhaust is away from any vents that enter the home. Always place it under a tent or other type of canopy.

PLUG IT IN, PLUG IT IN
Be sure and plug any appliances into the generator using heavy-duty extension cords that are outdoor-rated. Overloaded cords may place you at risk of fire or damage the appliance. Never run the cords under a rug.

GROUNDED AGAIN!
Be sure and check the manufacturer's instruction booklet for the proper grounding information.

KA-BOOM
Never store fuel indoors and be sure they are in safety containers and ventilated. Remember, the vapors can travel along the ground and even be ignited by a pilot light from a hot water heater in the garage. They can even be ignited by the electric arc created by just turning on a light switch. Never try to refuel an electric generator while it is still running.

GET OUT THE ALOE
Keep kids away from the generator while it is running since many of the parts are hot enough to give them a serious burn.

ROOF RETROFITTING

GABLED ROOFS
During a hurricane the end walls take a very bad beating, and if not properly braced, it can collapse. It is recommended that you install 2X4's the length of the roof, overlapping the ends of the 2X4's across two trusses. The gable end trusses are attached to the top of the gable end walls. The bottom of the truss needs to be securely nailed to the top of the wall and then braced to adjacent trusses. This will stop the wind from pushing or pulling the gable end at the critical points.

To secure the gable end wall, just fasten 8-foot long braces to the bottom chord of the gable truss and the adjacent trusses with 16d nails. Be sure that the braces are perpendicular to the truss and spaced at a maximum of 4-feet on center. Also be sure and tie back the gable truss with at least one 8-foot long brace along the ridge of the roof to several of the interior trusses.

SHINGLES

Normally shingles are not designed to withstand hurricane force winds. To make the shingles more secure you will need to cement the shingle tabs to the underlying shingles. Place two spots of quick-setting asphalt cement about the size of a quarter under each tab with a putty knife, or use a caulking gun. Press the tab onto the adhesive and be sure and cement all the tabs throughout the roof. Be careful not to bend them any farther than necessary when you apply the adhesive.

HURRICANE STRAPS

For added protection install metal hurricane straps to provide a measure of strength and safety for the roof to wall connection. The practice of toenailing the trusses or rafters is often not sufficient to hold the roof in place in high winds.

SHUTTERS

Impact-resistant shutters should be placed over all windows and doors to protect them from wind-borne objects but they can also reduce damage from sudden pressure changes if a window or door is broken.

SECURING ENTRY DOORS

Be sure and install head and foot bolts on the inactive door if you have double-entry doors. The doors should have three hinges and a dead bolt security lock, which has a minimum one-inch bolt throw length. The bolts should extend into the door header and through the threshold into the subfloor.

SECURITY

SECURITY TIPS

> Never leave house keys in common locations such as under the doormat or under a rock near the front door. Put a key in a small container and bury it under a plant.
> When you leave home place the phone ringer on low tone so it can't be heard from the outside.
> Use automatic timers to turn TV's, lights, and radios on at different times.
> Don't cancel your newspaper or mail delivery, have someone pick it up.

- Be sure that your door hinges are not on the outside.
- Place safety bars on all glass sliding doors.
- Cover your garage windows so that a thief cannot see if the cars are gone.
- Be sure that you have a secure deadbolt on all entry doors.
- Notify your alarm company that you will be gone for an extended period and provide an emergency number.

FAMILY DISASTER PLAN

- Be sure and list any type of hazard that might affect the family in case of storm surge, mudslide, earthquake, flooding, or wind.
- Locate a safe room in your home or the location of a community shelter.
- Determine escape routes from your home to a safe location as well as an alternate route.
- Be sure and have an out-of-state contact for all family members. Use just one contact.
- Make a plan for your pet if you have to evacuate.
- Make sure that all children know how to dial 911 and have emergency numbers near the telephone.
- Check your insurance coverage and remember flood insurance is a separate policy.
- Stock non-perishable emergency supplies in your disaster supply kit and have it handy so that it can be moved easily.
- Be sure that you have a NOAA weather radio and replace the batteries every 6 months.
- Make sure you have a good first aid kit and have taken a CPR and first aid class.

DISASTER KIT

- Water – at least 1 gallon per person for 3-6 days.
- Food – enough for 3-6 days. Non-perishable packaged or canned foods and a non-electric can opener. Snack foods, paper plates, utensils and cooking fuel and tools if applicable.
- Blankets & pillows.
- Clothing, seasonal rain gear, sturdy shoes.
- First aid kit, prescription drugs, general medicine.
- Special items – for any elderly or infant needs.
- Toiletries, hygiene items, moisture wipes.
- Flashlight & batteries.
- Radio, battery operated with TV if possible and extra batteries.
- Cash in small bills.
- Keys to house and car.
- Toys, books and games.

- Important documents in a waterproof container. Checkbooks, social security card, birth certificates, etc.
- Tools – Keep a small set in your kit.
- Vehicle fuel tank filled.
- Pet care items and records. Carrier or cage & current picture. If you have to take your pet to a shelter, you will need to have a current shot record.
- Medications.

LOCATION, LOCATION, LOCATION

- If ordered to evacuate never hesitate or delay your departure and if possible leave before the order is given. Even a slight delay may result in much longer travel times, as congestion will worsen.
- Best to select a destination that is as close as possible to your home, preferably in the same county or minimize the distance you need to travel to reach the shelter. Remember hotels and motels will fill up fast.
- If you have to evacuate to another county or far distance, be prepared with extra gas and supplies for a long ride with the possibility of no available gas station.
- If you can stay with a friend or relative near your home it would be best if their location were safe.
- If going to a hotel or motel, make reservations as soon as possible.
- Use a shelter as the last resort, not your first choice.

TIPS TO STOP KITCHEN FIRES

- **Fire in a Pan** – Don't move the pan, turn off the burner and the fan in the range hood. Place an oven mitt on your hand or use a hot pad and slide a lid that is larger than the pan over the top to suffocate the fire. Be sure and slide it on, don't place it over the top. You can also pour baking soda on top of the fire to put it out.

- ➢ **Fire on Stove Top** – If the fire has spread to the stovetop, immediately turn off the burner and fan in the hood, and pour a generous amount of baking soda on the fire until it is out. A fire extinguisher is the first choice.
- ➢ **Fire in the Oven** – Turn off the oven and close the door. This will sometimes put out the fire. If not, have a fire extinguisher handy and use it.
- ➢ **Fire in Electrical Outlet** – Put out the fire with a fire extinguisher then turn off the main power to the house and call fire department.
- ➢ **Fire in a Wall Switch** – Stand clear of the switch and turn it off with a long handled wooden spoon or broom handle. Shut off all power to the house and call an electrician before you restore power.

WATER STORAGE FOR EMERGENCIES

Remember, in case of emergency, you can live without food for a period of time, but you cannot live without water.

- ➢ There are two types of water: commercial and tap. Bottled water is safer to store for drinking purposes and emergency storage, but the bulk of your water supply will probably be tap water due to the cost.
- ➢ One gallon of water a day is considered the minimum supply for drinking and 1 gallon per person per day for cooking, washing, etc. Two people will require about 56 gallons of water to survive for two weeks. Forget the daily showers.

- ➢ Choose your water containers carefully and pick ones that will not leach chemicals into the water. Glass is excellent and plastic is fine as long as both are thoroughly cleaned before being used. Camping jugs and empty soda bottles are fine. A 2-liter soda bottle holds about 2-quarts of water.
- ➢ If you are unsure of the quality of the water or need to use suspect water in an emergency, place 10 drops of liquid chlorine bleach into 1-gallon of water. Adjust the number of drops for smaller containers. Boiling the water is always preferred if you have the heat available.
- ➢ Emergency water sources may be from a waterbed, pond, pool or hot tub, but should always be purified before drinking. These sources may best be used for toilet flushing. The water in your hot-water heater or toilet tank (not the toilet) may be used for drinking after purification. If you suspect a water shortage clean the bathtub until it is spotless then fill it with cold water.
- ➢ Stored water should be rotated at least every six months. The containers should be emptied and cleaned thoroughly before you refill them.

WHERE OH WHERE HAS THE WATER GONE?

- To produce food for one year............................. 1 million gallons
- To grow one large potato............................... 18 gallons
- To produce one-pat of margarine.....................85 gallons
- To produce one loaf of bread...........................56 gallons
- To manufacture one pint of whiskey..................... 110 gallons
- To produce one pound of flour.........................350 gallons
- To produce one pound of beef..........................4,850 gallons
- To grow one ear of corn................................ 61 gallons
- To produce a lettuce dinner salad......................... 6 gallons
- To grow one tomato..................................... 3 gallons
- To produce one cola soft drink.......................10 gallons
- Taking a bath... 30 gallons
- Watering the lawn...................................... 200 gallons
- Brushing your teeth..................................1 gallon
- Washing a car.. 100 gallons

SAFE WATER DRINKING HOTLINE - (800) 426-4791 (ask for free booklet)

GREENPEACE INTERNATIONAL - (202) 462-1177

CHAPTER 25

HOUSEHOLD TIPS

OFF WITH THEIR SHOES

Approximately 75% of all dirt in the home is brought in on people's shoes. If you think about all the places you have been during the day and what you have stepped in, you start to realize that some of that dirt, grime, lawn chemicals, sand, gum, feces, mud, soot and even rubber from car tires may be on the soles of your shoes. The thicker the soles and the type of special soles that are deep cut are perfect to carry all sorts of garbage into your home.

Many of the churches of the world and museums will not allow people to enter unless they remove their shoes or at least wear special disposable slippers or other type of shoe coverings to protect the carpeting and exhibits. In every oriental culture, shoes are not allowed in the house.

Grandma had a small cabinet near her front door as you entered with slippers she kept cleaned.

SHOE RULES FOR PEOPLE & PETS

- Use the mat outside the door to scuff your shoes.
- Put on a pair of slippers or go in your stocking feet.
- All company had the same rules, which were on a little plaque by the front door.
- There was a boot brush hanging by the back door, which is where any workers entered.
- In winter you had to brush the bottoms of your clothing to get off any salt and snow, which may damage the carpets or furniture.
- Use a lint roller on your pet when it comes in from the outside to remove any debris it picked up as well as fleas.

336

EASY TO CARE HOUSE PLANTS

I've got a green thumb.

HOUSE PLANTS THAT ARE EASY TO CARE FOR

Philodendron
This is one of the easiest plants to care for and really hard to kill unless you never water it. There are over 300 varieties and the plant will thrive in air-conditioned spaces as well as dimly lit areas.

Cactus
It is a member of the succulent family of plants and stores water in case you forget to water it occasionally. There are many varieties, some of which have prickly spines and colorful flowers. It does need sun and dry soil to do well.

Spider Plant
Looks like a big spider and likes warm, dry air with lots of sunlight and water, however, it will put up with tougher conditions.

Dracaena
Available in a number of varieties, however, the most popular is similar to a palm. It can grow as high as 15 feet and it thrives in a variety of light conditions ranging from full sun to deep shade.

Aspidistra
This is a very rugged plant that has large glossy leaves and will thrive in a dark, forgotten corner, but likes a little sunlight occasionally. Found in the outdoor section of the nurseries, but well indoors.

NO DUST ARTIFICIAL PLANT
You will never have to dust an artificial plant if you spray the plant with hairspray about every 2 months. They will not attract dust and retain their vivid colors.

EGG WATER BOOSTER

After the water cools from boiling eggs, use it to water your plants. The water contains growth-stimulating minerals. Crushed eggshells are good too on top of the soil.

SNOW FOR PLANTS

Try melting snow and allow it to come to room temperature before using it to water your plants. Snow contains trace minerals that the plant can use.

RAINDROPS KEEP FALLING............................

It's a good idea to collect rainwater and water your plants with it. The plants will get a healthy boost and the leaves will sparkle.

TOGETHERNESS

If you place a number of plants next to each other or at least near each other, they will create a moist environment and be healthier.

POOR SICK PLANT

If you have a houseplant that appears to be sick, just place a clove of garlic in with the plant and cover the plant with a plastic bag. Be sure and keep the soil moist and don't seal up the bag. Also, keep the plant out of the sunlight.

FEED ME, FEED ME

Houseplants need to be fed regularly with fertilizer or they may become nutrient deficient. Just use a commercial plant food and follow directions.

HOME ODOR & CLEANING PROBLEMS

In The Kitchen

- ❖ Be sure and air out the house regularly by opening windows and doors if screened.
- ❖ Bowls of white vinegar, charcoal briquettes, or coffee grounds placed around will absorb odors.
- ❖ Be sure and change furnace and air conditioner filters regularly.
- ❖ When vacuuming, place a few drops of eucalyptus oil in the bag.
- ❖ Rub a half of a lemon over a cutting board when done.

- Run the disposal every time you place food in and run plenty of water to wash it away.
- Grind up a few slices or ½ a lemon in the disposal occasionally.
- Run hot water in your kitchen drains every day.
- Wash out all cans before placing them into the garbage or trash compactor.
- If you don't use the dishwasher every day, place some baking soda on the bottom.
- Never buy a glass-top kitchen table since it scratches too easily. If you do buy glass, make sure it is colored to hide some of the damage.
- The cushions on kitchen chairs should be easily removed for fabric replacement.
- Have plastic covers for the chairs when the grandkids come over.
- Store all glassware upside down to prevent dust and critters from getting in.
- Be sure that you do not use liners for your cabinets; that has a bug deterrent in it.
- Never dry silver on a rubber mat since it causes the silver to become darker.
- Never wash crystal in hot water and then rinse with cold water or it may crack.
- If china has a gold trim, be sure and never wash it in very hot water since the gold may run.

In The Closet

- Place cedar shavings in an old stocking and hang it in the closet.
- Never place smelly clothes back in the closet. If you wear them, wash them!
- Allow closet doors to remain open occasionally to let them air out.
- Place a few drops of your favorite fragrant essential oil on a cotton ball and place it into the closet.

In The Bathroom

- Every week, place a small handful of baking soda down the shower drain followed by some white vinegar. Wait 10 minutes and then flush with hot water.
- Unwrap fragrant soaps and leave them in a basket. This will make the bathroom smell better and will make the soap last twice as long by reducing the moisture in the bar.

339

- Keep a scented candle and matches in the toilet area.
- Never wallpaper a bathroom that gets easily steamed.
- Always paint using high-gloss finish paint since it cleans easily and repels soil.
- Avoid water getting on the floor by weighting down the bottom of the shower curtain.

In The Kid's Room

- Avoid toy boxes and trunks since toys always get jumbled and the one they want always end up on the bottom.
- Try and rotate toys every 6 months so that the child will not get tired of them.
- Be sure and lower the closet rods to the child's height.
- Mount a battery-operated light in the closet if there is no light and easily reached switch.
- Buy a bed with built-in storage drawers.
- Purchase children's furniture that sits on the floor and has no legs raising it up so that toys and dirt can get underneath.
- Never wallpaper a kid's room. Paint with washable paint.
- Be sure and only purchase washable art supplies.
- If you have vinyl flooring in the room, be sure and place a washable carpet over a large area.

In The Bedroom

- Place a used fabric-softener sheet between the mattress and box spring.
- Place fresh flowers in the bedroom.
- Place some lemon peels in a small porous cloth bag and place in drawers.
- Never allow food in kid's rooms.
- Do not allow pets to sleep in the bedroom or bed.
- Place a bar of fragrant soap in a drawer to keep it smelling great.
- Purchase quality linens with a thread count of at least two hundred per square inch and be sure that it is non-ironing.
- The mattress should be turned twice a year.

In The Pet's Bed

- ❖ Brush some baking soda on the pet's coat between baths.
- ❖ Place a few drops of essential lavender oil in the pets bedding to get rid of fleas and make it smell nice.
- ❖ Place a thin layer of baking soda in the litter box before adding the litter.

In The Fireplace

- ❖ Make the wood smell fragrant by placing a log of sweet-smelling citrus or juniper on the fire.
- ❖ Before lighting, add a few peels of dried citrus, cinnamon sticks, or pine cones among the logs before you light them.
- ❖ Use some dried fragrant herbs as part of your kindling.

I CAN HELP, DON'T THROW ME OUT

Don't dispose of all the ashes. A good fire needs a two-inches carpet of ash under the grate. This will help the fire start faster and help to radiate heat into the room.

Miscellaneous Tips

- ❖ Hang an old stocking filled with charcoal briquettes in the garage or basement.
- ❖ Keep a few cinnamon sticks wrapped in cheesecloth in cupboards.
- ❖ Place a fabric-softener sheet in suitcases that are not used very often.
- ❖ After you finish a bottle of perfume, leave it open in a drawer that might have an odor.
- ❖ Place a charcoal briquette in a filing cabinet to keep the papers from becoming musty.

YUK, DIRTY ASHTRAY

With the exception of glass and crystal, you can spray furniture polish on the bottom of ashtrays and the residues of the ashes will not stick to the ashtray.

KITCHEN CLEAN-UP EASY

❖ To clean the microwave easily, just place a cup of water with 2 tablespoons of baking soda in it and run the microwave for a few minutes then just clean the fallout.
❖ Use a grout sealer on all grout.
❖ Avoid glass doors on all appliances since they are hard to clean.
❖ Never use flocked or grass-covered wallpaper in the kitchen since they absorb grease.
❖ The best kitchen floor for easy cleaning is a vinyl floor with a low-gloss finish.
❖ Have glasses with the kid's names on them.
❖ Place honey or cooking oil on a plate when stored in the cabinet.
❖ Clean the blender with a soap shake.
❖ Use aluminum liners in the oven.

PROTECT ME! COVER ME UP

Grandma always protected her wall-to-wall carpet and hated to wash it. Whenever the grandkids came over she always had an old, clean piece of carpeting that was rolled out for the kids to play on.

GUARD ME

Protect all fabrics with a Scotch-guard coating. Costs a little, but is worth every cent. Spills will not seep into the fabric before you are able to clean them up.

CHEAP WINES STAIN MORE

It is best to serve only quality wines, especially red wines. The inexpensive wines will stain the fabrics and carpets more easily since they contain higher concentration of colorant.

NEW GLASS FOR CLEANER WINDOWS

Weather Shield Manufacturing is making a glass called Kleen-Shield that has the ability to repel dirt, bugs and even water spotting using polymer that is like Teflon.

Natural Fabrics

Cotton
It is a very strong and versatile fabric that has excellent pilling resistance and good resistance to abrasion. If blended with any synthetic it will stand up to soil better.

Leather
Not a fiber but is very strong and resistant to abrasion. Dust and grime will cause it to crack eventually if it is not conditioned to stay supple.

Linen
This fabric is crisp and cool to the touch but it will stretch and wrinkle easily unless it is blended with other fabrics. It will resist moths and soil as well as being anti-static.

Silk
Strong, supple and drapes easily. It is easy to dye and will add luster when combined with other fabrics. It has poor abrasion resistance, spots easily and can be very difficult to clean.

Wool
Very resistant to abrasion, resilient and warm and is susceptible to moths and mildew. It is easy to keep up, especially when added to other fabrics.

Synthetic Fabrics

Acetate
Inexpensive, sunfast, drapes well but wrinkles easily and will damage easily unless it is blended with a stronger fabric.

Acrylic
It has good wrinkle and abrasion resistance qualities as well as being soft and retaining its shape well. Tends to darken when exposed to sunlight, however, it will repel soil, cleans up easily and blends well with many fibers.

Nylon
It is an excellent fabric that is soil, abrasion, and mildew resistant. It is very versatile and can be produced in tweed to silky velvets. But it does have a tendency to pill and fade over time but adds strength to any other fabric.

Olefin
Very resistant to soil, abrasion, and sunlight, but it is occasionally scratchy when touched.

Polyester
Relatively wrinkle-free and can handle sunlight well as being abrasion and water-based stain resistant. Sometimes feels a little stiff, absorbs grease stains but is stronger when cotton is added to it.

Rayon
It is a very silky and inexpensive fabric with the look and feel of a natural with the advantages of a synthetic. It will drape well, resists moths but may easily be subject to abrasion, fades easily, and wrinkles. It is best to purchase it when it is combined with nylon, cotton, or wool.

Vinyl
This is actually a fabric-backed plastic that will resist most stains, however, body oils and perspiration will cause it to harden. It tends to feel cold, which makes it a poor choice for a sofa covering but excellent for chair seats and benches. If there is an animal with claws around, never buy this type of fabric.

TO STAIN OR NOT TO STAIN
Spray on fabric protection will only make the fabric stain-resistant and not stain-proof. They will make spills and dirt stay on the fabric for a period of time allowing them to be cleaned up before they soak into the fabric. The protectors are available in two types: **silicone**, which can resist water-based stains, such as wine, juice, and milk and **fluorochemical**, which can resist both water-based as well as oil-based stains (mayonnaise, margarine, etc.).

WHY PAY WHEN IT'S FREE?

The majority of upholstery fabric manufacturer's spray their goods before they sell the fabric. When you purchase a sofa and the salesperson sells you the *"extra protection"* such as Scotchguard™, it may already be on the fabric.

NO DUST PICTURE HANGING
To prevent crumbles and drywall dust when hammering a nail into the wall, just place a cross of tape over the spot and pound away.

NO SCRATCHES, MY LADY
Always glue small felt pads on the bottoms of all lamps, ashtrays, vases or other knick-knack that you place on a glass tabletop to avoid scratches.

CHAPTER 26

WALLPAPER SECRETS

GENERAL INFORMATION:

There are many different kinds of wallpaper and you need to know what kind you are dealing with to solve any problem associated with repairing or cleaning it. If you are not familiar with the type of paper you have, try and bring a small piece to someone at a local paint and wallpaper store to identify the type of paper. Wallpaper will be either: washable, non-washable, or scrubbable. Wallpaper is easily damaged and best to know what you are doing if you try and repair it.

TIPS ON CHOOSING WALLPAPER

Burlap/Grass Cloth

May be used anywhere except in a hard use area where grease, moisture, or dirt may come into contact with the paper. Use mixed vinyl adhesive with ½ pint less water than the directions asks for. Apply two coats of the adhesive using a mohair paint roller cover for the best results. The cost is expensive for this type of paper.

Cloth-backed vinyl

This is one of the best papers for high traffic and high-humidity areas. Able to be stripped but is stiff and difficult to shape to the wall or high ceiling surfaces. If you purchase lightweight paper, it is best to use a wheat-paste adhesive and if the paper is heavy weight, use a vinyl adhesive.

Foil

It is used mainly in kitchens, bathrooms, and laundry areas since it is easy to clean. It is best to get a professional to hang this paper unless you have done it before. Be sure not to crease the paper when you are pasting and hanging it and be very careful around the electrical outlets and switches.

Flocked

Best not to use in high traffic or difficult to clean areas! Be sure and keep the adhesive from getting on the face of the paper. If it does it must be removed immediately with clear water and just blot it dry, never rub it. If the flocking does mat, use a suede brush to gently go over the area.

Hand-screened paper

Used to achieve a very stylish effect, but it is very expensive and usually made of paper that is easily damaged. Best to have a professional do the papering.

Paper-backed vinyl

Best used in high-traffic areas or locations that may have high moisture content. Can be stripped and the hand-printed vinyl must be trimmed. Be sure and use a lot of adhesive and do not stretch it when hanging it. If the seams do curl, paste them down with vinyl-to-vinyl adhesive and be sure and remove any excess adhesive immediately.

Solid paper

This is the lowest price wallpaper and can easily be damaged if scrubbed too hard. Best to only use it in low traffic areas and it is hard to strip. It should be hung with wheat-based adhesive. Work very carefully since the material will tear easily. Be sure and butt edges and roll all seams then clean immediately using a damp sponge.

Vinyl-coated paper

Can be used almost anywhere as long as it is not around too much moisture. It is more durable than solid paper and is usually hung one strip at a time. The excess adhesive needs to be cleaned immediately after each seam is rolled.

Wet-look vinyl

Best used in kitchens, laundry rooms and mudrooms, however, it may be best to apply a lining paper first since any surface imperfections will show through.

HIDE BEHIND THE DOOR

When you are going to wallpaper an entire room, it would be best to start behind a door with the first piece. It should be a spot that is not noticeable when a person first walks into a room. As you work your way around the room, you may have a mismatched pattern at the last corner. It won't be noticeable if you start at an inconspicuous location.

WALLPAPER REMOVAL METHODS

Removing wallpaper with no coating, such as vinyl

Step One: Apply a commercial stripper, which are usually sold in concentrated form. Use the manufacturer's guidelines and add the right amount of water. You may use a stripper with enzymes to break down the adhesive if you prefer. Use a sprayer or large sponge when using a liquid stripper or a roller for a gel.

Step Two: Remove the paper starting at the top using a putty knife or any broad knife and scrape gently. You must be careful or you will gouge the wall and that will mean another repair job.

Removing multiple layers of wallpaper that may have been painted over

Step One: First, use a scoring tool to score through the layer so that the stripper can get to the adhesive.

Step Two: Apply the stripper, allow it to remain for a short period then remove the paper with a putty knife or broad knife.

TAKE IT ALL OFF

As soon as the paper has been removed, you will need to remove the leftover adhesive residue. Dilute the stripper and wash the walls then rinse with clean water. You may still have to sand some areas if the adhesive has dried and really hardened over the years.

Removing strippable wallpaper

Step One: Just loosen the bottom of the wallpaper with a putty knife and gently pull the paper off from the loosened end. It should come off easily, if not you will have to use stripper.

Step Two: The majority of strippable wallpaper will leave a paper or fabric mesh backing on the wall. This will need to be removed using a stripper solution and be sure you follow the directions for removing wallpaper that has no coating.

NO HAMMER & CHISEL NEEDED

One of the best methods of removing wallpaper is to rent a steamer, which works very well, especially on plaster walls. However, steamers should only be used in the winter months (too hot in summer). Remember, the water dripping from the steamer is as hot as boiling water. Be sure and protect yourself when using a steamer.

SMOOTHIE

When applying wallpaper try using a paint roller instead of a sponge to smooth the paper out.

DON'T USE THE WRONG METHOD

Always test an inconspicuous area first (behind a door or a piece of furniture) before trying to clean wallpaper. Wallpaper should be vacuumed regularly to keep the dust off. Dust wallpaper downward from the ceiling with a vacuum or long-handled soft-bristled brush. You can also use a clean cloth tied around a broom handle. If cleaning flocked paper only use a vacuum soft-bristled brush.

HELP! I'M FALLING AWAY

If the wallpaper is loose, you will need to know the type of paper so that you can use the right paste to re-paste it. Check with the wallpaper store for the correct paste, especially for plastic-coated wallpapers. Normally, ordinary rubber cement will do the job on almost all papers.

MY WALLPAPER IS BUBBLING UP

You will need to cut across the blister (keeping within the pattern) with a very sharp single-edge razor or sharp X-Acto™ knife then lift the edges and place glue inside and smooth down with a damp cloth or sponge.

NEED A CHANGE HERE

When wallpapering be sure and change the water frequently since there is an adhesive buildup that will make the job more difficult.

BUY DOUGH OR PAY DOUGH

Commercial wallpaper cleaners, which look like a glob of dough, are available through most hardware and paint stores but it is still advisable to test an area first and then vacuum the area cleaned afterwards.

CLEANING WASHABLE WALLPAPER

These are papers with a plastic coating, which can be cleaned using minimal water on a clean cloth or sponge. Use the water very sparingly and never saturate the paper.

- **Grease Stain** - Hold several layers of white paper towels over the spot and press with a warm iron until the grease is absorbed.
- **Crayon Stain** - This means that you have to remove grease, wax and color. Try and first scrape off any excess with a dull butter knife then use a warm iron and the same method for grease stains. ***Best to buy washable crayons for kids.***

KEEPING GREASE IN ITS PLACE

If you have grease spots after removing old wallpaper, try applying a coat of clear varnish to the spots. The grease won't soak through to the new paper.

CLEANING SCRUBBABLE WALLPAPER

These papers are made from vinyl or special vinyl-impregnated paper and can be scrubbed with a foam cleaner or all-purpose detergent. Be sure and use a soft cloth or a sponge and rinse well. Never use any abrasive cleaners or you will scratch the finish. These are good papers for kids' rooms or rooms that will get a lot of use.

CLEANING FABRIC WALLPAPER

If they are vinyl-coated they will be easy to clean with a sponge dampened in soapy, water. If they are burlap or grass cloth, best to go by the manufacturers suggestions.

CLEANING VINYL WALLPAPER

Never use an abrasive cleaner, even a soft-scrub type. Also, never use any type of solvent cleaner or it will dissolve the ink. Use a mild dishwasher detergent and water for the best results.

I'M COMING APART AT THE SEAMS

If one or more of the seams are opening, just fill a plastic squeeze bottle with wallpaper paste. The spout should be small so that it will fit under the edge of the seam. Just one squirt and a little pressure on the area should solve the problem. Make sure you remove any excess with a damp cloth and smooth the area down with a roller.

HOW TO REPAIR WALLPAPER

Re-pasting

Lift the loose wallpaper and dampen with water, then spread a thin wallpaper paste underneath and smooth down with a clean damp cloth. Use a paste that is recommended for that particular type of paper.

To Remove a Blister (bubble)

Cut across the blister with a very sharp single-edged razor blade or X-acto knife along a line in the pattern. Lift the edges carefully then spread a thin layer of wallpaper paste underneath and smooth down with a damp, clean cloth.

Repairing Tears or Holes

Use a piece of leftover paper and tear a small piece to fit over the hole. Don't cut a piece since irregular edges will not be seen as easily as a sharp edge. Place wallpaper paste on it and paste it down.

PUSHPINS TO THE RESCUE

When you hang a sheet of wallpaper, especially the heavier or wider paper, try pushing several pushpins in to secure each strip near the ceiling while you are smoothing the paper downward. You can then remove the pins, cut away the excess paper, and smooth it out.

THE PROPER METHOD OF HANGING WALLPAPER

1. Purchase pre-pasted and strippable paper. Watch out for difficult patterns that may be hard to match.
2. Make sure that you repair any holes or cracks and sand them, if needed, making sure that the areas are perfectly smooth.
3. Be sure that the surface to be covered is clean and dry.
4. Before applying the wallpaper, make sure to paint any areas that will come into contact with the surface being covered. These include ceiling areas, moldings, window and door frames.
5. Best to apply a primer/size but there are a number of benefits to this step. First, it allows you to slide the paper onto the wall and reposition it easier. Second, it will make the bond stronger between the paper and the wall. Third, it will make it much easier to remove the paper when you want to remove it.

6. Next take a measurement and measure the width of your paper strip then subtract ½ inch. Near the top of the wall, you will need to measure the distance out from the corner and mark it with a pencil. Never use ink or it may bleed through the paper.

7. Drop a plumb line along the pencil mark (vertical line is needed from the top to the floor to hang the first strip). Tack a chalk-coated string at the pencil mark and tie a weight to the bottom of the string. When the weight stops moving, hold the bottom next to the wall and pull it away leaving a mark to go by. Remove the string now that you have made a plumb line.

8. Since wall and ceiling joints are rarely straight, make sure you drop a new plumb line whenever you turn a corner.

9. Cut the wallpaper in strips of paper 6 inches longer than the wall height, which will give you three inches of overhang at the top and the bottom of the wall. The extra paper will allow for the unevenness of walls and ceilings. Be sure and match the pattern of every strip, with the previous strip.

10. If you cut several strips at a time, be sure and number the strips as you cut them on the backside with a pencil. The strips must be hung in the right order so that the patterns will match up.

11. Wet the pre-pasted paper by rolling the paper from bottom to top keeping the pattern on the inside. Be sure and place the paper in the water tray gently and push it to get rid of the air bubbles. Allow the paper to remain in the water for the time recommended on the manufacturer's instructions.

12. When you remove the paper from the water do it very slowly and make sure that the adhesive back is wet and that there are no dry spots.

13. You now have to "book" the paper. This is done by simply folding the bottom of the paper to the middle (on the adhesive side) and then the top to the middle (looks like a book). Make sure that you do not crease the paper. The reason for this step is when the paper is placed into the water it expands unevenly and will spread at the seams if it is hung immediately. The booking step allows the paper to stabilize and the adhesive to become activated. The instructions from the manufacturer should tell you how long to keep the pieces booked.

14. To start hanging the first strip of paper, unbook the top half, remembering to leave the three inches on top, and be sure and line the edge of the paper with the plumb line before sliding it gently into place. If you pull it into place, you may damage the paper.

15. Use a smoothing tool to smooth out the paper. Always, start from the center of the paper moving up and down then smooth out the sides. This should eliminate all the air bubbles.

16. Trim off the excess paper on the top and bottom with a straight edge and a sharp utility knife or single edge razor blade device. Clean off the ceiling with a damp sponge from any adhesive that may have gotten there from the excess paper.

17. Now unfold the bottom half of the paper and smooth it out onto the wall. Make sure that it lines up with the plumb line.

18. Trim the corner and bottom excess paper and clean any surface such as the baseboards and floor where the adhesive might spread.

19. Use your damp sponge to wipe down the wallpaper making sure that there is no adhesive residue on the paper.

20. You need to remember to book each strip and hang the top of the next strip first, placing it as close to the first strip as possible. Always use both hands to slide the strips into their place, matching up the patterns as you go.

21. Continue doing exactly as you did for the previous pieces making sure you clean up the areas and paper before moving on.

22. After the paper has been on the wall for 15 minutes, lightly roll the seams using a seam-roller. Never push down on the roller hard or you will squeeze the adhesive out and the seams will eventually loosen up.

BE A SCRAP COLLECTOR

Always save scraps of wallpaper in case you will need to repair and area at a later date. You may also want the scraps to paper an outlet.

BORDER BEWARE

If you are going to hang a border, be sure and allow the wallpaper to dry for 2 days before adding the border. It is best to use a vinyl-over-vinyl adhesive instead of wetting the paper. Be sure and follow the directions to the letter and let the border sit for the recommended amount of time.

50 WAYS TO SAVE ELECTRICITY

KEEP YOUR ELECTRICITY BILLS DOWN AND SAVE ENERGY FOR THE FUTURE BY BEING AWARE OF THE MOST EFFICIENT WAYS TO USE ELECTRICITY.

COOKING

Keep the oven door closed. Every time you open it the temperature drops about 20^0F.

Cook several dishes at the one time. If you are cooking small items use the fry pan.

Keep food warm at 70-80^{0}F since higher temperatures waste electricity and over cook food.

Use oven heat for plate warming after cooking.

Use utensils that have flat bottoms and well-fitting lids! Make sure they cover hotplates.

To cook vegetables the water doesn't need to be boiling furiously - a gentle simmer is enough.

Use bright clean hotplate reflectors to send the heat upwards where it is wanted.

Pressure cookers can save up to 25% of power.

Thaw frozen foods before cooking - this saves about 15 minutes cooking per pound.

Don't boil water on a hotplate - use an electric kettle.

Make sure your oven door seals properly.

HEATING AND COOLING.

Have the ceiling insulated with at least 50mm of fibrous or foam insulation.

In timber framed or brick homes the walls should also be insulated. Block off any chimneys not being used - a lot of heat is lost there.

Unless you have full home conditioning close the doors of the room/s being heated or cooled. Doors and windows should fit well because draughts can waste a lot of energy. Close curtains to stop heat escaping.

See that air conditioner filters and condenser coils are kept clean.

Reverse cycle air-conditioners provide 2 to 2.5 times as much heat as an element type heater for the same electricity consumption.

It is best to shade windows during summer to keep sun off the glass.

Don't leave heating or cooling appliances on when rooms are unoccupied.

Use personal fans and ceiling fans for relief from hot weather. Fans cost much less to run than air conditioners.

Leave room conditioner "fresh air" and "exhaust air" controls in the closed positions unless you want to freshen the room air.

Set fan at high speed for a room conditioner to work most efficiently.

Evaporative coolers are very effective when installed correctly. The operating cost of an evaporative cooler is only a fraction of that of a refrigerated unit.

A student can be kept warm with a 150 watt infrared lamp fitted under the desk.

Electric blankets are the cheapest form of bedroom heating.

REFRIGERATION

Select a fridge that uses waste heat for defrosting etc. These fridges are usually cheaper to operate.

Buy the size you need. Extra capacity uses extra power.

If you already have a chest or upright freezer, buy just a refrigerator instead of a fridge freezer combination.

Defrost before the ice buildup is ¼-inch thick.

Open the door only when necessary.

Make sure the door seals well. If a piece of paper will slide easily between the cabinet and the door seal is not good enough.

Keep dust and fluff brushed off the coils on the back or bottom of the fridge.

Put the fridge in a well-ventilated position.

Place your fridge away from direct sunlight or any source of heat. Don't put hot food into a fridge or freezer.

CLOTHES AND WASHING

Don't buy a large machine if you don't need it. For the occasional big wash an extra cycle or two is cheaper than using a large washer.

Adjust the water level to economically wash a partial load. Otherwise it is better to wait until you have a full load, but don't overload your machine.

Your washer may have features than can save your money. Soak cycles remove stubborn stains in wash cycle. Suds savers allow you to reuse hot water.

Use correct type of detergent and cold or tepid water will wash clothes effectively.

LIGHTING

Good lighting means avoiding glare and gloom by using the right amount of light in the right way.

Use light translucent shades - opaque or dark shades require bigger lamps.

Use a good local light near the task. It is more effective and more efficient than a large central light.

Use fluorescent tubes since they use about a quarter of electricity used by ordinary globes and they last about eight times as long. They CAN be switched on and off as often as you need without affecting operating cost.

CLOTHES DRYING

Use solar energy to dry your clothes - it costs nothing.

Operate your dryer using the fan alone. Only switch the heater on if it is really necessary. Vent the dryer outside the house and don't let lint block the vent.

Never overload or under-load the dryer - you get most economical operation with the correct load.

Switch off when the clothes are dry enough - over drying makes them feel harsh and wastes electricity.

Tumble dryers are more effective than cabinet dryers.

WATER HEATING

Water restrictors and low flow shower nozzles will help to save water.

Insulate hot water pipes from storage heaters for at least a yard from the heater, since heat can be conducted along these pipes and lost to the atmosphere.

Normally you will use less water for shower than bath.

Place an insulated blanket around your hot water heater.

APPENDIX A

APPLIANCE LIFE EXPECTANCIES IN YEARS

APPLIANCE	AVERAGE LIFE EXPECTANCY
Air Conditioner (room)	11
Calculator (electric)	7
Can Opener (electric)	7
Charcoal grill	6
Clock (electric)	8
Coffee maker (perc)	6
Dishwasher	11
Dryer (electric)	13
Dryer (gas)	14
Electric Blanket	8
Electric Fan	16
Fax Machine	8
Floor Polisher	11
Furnace (electric)	18
Furnace (gas)	16
Garbage Disposal	10
Hair Dryer	4
Hi-Fi System	6
Humidifier	8
Ice Cream Maker (electric)	9
Iron (electric)	9
Lawn Mower (gasoline)	8
Microwave Oven	11
Personal Computer	6
Popcorn Popper	5
Range (electric)	15
Range (gas)	15
Refrigerator	13
Security Alarm System	14
Shaver (electric)	4
Smoke Detector	10

Telephone Answering Machine	5
Television (color)	8
Television (B&W)	9
Toaster	8
Trash Compactor	10
Vacuum Cleaner	11
Washing Machine	12
Water Heater (electric)	12
Water Heater (gas)	10

INDEX

children, 103